Flies for Fish and Fishermen

Flies for Fish

and Fishermen

THE WET FLIES

Helen Shaw

with photographs by
Hermann Kessler

STACKPOLE
BOOKS

Published by
STACKPOLE BOOKS
Cameron and Kelker Streets
P.O. Box 1831
Harrisburg, PA 17105

Printed in the United States of America

10 9 8 7 6 5 4 3 2 1

First edition

Jacket design by Tracy Patterson
Book design by Art Unlimited

Front Matter

Library of Congress Cataloging-in-Publication Data

Shaw, Helen.
    Flies for fish and fishermen : the wet flies / Helen Shaw ; with
photographs by Hermann Kessler. — 1st ed.
        p.   cm.
    Includes index.
    ISBN 0-8117-0607-9
    1. Fly tying. I. Title.
SH451.S49   1988
688.7'912 — dc20   89-32377
                                                              CIP

Author's Note

This book evolved during the early 1970s through many discussions with my husband, Hermann Kessler, an art director with many years of experience in publishing. It presents literal ideas in a visual manner. He showed me how to organize this information in a simple and straightforward way, beginning, as he suggested, with a silhouette of a simple *fly form* and following it with actual patterns in color, as illustrated in the color plates.

To
Donato Leo,
photographer
and dear friend,
whose full-page color photographs
precede each chapter.

TABLE OF CONTENTS

Oh, for a touch of the light bamboo,
And the sound of the spinning reel,
And a day in the dear old haunts with you,
With a rod and a well-filled creel.

Fayette Dublin, "The Winding Stream"

Preface

The term *hand-tied fly* is often used for emphasis. Flies for fishing are always hand-tied; they cannot be made any other way. Other lures can be manufactured by machine, but to this date only the human machine is capable of sorting and selecting perfect feathers, determining quality and color, and, most important, deciding the particular effect that is to be achieved.

It is true that dubbing can be blended by machine, and this can be a convenience when large quantities of it are needed. But the color and components of the blend are determined by you, the tyer, in the proportions you desire, for the particular patterns you prefer. You will apply that dubbing by hand to hooks of whatever size you choose, in the amounts you want to use.

Fortunately, fly tying is a craft that has not been overtaken by the machine-and-computer age. The individual is still important in fly tying. In it you can find self-expression and thus personal satisfaction in your ability to master the use of diverse materials with skill acquired through dexterity. The level of skill you will attain and the quality of the flies you will tie depend solely upon your determination to devote the time to practice with the materials. Each one has its own characteristics. You must become accustomed to the way these materials feel and behave while you are working with them. Practicing attaching them to a hook and fashioning them into a part of a specific pattern is very important. The need to practice with each material separately cannot be overemphasized. "Practice makes perfect" is a truism not to be ignored, no matter what skill you want to acquire.

Flies for Fish and Fishermen presents to the earnest tyer an orderly and simplified system for learning how to tie many fly patterns through focusing attention on the use of one body material at a time. The patterns with bodies made of one material comprise a *fly form*. There are seven fly forms. All of the flies in each fly form are shown in the color plates.

Each horizontal row of flies on the color pages represents a *stage* in the development of the patterns using one basic material for the body. Each fly form has six stages of development. You will progress from patterns having the least material and the simplest construction through six stages, in each of which a new element is added. Your proficiency in manipulating the constant body material increases with each pattern you tie. The first fly on the left in each horizontal row on the color plates is a *silhouette* of the patterns that follow in that row. It emphasizes their component parts and is not a pattern. The patterns are in color.

After tying the first pattern in the first row, you are able to tie all of the patterns that follow in that row. By developing the first patterns through the subsequent stages in which additional materials are introduced, you will be able to tie thirty-six different patterns in the first fly form alone. With each stage you master, you will acquire the skill to carry you on through the stages of the fly forms that follow.

Sometimes a particular pattern will differ in some small detail from the other patterns in the stage. A wing or a tail may require special treatment. These details are explained to you as the patterns progress.

The black-and-white photographs show steps that are fundamental to the fly patterns, but they will not necessarily be repeated. You can always refer back to appropriate shots. The flies in the color plates are tied on #10 hooks. For a clearer demonstration of tying details, a #6 hook is used in the black-and-white photographs.

For your convenience and quick reference, a list of the patterns described follows at the end of each stage in the fly form. The materials used for each pattern are listed too, in the order in which they are applied to the hook. Additional patterns in the same fly form are listed there also.

Fly patterns have always held a fascination for me—there are so many! When the compilation of this book was begun, in the early years of my fly tying, I thought of it as a "game of variations." Every beginner in fly tying becomes aware of the seemingly infinite number of patterns. Every year new patterns are "invented" or "originated," and the long list is increased. Some of these "new" patterns are ingenious further developments of an old standard pattern. Some are called new because of the application of materials that were not available in the earlier days of the craft. Some vary so slightly from one another that the difference is not immediately discernable.

When and where the patterns originated is speculative in a great many instances. Their origins are relatively unimportant to today's fly tyer, for the patterns are here to be reproduced by skillful fingers, to be adapted or altered to individual needs, and to be enjoyed. The game is still one of variations.

Fly patterns are perennial. By now, with thousands from which to choose, many tyers find the mass of information about them a little overwhelming. Wherever fishermen gather, flies that have been developed locally and used with success quickly become popular in that area. But when one is learning to tie, the question of which pattern to try first always arises: those with familiar names, or the latest and newest pattern just originated?

The answer, of course, is to start with the simplest ones—those having the fewest materials—and to perfect them. Other patterns, which require more materials to be applied in a more intricate manner, will be easier to tie later on.

Although materials carelessly bound to a hook may be used as a fly for fishing, the real enjoyment of any craft is found in striving for excellence. Fly tying is no exception. Do not be satisfied with poorly tied flies. With a little more patience—and practice—you can achieve handsome ones that are securely bound, pleasingly proportioned, and quite uniform as successive flies of the same pattern are tied: flies of which you can feel justly proud.

Instructions in fly tying are, of necessity, filled with repetitions of the proportionate amounts of the various materials being used. These, also of necessity, vary according to the size of the hook and the pattern being tied. Most of the proportions, therefore, must be approximate, rather than so precise that one must adhere to them without deviation. After all, we are dealing with materials that may not be uniform for everyone receiving the instructions.

Strand can mean a single filament, as a strand of tinsel. Or it can mean an undivided length of floss or yarn made up of many filaments, or fibers, that can be divided into several smaller strands.

When we refer to a *flue*, it is a barb of a feather, whether that feather is a goose or duck quill, a hackle, or a flank feather of wood duck, teal, or mallard. However, *barb* also refers to the raised projection behind the point of a hook.

A *wisp* is a small bunch. It refers to a small amount of the material in question.

A *strip* is a narrow piece of material made of feathers such as goose, duck, or turkey, to be used for tails or wings. In reference to small pieces, it indicates several flues (or barbs) of the feather that are to be removed together, as a single piece.

Sparse refers to a few thinly scattered elements. In fly tying it is used to indicate a thinly wound hackle: a hackle wound once or twice around the hook. Such as a hackle is "sparsely" wound in order to distribute its flues or barbs thinly around the hook.

Spare means to use with restraint or moderation. It also refers to a thinly wound hackle: a hackle wound sparingly or sparsely.

Gape refers to the width between the hook shank and the point of the hook, the amount of clearance between the hook shank and the point.

Gap or *gaps* refers to the spaces inadvertently left between the windings on an all-tinsel or all-quill body.

Tippet refers to a ruff of feathers on a bird. For fly-tying purposes it refers to the orange-and-black cape feathers of the golden pheasant.

To measure the flues of a hackle for length from the central stem or quill to the tips of the flues, lay the hackle across the hook where it will be tied on later, and permit the flues to fan out. If they are to reach from the wing position to the bend of the hook, that will be approximately twice the width of the hook's gape. With the hackle flues spread out in this manner as you hold it across the hook, you can determine whether the hackle you have selected has flues that are too long, too short, or just right for your purpose.

We will refer to materials mostly in generic terms: yarn, instead of wool or mohair yarn; chenille, instead of silk or cotton chenille; floss, instead of silk or rayon floss. However, the natural material sometimes may be indicated in a pattern. There are many synthetic substitutes for natural fibers in use today, and you will use whatever kind is available for your purpose.

Brown Hackle Peacock	Grizzly Hackle Peacock	Black Hackle Peacock	Green Insect	Grouse and Peacock	George Harvey Hackle
Coachman	Leadwing Coachman	Dark Alder	Gray Alder	Gray Gnat	Winged Peacock
Barrington	Pea Hen	Yellow Coachman	Chantry	Green Peacock	Dark Olive Gnat
Governor	Green Governor	Prime Gnat	Caddis	Bennett	Lowery
Marston	Swiftwater	Bog Fly	Grackle	Rio Grande King	White's Mosquito
Dark Turkey	Howell	Hardy's Favorite	Light Caddis	Warwick	Francis Fly

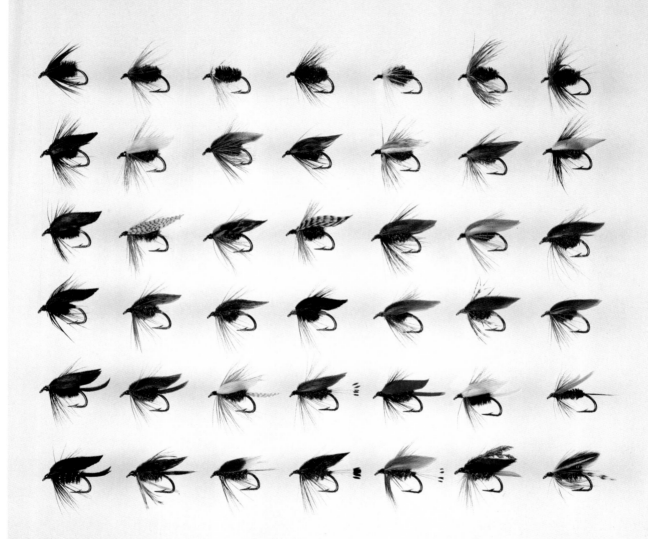

Herl Body
The First Fly Form

First Stage: Body and Hackle

All of the flies in the first fly form have herl bodies, either peacock or ostrich herl, both of which are applied to the hook in the same manner: with the quill tied against the hook so as to precede the herl as it flares around the hook, hiding the quill completely as you wind it on.

The first pattern requires a brown hackle. Brown hackles are often referred to as "red." This is one of the ambiguities accepted in fly-tying terminology. Red should be used to mean the primary color, but whenever you come across the term "red" in reference to a bright brown hackle, a brown one from a chicken known as Rhode Island Red is indicated. When a brown feather is required, "brown" should be the word used. This can be qualified easily when necessary with red-brown, reddish brown, light or dark brown, and a small confusion will be eliminated.

For the first pattern, then, select a medium brown wet-fly hackle, with soft and webby flues, that will reach to the bend of the hook. After you have wound the peacock herl carefully onto the hook, tie on the brown hackle with its dull side away from the eye of the hook. As you wind it on,

the natural curve of the soft webby feather will cause the flues to arch back over the herl body. This curve is more apparent with some feathers than with others, but all will lie back when the fly has been in the water. For wet flies a sparsely tied hackle is best; a few turns around the hook—two, or three at most—is all that is necessary.

A wrap knot, forming the head of the fly, will cover the trimmed end of the hackle's quill stem, and the first herl-bodied fly is complete when the head has been given several thin coats of a waterproof clear lacquer or fly head varnish.

The resultant fly will sink quickly beneath the surface when cast, and the soft webby fibers of the hackle will move seductively in the water currents as the fly drifts in a stream or is manipulated carefully through the quiet water of a lake or pond.

Having mastered this excellent, simple pattern, the Brown Hackle Peacock, you are now able to tie the patterns that follow, all of which belong to the same first stage of construction. The next three patterns differ only in the color or the hackles.

For the second pattern, select a medium-dark grizzly hackle. Grizzly hackles are barred in dark

All of the herl-bodied flies have a full oval body of prime peacock herl. Here, a brown hackle is wound on with its flues turning back over the body. When the excess hackle has been secured and clipped off and the tying has been completed with a wrap-knot head, this fly will be a Brown Hackle Peacock, the first pattern in the first stage of the first fly form.

gray and white and originate with the fowl known as a Plymouth Rock or barred Plymouth Rock. Although some grizzly hackles can be obtained with a very dark barring, they are never barred in a true black. The bars may be dark, fine, and closely spaced, giving a dark appearance to the feather as a whole, or they may be a paler gray and widely separated. The latter are sometimes referred to as *chinchilla hackles*. The Plymouth Rock breed of fowl is the most common source of these barred feathers, although one or two less-common breeds of domestic fowl have feathers with similar markings — the Campine, for instance.

Beginning with a second peacock herl body, add the grizzly hackle. Tie it on, and finish the head as you did for your first fly in this stage. You now have a Grizzly Hackle Peacock, an excellent and well-known wet fly.

For the third pattern, choose a natural black wet-fly hackle, or a white one that has been dyed black. (Naturally black hackles have a brownish

tinge on their dull sides.) Begin this fly with another peacock herl body. Tie on the black hackle with its dull side away from the eye of the hook. Wind it on, and finish with a wrap knot as you did the first two patterns. This one is the Black Hackle Peacock. A change in the color of the hackle is the only change that has been made, and already you have tied flies of three different patterns.

While it is not always possible to find the exact color, size, and length of hackle that would be the perfect one for each fly, it is worthwhile to try. Remember that hackles, as well as other feathers, are not always absolutely uniform in every respect.

Not all fly patterns will have names as descriptive of the materials used to fashion them as have these first three basic patterns. The fourth pattern, instead of being called a "Cream Hackle Peacock," is called the Green Insect. It is made simply by using a cream-colored hackle with the peacock herl body. "Cream" can mean almost any light tint of warm yellow, from an off-white to a pale honey or very light ginger.

When two hackles of different colors are to be used, as in the fifth and sixth patterns, the first hackle should be tied on a little farther back from the hook eye than it is when a single hackle is used. Estimate space behind the hook eye to accommodate one or two turns of the second hackle as well, in order to leave enough room for a neatly tied head that is not crowded against the eye of the hook. The thickness of a hackle quill may sometimes determine the size of the fly's head as the wrap knot is bound over it.

For the fifth pattern, then, begin by tying another Brown Hackle Peacock — your first fly in this first stage of the herl-bodied wet flies — remembering to place the brown hackle just a little farther away from the eye of the hook than you did the first time because you will be adding another one or two turns of a second hackle. When the brown hackle is in place, tie on a grouse feather and wind it between the brown one and the eye of the hook. Finish with a wrap-knot head. You now have a Grouse and Peacock, named for the kind of hackle used. (The name does not mention, however, that a combination of hackles was used.)

Both grouse and partridge body feathers make excellent wet-fly hackles. They are soft, webby, and finely marked in muted tones of tans, browns, and grays. For fly-tying purposes, the grouse is darker and more boldly marked than is the partridge.

The sixth pattern, with a double hackle, is the George Harvey Hackle. The basic pattern for this is the Black Hackle Peacock with a brown hackle tied on after the black one is in place — inserted, as it were, between the black hackle and the eye of the hook, just as you did with the grouse hackle in the preceding pattern.

Having perfected the first fly of the first stage, you now have six different patterns at your command: all are part of the first stage in tying the herl-bodied flies. There are additional patterns in this same category.

The fifth and sixth patterns require two hackles. In addition to the brown hackle, a grouse feather is used for the second hackle. Enough space has been estimated between the brown hackle and the hook's eye to accommodate two more turns of this second hackle.

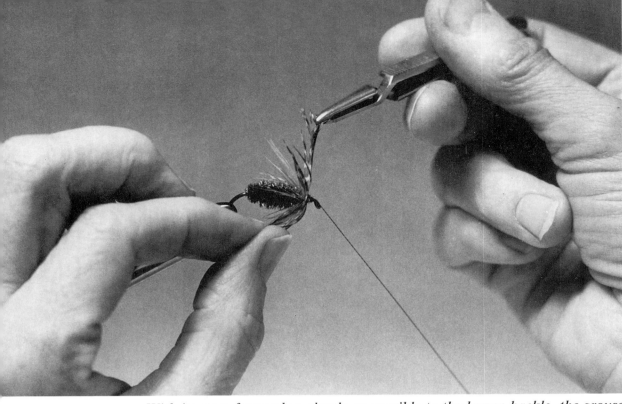

With its stem fastened as closely as possible to the brown hackle, the grouse feather is wound around the hook as though it were a continuation of the brown one. When the tying is finished, this fly will be a Grouse and Peacock.

Name of Pattern	Body	Hackle
Brown Hackle Peacock	Peacock Herl	Brown
Grizzly Hackle Peacock	Peacock Herl	Grizzly
Black Hackle Peacock	Peacock Herl	Black
Green Insect	Peacock Herl	Cream
Grouse and Peacock	Peacock Herl	Brown Hackle Faced with Grouse
George Harvey Hackle	Peacock Herl	Black Hackle Faced with Brown
Additional Patterns		
Witchery	Peacock Herl	Badger (List)
Coch-y-Bondhu	Peacock Herl	Furnace
Ginger Hackle	Peacock Herl	Ginger
Grouse Hackle	Peacock Herl	Grouse
Olive Partridge	Peacock Herl	Partridge Tinted Olive Green
Partridge Hackle	Peacock Herl	Partridge

The badger hackle, which is a dark gray with white or cream edges, is sometimes called a "list" hackle—a list being a border or edging. In fact, the list hackle may have its white or cream flues touched with a darker tone at the tips.

A furnace hackle is a brown version of the badger or list hackle, having a dark center bordered with fiery brown, and sometimes its brown edging has darker tips.

The natural colors found in hackles available for fly tying run from white through cream, ginger, brown, and black. There are hackles that are barred in gray and white (grizzly), brown barred with lighter brown (brown grizzly), ginger barred with white, white with ginger tips, cream with gray centers, and some hackles that are barred with multiple colors of gray, ginger, brown, and white. Of all the natural colors in hackles, the Andalusian hackle (a soft, smoky, darkish blue-gray, an elusive color difficult to describe accurately) is the rarest.

Of the Andalusian breed, under "The Races of Domestic Fowl," the 1927 *National Geographic* has this to say in part:

> The Andalusian was first known as the Blue Minorca. The color of the plumage is slate blue, laced with darker blue. The male's hackle, back, saddle and tail are bluish black. One interesting fact in the breeding of the Blue Andalusians is that the color might be called a hybrid—that is, when the blue male is mated to a blue female, only half the progeny are blue, one-quarter are black and one-quarter are white.

> To produce progeny which are all blue, it is necessary to cross black Andalusians with white ones. This situation is interesting from the biological standpoint, largely because as a result of a study of various matings, it has been discovered that the blue coloration is due to the particular shape and manner in which the black pigment granules are laid down in the feathers.

The color can be imitated, if not exactly matched, quite acceptably for fly-tying purposes by a process using silver nitrate. Since the quality of the hackles and the uniformity of color can be maintained to a great degree in the dyed feathers, they are a more dependable source than are the natural Andalusians, which are difficult to obtain.

Natural black hackles, which are not really jet black, can be dipped in blue dye, and the result is sometimes quite satisfactory, but the results of the silver nitrate process are superior. If you want to dye hackles, remember that not all feathers accept the dye at the same rate; it is best to dye small quantities at a time.

Second Stage: With Wing

In the second stage of the same fly form, other patterns evolve from the first basic patterns of herl body and hackle. After the hackle has been tied onto the herl body, a wing for a standard wet fly is added, to lie back over the body of the fly. It may be made of feather or hair. The difference in wing material does not necessarily change the name of the pattern, except perhaps to give it the designation of *feather wing* or *hair wing*, if a preference for either type of wing is indicated for a specific pattern.

For fly-tying purposes, the use of the words "wing" or "wings" has little to do with how many feathers, strips of feathers, or hairs are being used. For example, a pair of matched strips of feathers or a pair of matched hackles, tied on back-to-back so as to remain closed as a single unit, can be referred to as a "wing." When the pair is separated either horizontally or vertically, and spread apart into a V so that each half is visible at the same time, reference is made to "wings." But when two hackles are tied on flat and spread apart horizontally, at right angles to the fly body, the result is a *spent-wing* pattern.

When a wing is made with hair, the application of "wing" or "wings" is more obvious, for although many individual hairs are bunched together, the effect is that of the single unit. This, then, is a wing. When the bunch of hair is divided, the wings are evident immediately. However, one may also refer to the fly with these wings as a *divided-wing* pattern.

For feather wings, the white and slate gray feathers from goose or duck wings are used, as are the speckled tan and brown turkey wing feathers. Suppliers of fly-tying materials refer to these feathers as quills. Some have broad, rounded tips and are referred to as *broad quills.* Some taper toward the tips, ending in slim points, and these are called *pointer quills,* or *pointers.* However, since a quill is a separate, specific material used for fly tying and is obtained from the shafts of these and other feathers, we will refer to the fly-wing material as goose, duck, or turkey.

The gray color of goose wing feathers is called "slate" as well as gray. The gradation of tone on many may be quite marked, shading from a dark tip to pale gray at the base. Others may be uniform gray throughout. Well-paired feathers will furnish tone-matched wings when the sections for the wings are cut from corresponding positions on the feathers. The paired feathers should be of the same width in order to have their natural curvature of the same strength when strips of them are placed together as wings.

Feathers such as white or gray goose and tan or brown mottled turkey are a joy to use for winging wet flies. Their natural curves and sturdiness of texture make wet-fly wings that fit together neatly and positively, to fashion a firm, strong pair.

At this point, observe the differences in character between the goose and turkey feathers. The goose feather has a very narrow side and a broad one. It is the broad side that will furnish material for wet-fly wings. The turkey feather has flues of about the same width on both sides of its central shaft. Even though the colors may be muted, one side is more highly colored than is the other. It is this highly colored side that will furnish material for the wings of our wet flies.

Hold a goose feather and a turkey feather by their central shafts, side-by-side, their tips vertical. With the undersides of both feathers turned away from you, notice that the top side of the goose feather flares toward you at the outer edge of its flues, while the flues of the highly colored side of the turkey feather arch smoothly away from the central shaft, and away from you.

When sections of flues have been cut from a matched pair of goose feathers and placed together so that their tips curve inward, toward each other, the underside of the feather, which is shiny, will become the outside of the fly wing. Just the reverse is evident when sections of the flues are

taken from matching turkey feathers and are held with their tips together. The top side, which is the highly colored side, will still be on the outside of the pair. Making use of the natural contours of the feather you use will enhance your enjoyment in the craft of fly tying.

The markings on turkey wing and tail feathers are extremely varied. By carefully sorting and matching these feathers it is possible to find pairs with bold markings or subtle designs, and it is satisfying to keep these pairs together to use, knowing that the patterns on the wings you make from them will be uniform on both sides of the fly. The colors range from light mottled gray through cream and tan to dark brown. They may also be plain, or mottled with lighter tints or darker shades, heavily mottled or lightly speckled. Some of the dark brown tail feathers are tipped with a band of cream or white.

The wet flies on the color plates are uniform in size, and unless otherwise specified in a particular pattern, the proportions of tail, body, and wing are uniform also, with the wing tips extending beyond the hook no more than the width of the gape. With practice, these proportions will be maintained with ease when you are using hooks of smaller or larger size.

For the first pattern to have a wing in this second stage, we will choose a Coachman. Just the addition of a white goose-feather wing to the Brown Hackle Peacock will give us this very famous fly pattern. If a white wing made of calf-tail hair were used here, the pattern would be called a Hairwing Coachman.

By using a slate-colored goose-feather wing instead of the white one, another well-known pattern, the Leadwing Coachman, will emerge as our second pattern in this second stage.

When a brown furnace hackle (one having a dark, almost black center) is used instead of a plain brown hackle, and a wing of dark brown turkey is added, you will have a Dark Alder as the third pattern.

By using a light gray wing made from a mottled gray turkey feather over the Grizzly Hackle Peacock, we will have a pattern called Gray Alder. A dark slate goose wing over the same basic pattern will produce a Gray Gnat.

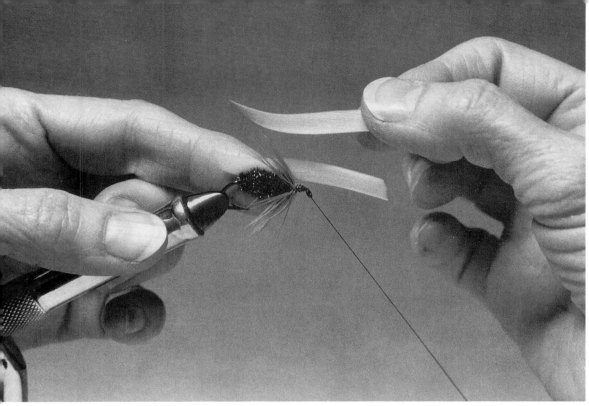

Two strips of white goose for a wing are added to the Brown Hackle Peacock. The finished fly will bear a name well known to fishermen, and to many who have never fished at all.

Measured for length against the body and hook, the wings are grasped by the fingers of the left hand and held in place to free the right hand for tying. The wing tips extend the width of the gape beyond the bend of the hook. Found in almost every fisherman's fly box, mentioned innumerable times in fishing classics, this is the Coachman pattern.

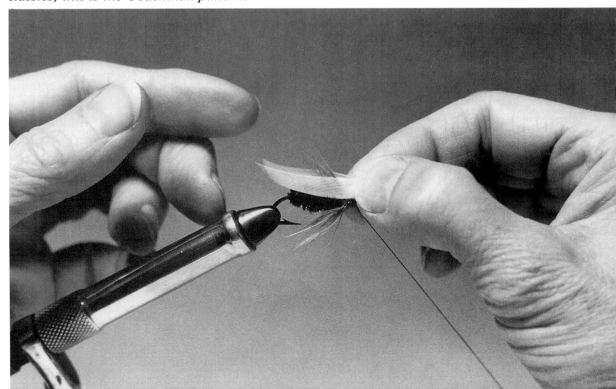

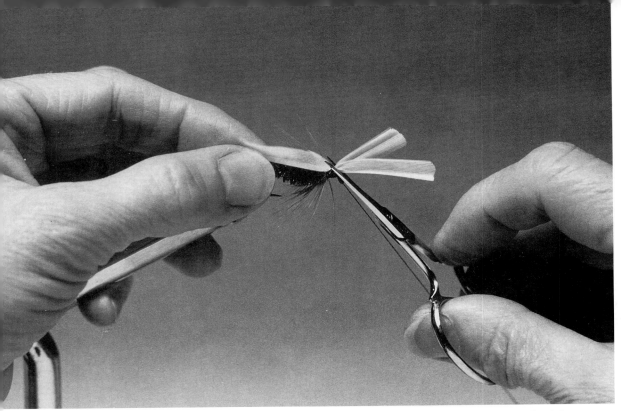

Taper the stubs as they are being clipped off. Finish the head with a wrap knot, covering the stub ends neatly and completely. When a pair of gray strips from slate-colored goose are substituted for the white you will have a Leadwing Coachman.

Name of Pattern	Body	Hackle	Wing
Coachman	Peacock Herl	Brown	White Goose
Leadwing Coachman	Peacock Herl	Brown	Slate Goose
Dark Alder	Peacock Herl	Furnace	Dark Brown Turkey
Gray Alder	Peacock Herl	Grizzly	Light Gray Mottled Turkey
Gray Gnat	Peacock Herl	Grizzly	Dark Slate Goose
Winged Peacock	Peacock Herl	Black	Silver Gray Duck
Additional Patterns			
Winged Insect	Peacock Herl	Cream	Speckled Mallard
Isonychia Bicolor (Jennings)	Peacock Herl	Light Ginger	Dark Slate Goose
Brown Mallard	Peacock Herl	Light Brown	Brown Mallard
Deer Fly	Peacock Herl	Brown	Barred Wood Duck
Gerry	Peacock Herl	Ginger	Slate Goose
White Wing	Green Ostrich Herl	Brown	White Goose

With a wing made from silvery gray duck tied on over the Black Hackle Peacock, the pattern will be a Winged Peacock.

Wings only have been added to the first three wet-fly patterns of the first stage, but six more patterns have resulted.

Of the additional patterns, the Winged Insect can be recognized as the Green Insect of the first stage with a wing added. The Isonychia Bicolor has also been called a Leadwing Coachman, or a Ginger Leadwing Coachman, which is more accurate. This could be shortened to Ginger Leadwing, but by whatever name, it is an excellent wet-fly pattern.

Third Stage: With Tag

The next fly patterns are still without tails. Now that the original herl-body-and-hackle fly has been winged, another material is added to the original structure. This addition, usually of tinsel, is called a *tag*, and it is tied on the hook before the body is made. It will provide the first bit of sparkle not inherent in the natural gloss or sheen of the peacock-herl body.

The tag is placed on the uppermost curve of the bend of the hook, just where the hook shank be-

gins to round downward to form the heel. Cut the end of the tinsel into a taper and tie it on above and approximately midway between the barb and point. Bend the tiny pointed end back over the tying thread to secure it. Wind the tinsel three or four turns down on the bend of the hook—no more—and back to the place you tied it on. This gives the fly its tiny light-catching tag. Again, taper the tinsel when you cut off the excess and bend that tiny point back over your tying thread to secure it. While you are winding the tinsel, keep the turns of it edge-to-edge, without a gap and without overlapping. The body material will cover the tying thread that binds the tinsel in place.

Actually, the number of turns of tinsel to use for a tag depends on the width of the tinsel being used. If the tinsel is fine and narrow, four or five turns will be ample for a tag the size of those shown in the color plates. A larger hook would permit a few more turns of the narrow tinsel, or a wider one could be used. Two or three turns of a fine tinsel are adequate for smaller-sized hooks or when a short tag is specified for a particular pattern.

With the tag in place, the herl body now begins as though it were a continuation of the tag. Not

The tapered end of the tinsel strand (for a tag) is tied on the hook shank midway above the barb and point.

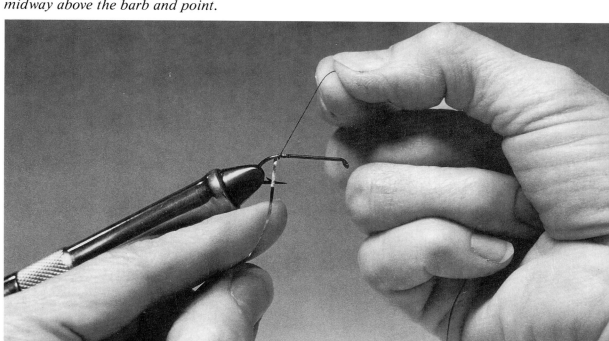

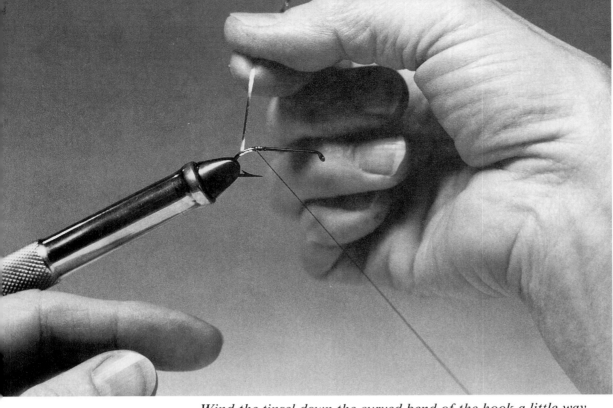

Wind the tinsel down the curved bend of the hook a little way . . .

. . . and carefully wind it upward again, to the place where it was tied on. Secure it here and cut off the long strand of excess tinsel. When the same kind of tinsel is specified for both tag and rib, the continuous tinsel *technique can apply. Do not cut the tinsel off here, just hold it out of your way for use later, after you have tied the body.*

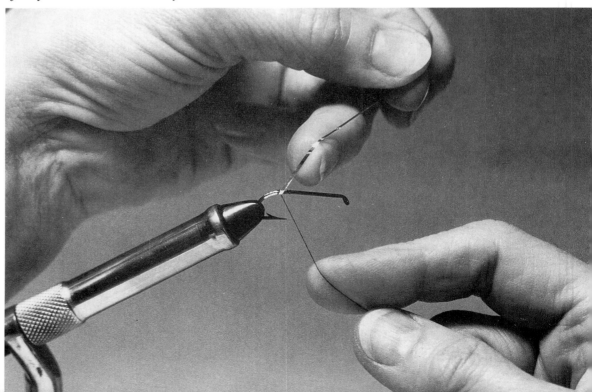

one turn of tying thread should be visible where tinsel tag and herl body meet above the barb of the hook.

The following patterns in this third stage are all of the same construction as are the previous ones in this fly form—the only new element is the tinsel tag. The only changes are a difference in the color of the wing or in the material from which the wing is made, and in two instances in the color of the hackle.

By adding a small gold tinsel tag and a gray speckled mallard-feather wing to the Brown Hackle Peacock, that pattern of the first stage has been changed into a Barrington.

Another gold tag, this time with a mottled brown wing of white goose dyed a ginger brown, will convert that same first pattern into a fly called the Pea-Hen.

When you add a gold tag and a wing of yellow-tinted gray barred teal to that basic Brown Hackle Peacock, you will have changed it this time into a Yellow Coachman.

To the Black Hackle Peacock of the first stage, the addition of a gold tag and a wing of dark slate duck will alter that pattern (and the Winged Peacock of the second stage) into the Chantry. Only the gold tag and a darker wing make the difference between the latter two patterns.

A silver tag on the peacock-herl body, a hackle that has been tinted a light olive green, and a wing made of a light slate-colored duck wing feather, will alter the Gray Gnat to a Green Peacock. The wing material, just a tint lighter, and the body are the same. Only a tag and the color of the hackle have made this change.

Darken both the olive hackle and the wing, and the pattern will then be a Dark Olive Gnat—one version of an Olive Gnat (listed with the additional patterns).

If you add a tag to the Winged Peacock of the second stage and compare it to the Chantry and the Dark Alder, little or no difference can be ascertained at once. This is a good example of three names for what is essentially the same pattern.

Tie the body material on over the ends of tinsel and thread that binds them to the hook.

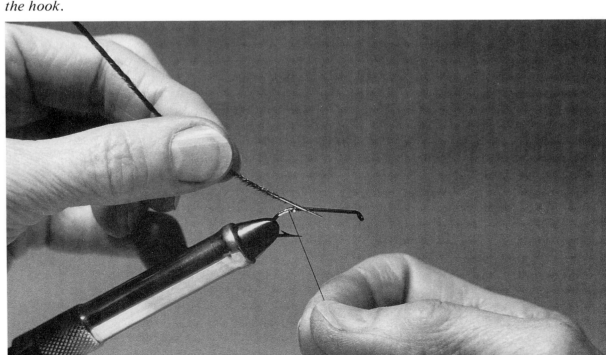

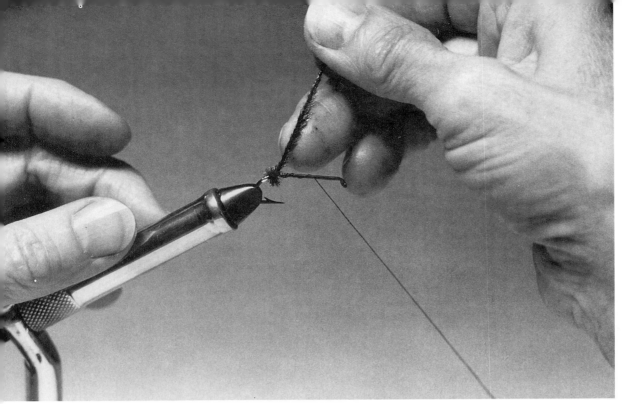

With the body herl covering the cut ends of the tinsel tag, wind it forward from above the barb, leaving three or four turns of the tinsel tag showing. Finish the herl body, and it will be ready for your next hackle and wing.

Name of Pattern	Tag	Body	Hackle	Wing
Barrington	Gold	Peacock Herl	Brown	Gray Mallard
Pea-Hen	Gold	Peacock Herl	Brown	Brown Mottled Game Hen
Yellow Coachman	Gold	Peacock Herl	Brown	Gray Barred Teal Tinted Yellow
Chantry	Gold	Peacock Herl	Black	Dark Slate Goose or Duck
Green Peacock	Silver	Peacock Herl	Olive	Light Slate Duck
Dark Olive Gnat	Gold	Peacock Herl	Dark Olive	Dark Slate Goose
Additional Patterns				
Dark Alder	Gold	Peacock Herl	Black	Slate Goose or Duck
Black June	Gold	Peacock Herl	Black (natural)	Slate Goose Dyed Black, with Head of Red Tying Thread
Olive Gnat	Gold	Peacock Herl	Furnace	Goose Dyed Olive Green
Green Beetle	Gold	Peacock Herl	Black	Slate Goose with Green Head
Alice	Silver	Peacock Herl	Chocolate Brown	Barred Wood Duck
Surprise	Red	Peacock Herl	Gray-Blue	Red Goose

Fourth Stage: With Tip

A confusing bit of terminology exists with "tag" and "tip." This is easily clarified by remembering that the tag is tagged on at the end of the hook. The tip is the tip-end of the fly body. It may be made of floss, chenille, or herl (either peacock or ostrich), depending upon pattern requirements.

Sometimes a herl tip is referred to as a *butt*. This term is more useful when it is applied to a fly pattern with a segmented body, that has herl between the segments. These segments are then said to be "butted" with herl. The back end of a fly body is still the tip of the body.

In many patterns the tip of the body is made of a different color than is the body itself and represents the egg sack of a mature female insect. In others it just forms an attractive color combination with the rest of the fly. In some patterns it is built up somewhat and is intended to give the fly an antlike form.

Many fly patterns that are used successfully for fishing are only approximations of actual insects. Some, which are completely fanciful, having no counterpart whatever in nature, appear to be fascinating to fish and fishermen alike.

The fourth stage of the first fly form, then, is the fashioning of a small tip at the end of the fly body. More fly patterns, still without tails and all having the same construction as the first three stages, will be added to your list of pattern accomplishments.

The tip of the body will occupy approximately a scant quarter of the body length. Whether or not a tag is part of the pattern, the tip will be formed on the hook where the end of the fly body would be normally. When a tag is present, whatever material from which the tip is made must cover the bound ends of the tag material as smoothly as possible. All but one of the patterns in the fourth stage of the first fly form have gold tags.

The tips of the following patterns are made of floss, and where floss is used for this purpose it is advisable to touch the finished tip with a drop of clear lacquer before proceeding to tie the rest of the fly. Floss has a way of slipping because not all the filaments in a strand are under the same amount of tension at all times. Allow the floss strand to spread slightly as you wind it around the hook while making a smooth tip. (Floss is our third fly form.)

Include a small tip of red floss in the Coachman pattern, substitute a brown turkey wing for the

Here, floss for a tip has been tied on over the tinsel ends of the tag. Wind it forward from above the barb and cover the tying threads smoothly.

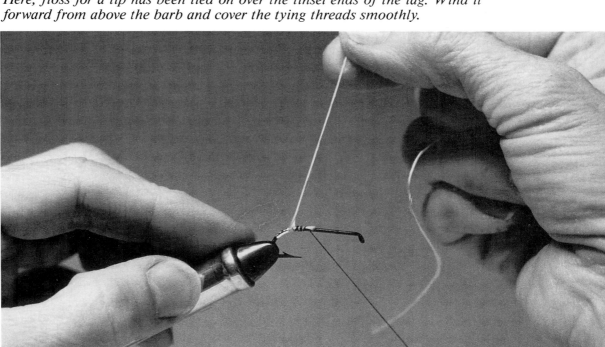

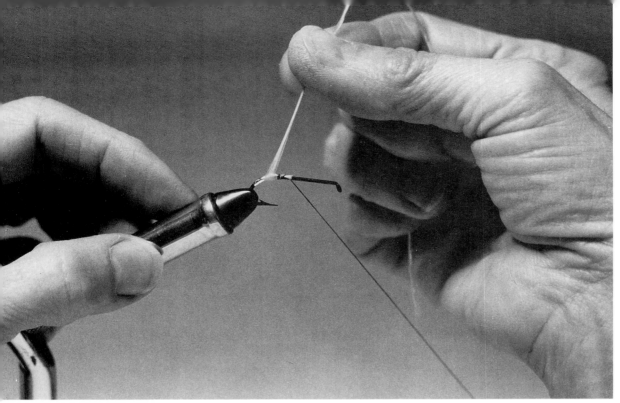

Allow the floss to spread slightly as you fashion a smooth and tapered tip. Keep it tight in order to prevent a single filament from slipping backward over the tinsel tag. This floss tip will form the end of the fly body.

With tinsel tag and floss tip in place, wind the body herl forward, entirely covering the area in which they were tied on.

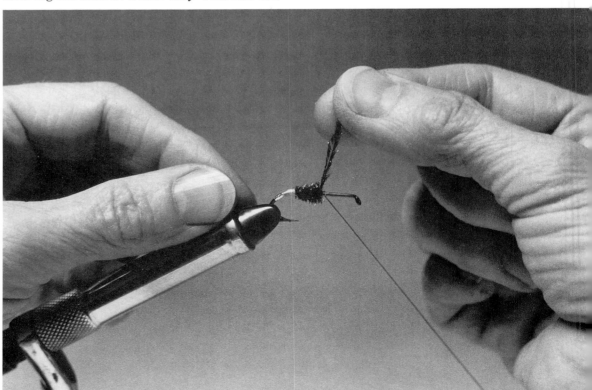

white one, and you will have changed that pattern into the well-known and popular Governor. Use a green floss tip instead of the red one, and the pattern will then be a Green Governor.

Just as the names of flies in the first stage indicate the materials to be used for them, so could the names for the Governors go right on through the spectrum, with tips of every hue. Some combinations would surely prove more successful than others in attracting fish, but in an experimental mood you might like to do your own testing and try them all.

The Prime Gnat, the third pattern in this fourth stage, also has a herl body, but this time it is made of black ostrich herl instead of peacock. The natural colors of ostrich herl—white, tan, gray, and black—are usually available wherever fly-tying materials are sold. The white can be dyed any color you desire. It is applied to the hook in exactly the same way peacock herl is used and tied in carefully to make sure the quill precedes the herl along the hook as it is being wound on.

The Prime Gnat is a beautiful dark fly without a tag, but with a tip of orange floss on the black

herl body. It has a black hackle and a wing of black-dyed goose. Orange tying thread may be used for the entire pattern in this case, and it will give the Prime Gnat its dark orange head.

For a pattern like this one, where the head of the fly is not black, thread of the specified head color may be used for tying the entire fly, thus eliminating the problem of changing thread in order to finish the fly properly. If the tip is of a lighter color, however, or of a different color than the tying thread, make sure the tip material covers the tying thread so that its color does not show through.

A tip of brown floss on a Leadwing Coachman pattern will create a Caddis. (The name "Caddis" is given to several patterns and is not intended to designate a replica of the insect.) Brown tying thread used throughout this pattern will form a brown head for this attractive fly.

With a yellow floss tip on the body of peacock herl, a hackle this time of a guinea fowl feather, and a wing of dark slate goose, you have a Bennett. This pattern is based on the Grizzly Hackle Peacock of the first stage. You have simply re-

Name of Pattern	Tag	Tip	Body	Hackle	Wing	Head
Governor	Gold	Scarlet Floss	Peacock Herl	Brown	Brown Turkey	Black
Green Governor	Gold	Green Floss	Peacock Herl	Brown	Brown Turkey	Black
Prime Gnat	Gold	Orange Floss	Black Ostrich Herl	Black	Black Goose	Dark Orange
Caddis	Gold	Brown Floss	Peacock Herl	Brown	Slate Goose	Brown
Bennett	Gold	Yellow Floss	Peacock Herl	Guinea	Dark Slate Goose	Gray
Lowery	Gold	Deep Yellow Floss	Peacock Herl	Brown	Cinnamon Turkey	Brown
Additional Patterns						
Orange Governor	Gold	Orange Floss	Peacock Herl	Ginger-Brown	Slate	Black
Fitzgerald's Choice	Gold	Orange Swan	Peacock Herl Dyed Magenta	Badger Dyed Dark Ruby	Light Widgeon	Black
Red Tag	Gold	Red Floss	Peacock Herl	Brown	Brown	Black
Red Tip Grackle	Silver	Scarlet Floss	Peacock Herl	Black	Red	Black
Green Knight	Gold	Green Floss	Peacock Herl	Brown	Cinnamon	Green
Potomac	Gold	Yellow Floss	Peacock Herl	Brown	Cinnamon	Brown

placed the grizzly hackle with the speckled guinea fowl feather and given the body a yellow tip. Gray tying thread used for this pattern will make the gray head.

With another tip of yellow floss and a wing made of cinnamon turkey, you will change the Brown Hackle Peacock into the Lowery. Use brown tying thread, for as with the Caddis the Lowery, too, has a brown head.

A strand from a swan's wing feather can be used in the same manner as a strand of peacock or ostrich herl. The body will be smaller in diameter than either, however. This is excellent for tiny flies or for a tip, as in the additional pattern above. For a fuller tip, ostrich herl can be used, dyed in any color specified for the pattern.

Fifth Stage: With Tail

A further embellishment for the fly patterns is the addition of a tail, the fifth stage in our development of the herl-bodied wet fly. Whether the tail is made of wisps or strands of feather, of hair, or just a tuft of floss or yarn, it is tied on the hook approximately above the barb.

Frequently, the addition of a tail to the basic structure of the second stage of the first fly form makes the only difference between one pattern and another. For instance, when a tail made of a few strands of slate goose is added to the Leadwing Coachman pattern to match its wing, the pattern then becomes a Marston.

A few strands of the speckled gray mallard feather used as a tail on the Coachman will give us still another pattern called the Swiftwater.

While the next pattern has the body and wing of the Leadwing Coachman, the color of its hackle is claret instead of brown. And when you add a tail made of a few strands of golden pheasant tippet, which is orange barred and tipped with black, you have made a Bog Fly.

In working with the tippet feather, it is advisable to use a few strands from both the right and the left of the feather's center to keep the bright orange of the strands showing on both sides of the tail. The feather is very dull on its underside, and when strands are taken from only one half of the feather some of the bright color will be concealed

when the tail is tied on.

Use a few wisps of dark scarlet hackle for a tail on the Black Hackle Peacock. Add a wing of dark scarlet goose, and a Grackle emerges from the third fly you tied in the first stage of this fly form.

As with the Prime Gnat of the fourth stage, the body of the next pattern is made with black ostrich herl. The tail for this fly will be a few strands of white goose that has been dyed yellow. With the brown hackle and white wing of the Coachman pattern, this fly is now the celebrated Rio Grande King.

In this way the patterns relate and change. The basic form of each is identical. Becoming familiar with the minute differences will enable you not only to recognize another pattern but also to add another excellent fly to your growing stock without difficulty. The actual construction of each one is the same. Your own experience in fishing with them will reveal their particular values on the waters you prefer to fish.

For the White's Mosquito, a few black wisps for the tail can be taken from a small soft feather that you will also use for the hackle on this fly. While the body is made of peacock herl, the herl itself is taken from the eye of the peacock frond so that the bright blue-green color will form the end, or tip, of the body. The wings for this pattern are very slender and of slate goose. Tie them on to lie back over the body with the tips curving outward and upward, away from each other. Tags are optional on these patterns.

Tails are used with patterns having tags and tips as well. Some of these are listed with the additional patterns for this stage. The Caddis pattern of the fourth stage for example, when made with a gold tag, a brown mallard tail, a brown floss tip, a brown grizzly hackle (instead of a plain brown one), with a darker slate-colored wing, has been changed into a Dark Caddis. It is our old friend the Leadwing Coachman with a tag, a tip, and a tail.

The pattern for the Academy is essentially the Grackle with an added tag and tip, while the Mascot has added a tail and a tip to the pattern for a Winged Peacock of the second stage of this first fly form.

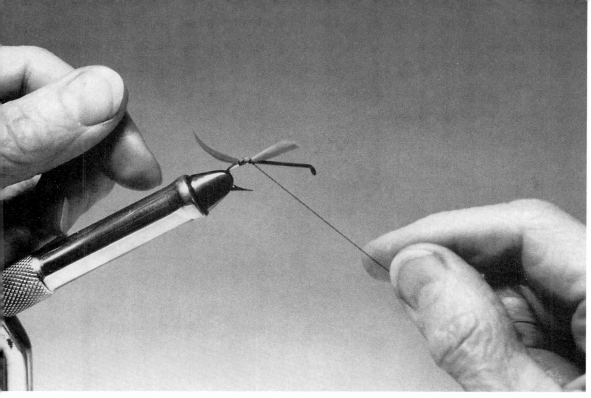

Short flues from the narrow edge of a goose feather can be used for tails and the wider side reserved for wing material. This uses the part of the feather that often goes to waste.

Matching flues from each side of the beautiful orange tippet feather of the golden pheasant should be used together to make tails for patterns like the Bog Fly, Hardy's Favorite, and Light Caddis.

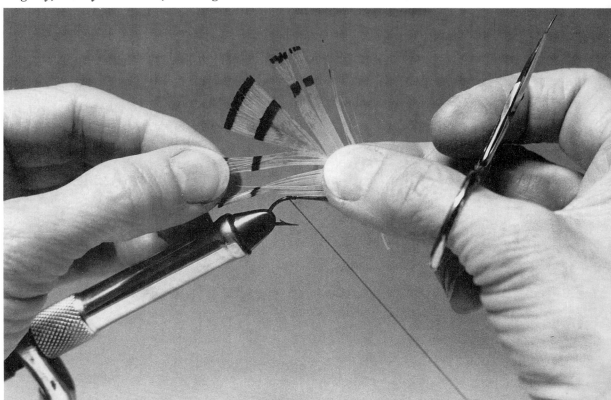

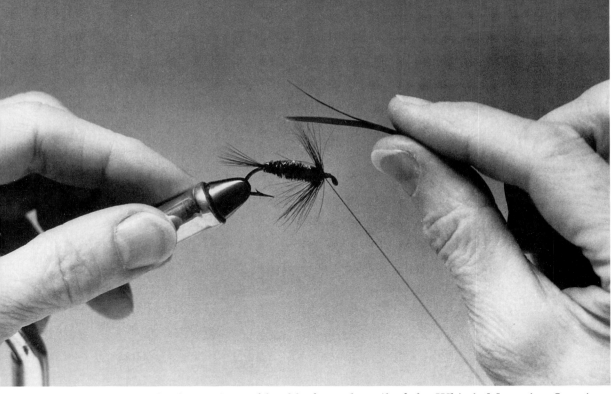

Fairly short wisps of hackle form the tail of the White's Mosquito. Its wings of slate goose strips are narrower than those for a standard wet fly. Matched dull side to dull side, the tips turn outward, away from the fly body.

Before they are tied on, the feather strips for a pair of narrow wings, held with the dull sides away from the hook, are measured for correct length against the body of the fly. Here, the tips, extending no more than the width of the gape behind the hook, reach just to the center of the tail. They will be held in place by the left hand . . .

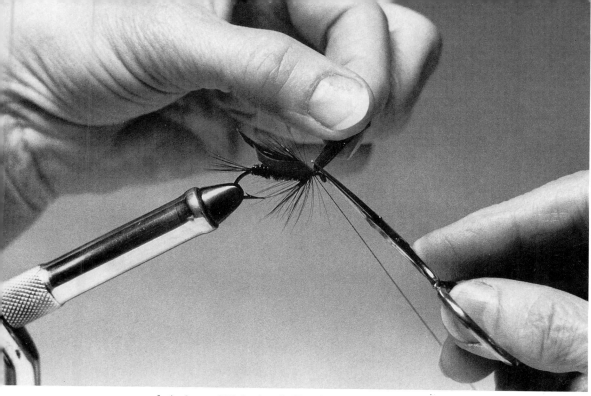

. . . and tied on. With the dull sides turned away from the hook, the natural curve of these feather strips will make a pair of wings with tips that sweep upward and away from the fly body.

Name of Pattern	Tail	Body	Hackle	Wing
Marston	Slate Goose	Peacock Herl	Brown	Slate Goose
Swiftwater	Gray Mallard	Peacock Herl	Brown	White Goose
Bog Fly	Tippet	Peacock Herl	Claret	Dark Slate Goose
Grackle	Dark Scarlet	Peacock Herl	Black	Dark Scarlet Goose
Rio Grande King	Yellow Goose	Black Ostrich	Brown	White Goose
White's Mosquito	Short Black Hackle Wisps	Green Herl from Peacock Eye	Black	Slate Goose, Narrow and Turned-out

Additional Patterns							
Name of Pattern	Tag	Tail	Tip	Body	Hackle	Wing	Head
Waters	Gold	Scarlet Tuft	———	Peacock Herl	Black or Dark Grizzly	Slate Goose	White Ostrich Herl
Olive Dun	Silver	Dark Olive Hackle Wisps	———	Peacock Herl	Green	Barred Wood Duck	Black
Governor Alvord	Silver	Dark Scarlet	Dark Scarlet Floss	Peacock Herl	Brown	Slate with Cinnamon Strip Over	Black
Dark Caddis	Gold	Brown Mallard	Brown Floss	Peacock Herl	Brown Grizzly	Dark Slate Goose	Black
Academy	Gold	Crimson	Red Floss	Peacock Herl	Black	Claret Goose	Black
Mascot	Gold	Red Goose	Yellow Floss	Peacock Herl	Black	Gray Duck	Black

The tail of the Waters is a short tuft of yarn above a tinsel tag. Its hackle and wing are the same as those of the Gray Gnat, but the Waters also has a white ostrich herl head. Select a strand of it for this detail . . .

. . . and attach it snugly in front of the wing. Wind it on carefully . . .

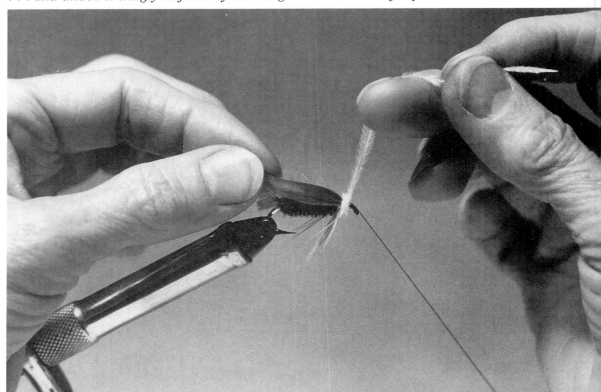

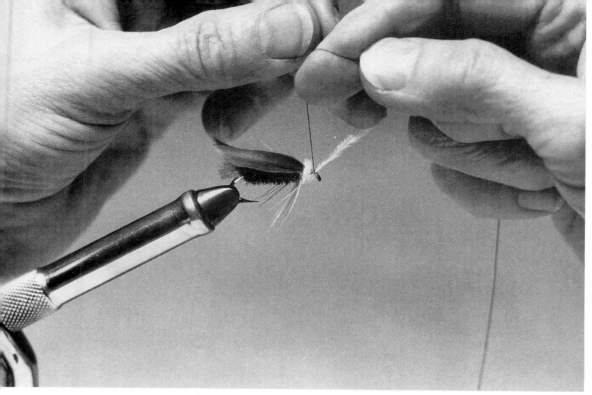

. . . and tie the white ostrich herl off, just behind the eye of the hook.

A short wrap knot over the end of the ostrich herl will leave enough space behind the eye to accommodate a fine leader. Apply clear lacquer to the head with care to prevent it from spreading into the herl.

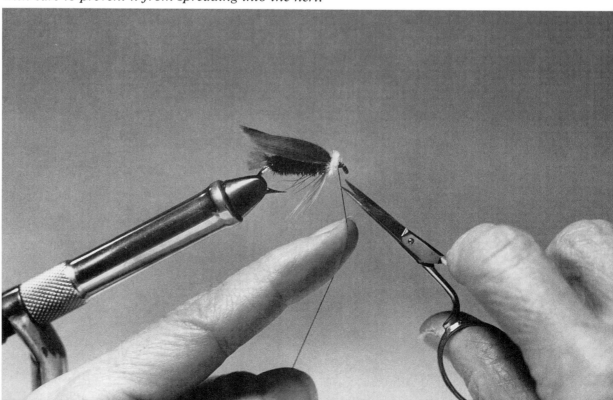

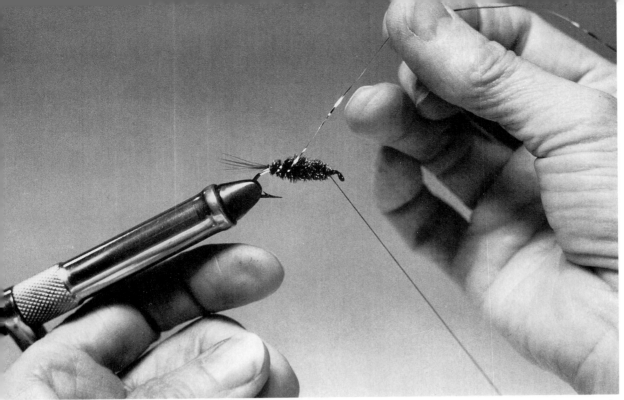

Plain, flat tinsel is used on many fly patterns. Here it is wound in evenly spaced ribs in the same direction as the body herl was wound.

Sixth Stage: With Ribs

To the first simple structure of body and hackle we have added other component parts: wings, tags, tips, and tails. In this stage, the ribbing now becomes an integral part of the patterns. A bright spiral of silver or gold tinsel, or of the many colored ones available, not only adds a decorative touch to a fly pattern but is functional as well. Its smooth, tough surface gives protection to a fly body.

A rib is usually wound on in the same direction as the body material, serving to stabilize a body made of fibers less tough. When it is wound counter to the direction in which the body material was wound, a rib insures greater durability for the windings then will cross *over* those of the body instead of paralleling them. A tinsel rib of fine wire used in this way after a regular rib has been made binds the whole body more securely. It could be added to any pattern without fundamentally altering it. The use of a tinsel rib on an otherwise unribbed pattern can be incorporated in the name of the pattern, as with the Gold-Ribbed Hare's Ear, which follows in the fifth fly form.

There are many bright-colored tinsels made of tarnish-proof metal for ribbing fly patterns, and also a synthetic material metallic in appearance that cannot tarnish. Round and oval tinsels of silver and gold are made with a thread core that determines their shape. Tinsels can be flat or embossed, in varying widths. They all are a useful part of the fly tyer's stock of materials. Solid wires are available in silver, gold, copper, or brass, in various weights.

When floss of a contrasting color is used for ribbing on a fly, the strand may be separated into several finer ones or used whole, depending on the size of the fly. The strand may be twisted into a slender cord while being wound on or it may be kept flat. The twisted strand will become a raised rib, while the flat strand will lie along the body in the manner of a strand of flat tinsel. Tying thread, sewing thread in silk or nylon, and buttonhole twist are sometimes used for ribbing. Multiple ribs of tinsel and combinations of tinsel with floss appear on some of the classic patterns of salmon flies.

Ribs for the patterns in this sixth stage of the first fly form are made with floss, thread, and tinsel. The strand is tied on after the tag and the tail are in place. It is then kept out of the way while the material for the body is attached over the

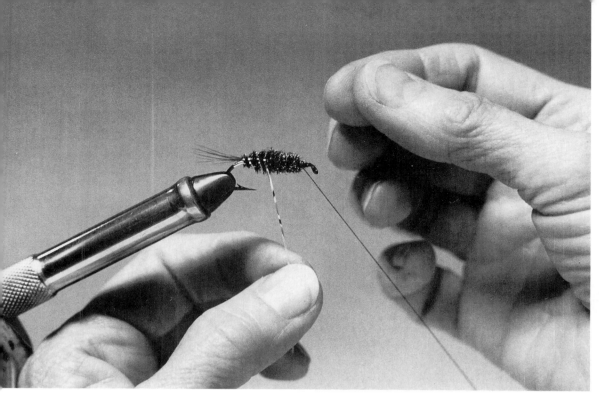

The flat tinsel here is being wound in reverse. It crosses over the body herl, which was wound in the opposite direction.

For the purpose of demonstration, in this sequence of photos a full strand from a skein of floss has been tied in, as though for a rib. When such a strand is untwisted and used as one broad, flat rib, there will be only a few ribs on the fly. Their bright segments alternating with the green herl over which they are wound will make a scintillating and attractive body.

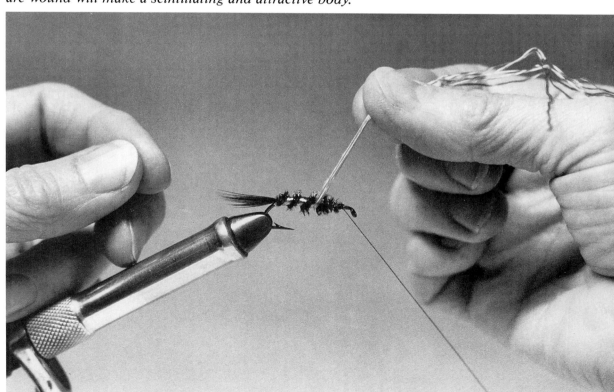

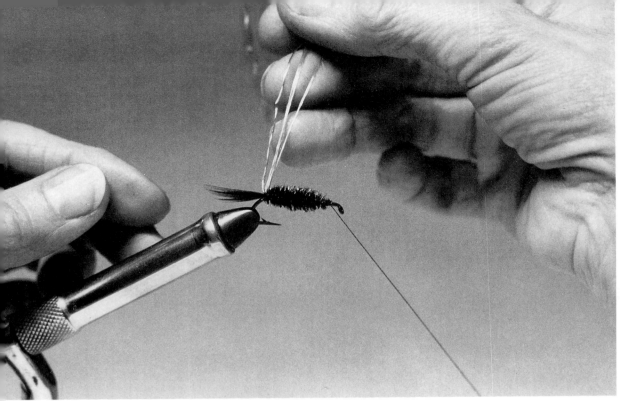

Here, the full strand has been separated into three finer ones. It could be
divided into more in order to have some fine enough for very small flies. Only
one single strand would be used for each small fly to make a narrow flat rib or
to be twisted into a slender cord to make a fine, raised rib.

Now, for demonstration only, two of the three strands are held back out of the
way. The remaining one has been twisted into a cord to make a raised rib over
the body of the peacock herl. Only the strand to be used for the rib should be
tied on. The width of a flat floss rib is determined by how many divisions
were made of the original strand. This also determines the diameter of the
floss cord. The number of ribs depends on the size of the fly and on how
tightly the strand is twisted.

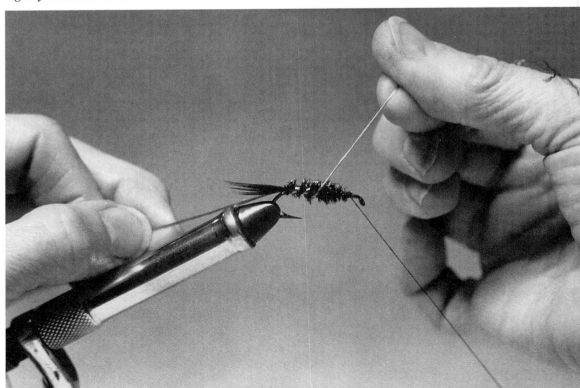

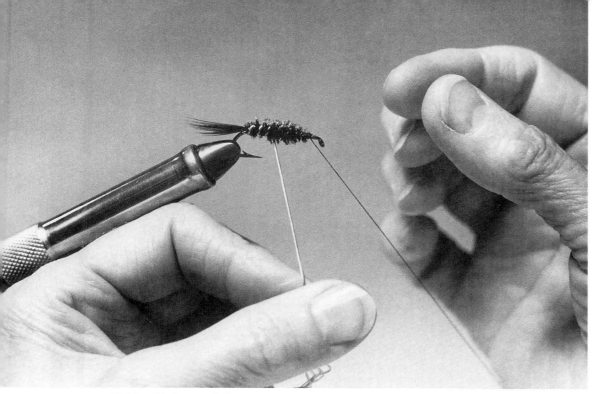

With all three of the strands twisted into a very tight cord, the floss ribs can be wound close together, making tiny bright ridges along the peacock herl.

stub ends. The rib is wound on after the body has been fashioned.

For the first fly in this sixth stage, our pattern will be a Dark Turkey. Make a short tag with fine, flat, gold tinsel. Select a few flues of brown turkey for the tail and use red silk thread for the rib. Wind it carefully over the body of peacock herl. As an alternative, a fine twisted strand of red floss is a good substitute for the thread. Make the hackle of dark grouse and the wing of dark brown turkey.

Although a variation of this pattern specifies a wing made of brown mallard, it is only logical that when "turkey" is in the name, a turkey feather should be used in the fly.

For the second pattern, the Howell, make a short tag of narrow, flat, gold tinsel, a tail of a few flues of claret-dyed hackle, and use the same strand of tinsel as a rib over the herl body. The hackle for this pattern should be dyed the color of deep red wine. Finish this fly with a wing of white-tipped turkey.

When tinsel for the tag and for the rib are the same color and the same width, as for the Howell, use the same strand of tinsel for both ("continuous tinsel" technique). Cutting the tinsel after the tag

has been wound would necessitate having to tie it on again in order to make the rib. So, after the tag is securely in place and the tail has been tied on, fold the tinsel strand carefully back, out of the way, to permit the body material to be tied on where tail and tinsel meet.

When the body material has been wound on and secured, pick up the strand of tinsel, making sure it does not kink, and wrap it once around the hook where tail and body meet. When you have done this, spiral the tinsel forward along the body and secure it.

Practice using "continuous tinsel" for tag and rib wherever a pattern indicates the same color and size of tinsel for both. It not only saves time, it requires fewer windings of tying thread in an area where you want to avoid bulk.

Now, with a tail of golden pheasant tippet added to the Brown Hackle Peacock, bind the herl body with a rib of red floss, finish with a wing of brown turkey, and you will have a Hardy's Favorite. This is an old fly pattern, probably predating the Hardy's catalog of 1921 in which it appears, along with the Coachman of earlier fame and many other patterns considered standards today.

Our next pattern, the Light Caddis, is based on

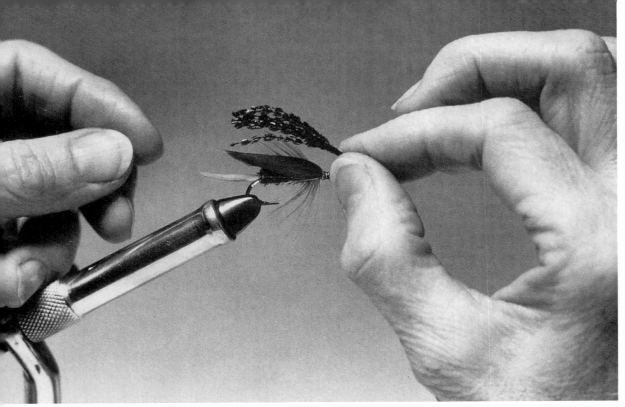

Whenever peacock sword feathers are used for a wing or for a decorative part of it, the herls must be chosen carefully so that they will all arch in the same direction. Measured to the length of the wet-fly wing, the sword feathers will make a very beautiful addition to this fly, a Warwick.

the Leadwing Coachman, with a tag, tail, and tip added. Begin by tying on a short silver tag and a golden pheasant-tippet tail. (Refer to the instructions for using the tippet feather for a tail on the Bog Fly, the third pattern in the fifth stage of this fly form.) This time, use an orange-floss rib instead of the red one you used on the Hardy's Favorite. Brown hackle and a light slate-colored wing of goose or duck will complete the pattern. Finish our herl-bodied fly with a black wrap-knot head.

The Warwick pattern has a fine silver-tinsel tag, a tail of goose dyed orange, and a rib of fine gold tinsel over the peacock-herl body. Use an orange hackle and make the wing of black-dyed goose. In addition, this pattern has a few strands of peacock-sword feathers as part of the wing. When you select the sword feathers, make sure that the natural curve is the same in all of them. Hold them to arch over the wing, with the tips meeting the end of the wing already in place. Grasp them with your left hand and tie them on. Carefully trim and taper the stub ends to leave as little bulk as pos-

sible. Finish with a neat and smoothly tied head. This is a very handsome fly and an effective one for fishing.

The sixth fly is based on the Grizzly Hackle Peacock of the first stage of these herl-bodied flies. The Francis Fly has no tip. It does have a tail of paired grizzly-hackle tips, or very small matching hackles. It has a dark red silk-thread rib over its herl body, and a grizzly hackle. It is winged with a pair of the gray body feathers from the jungle fowl, not the "eyed" ones. This handsome feather has a narrow light edge and a wide dark gray center with a white quill streaking through it. Carefully selected dark list, or badger, hackles, relatively short, can be substituted for the jungle fowl body feathers in order to have the dark center as wide as possible in proportion to the hook size. It is doubtful that a fish would hesitate to strike because of this substitution.

The last two patterns have brown tying-thread heads.

The Lynne and the Frame's Choice comprise all of the foregoing stages. The latter dates back to

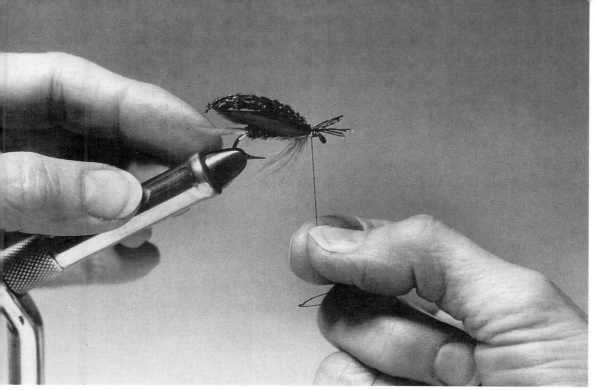

The peacock sword herls are tied in place over the wet-fly wing. Clip off the stub ends and finish the fly with a wrap-knot head.

Comparing badger hackles (left) *to body feathers of the jungle fowl* (right) *shows similarities and differences. To use a pair of badger hackles as an acceptable substitute for jungle-fowl feather wings, tie a narrow strip of white goose along each side of the wings to cover the central quill.*

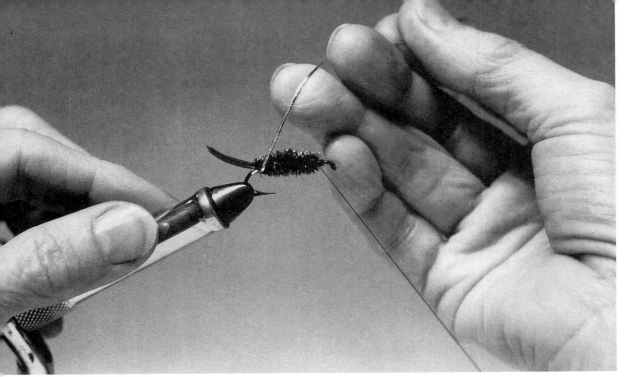

This is oval tinsel, to be used for ribbing on fly patterns that specify it, such as the Lynne and the Frame's Choice.

the turn of the century, and it is an excellent pattern used in the Midwest and on favorite streams across the country, often as a "starter" fly.

Variations

With everything there are variations, and fly tying is no exception. The variations here are other combinations of the component parts of the previous stages. Thus, a rib may be added to a pattern that has no tail, a tail may be added while a wing is omitted, or a pattern may be tied with a wing but no hackle.

Fly tying has always seemed to be a challenge to the individual tyer's ingenuity. No combination of color, material, or structure has been too strange or elaborate to escape a tyer's effort to achieve what he considers the ultimate in an irresistible lure—good at all times under all conditions!

Oval tinsel will make a heavier, bolder rib than will flat tinsel of the same width because it is thicker in diameter.

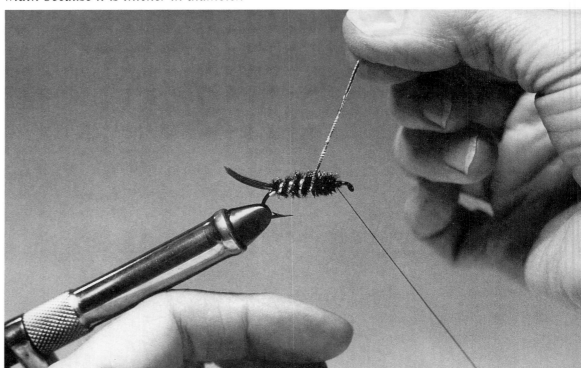

Herl Body

Name of Pattern	Tag	Tail	Rib	Body	Hackle	Wing
Dark Turkey	Gold	Brown Turkey	Red Thread	Peacock Herl	Dark Grouse	Brown Turkey
Howell	Gold	Light Claret	Fine Gold	Peacock Herl	Deep Wine	White Tippet Turkey
Hardy's Favorite	———	Tippet	Red Floss	Peacock Herl	Brown	Brown Turkey
Light Caddis	Silver	Tippet	Orange Floss	Peacock Herl	Brown	Light Slate Goose
Warwick	Silver	Orange Goose	Fine Gold	Peacock Herl	Orange	Peacock Sword over Black Goose
Francis Fly	———	Grizzly Hackle	Dark Red Floss	Peacock Herl	Grizzly	Jungle Fowl Body Feather, or Short Dark Badger Hackle

Additional Patterns							
Name of Pattern	Tag	Tail	Tip	Rib	Body	Hackle	Wing
Henshall	———	Peacock Sword	———	White Floss	Peacock Herl	Grizzly	Light Gray Mottled Turkey
Lynne	Silver	Slate Goose	Light Green Floss	Oval Silver	Peacock Herl	Honey Furnace	Pale Slate Goose
Frame's Choice	Gold	Lemon Yellow Goose	Lemon Yellow Floss	Oval Gold	Peacock Herl	Brown Grizzly	Pale Slate Goose
Scarlet Peacock	Gold	Scarlet Goose	Scarlet Floss	Flat Gold	Peacock Herl	Scarlet	Gray Goose
Lady M	Silver	Tippet	Black Ostrich	Silver	Peacock Herl	Gray	Cinnamon with Black
Gold-Ribbed Brown Shad	Gold	Brown Wisps	Brown Floss	Gold	Peacock Herl	Furnace	Dark Turkey

	Pattern	Tag	Tail	Tip	Rib	Body	Hackle	Wing
Tailless with Rib	American Alder	———	———	———	Rusty Red Sewing Silk	Peacock Herl	Black-Tipped Furnace	Black-Dyed Duck
	Shad Fly	———	———	———	Silver	Peacock Herl	Brown	Brown Turkey
Wingless with Tail	Orange Tag	———	Orange Floss Tuft	———	———	Peacock Herl	Ginger	———
Wingless with Tail and Rib	Mouse Hackle	———	Red, Brown Hackle Tips	———	Gold	Peacock Herl	Grizzly and Brown	———
	Speck	———	Guinea	———	Silver	Black Ostrich Herl	Black	———
Wingless with Tail, Tag, and Tip	Don's Dependable	Gold	Teal	Blue-Gray Floss	———	Peacock Herl	Honey Grizzly	———
	Dermot	Silver	Swords	Orange Floss	———	Peacock Herl	Orange	———
Wing and Tag without Hackle, Tail, or Rib	March Dun	Gold	———	———	———	Peacock Herl	———	Light Slate Goose
Wing and Rib without Tail or Hackle	Winged Shad	———	———	———	Green Floss	Peacock Herl	———	Mottled Brown Turkey
Body and Wing only	Light Olive Gnat	———	———	———	———	Peacock Herl	———	Slate Goose Tinted Olive

Brown Wren	Gray Hackle	Green Grub	Case Worm	Brown Sandy	None Such
Thacher	Cardinal	Claret Gnat	Fosnot	House Fly	Forest Fly
Black Imp	Beeman	Yellow Moth	White Moth	Red Oak Fly	Black Cap
Perry	Nez Perce	Proctor	White Miller	Riley Fly	Grannom Gray
Gray Moth	Yellowstone	Blue Miller	Rio Grande Queen	Rube Wood	Ben Bent
Ingersoll	Florence	Orange Miller	Green Turkey	Blue Turkey	P.J.

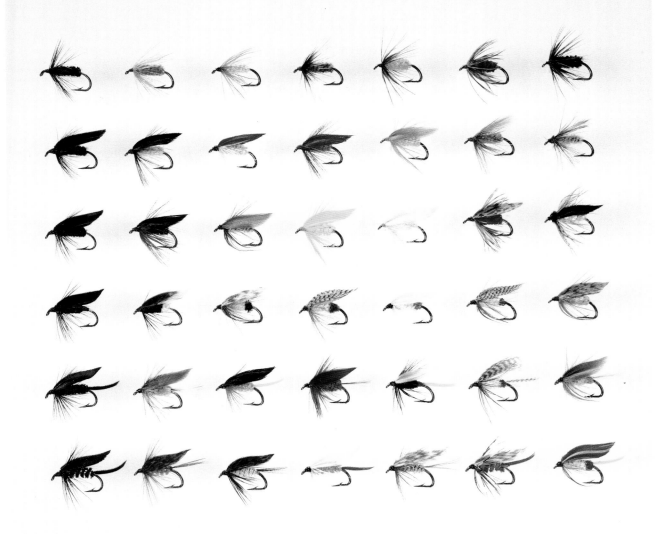

Only an idle little stream
Whose amber waters softly gleam
Where I may wade, through woodland shade
And cast the fly — and loaf — and dream

Henry Van Dyke, "When Tulips Bloom"

Chenille Body
The Second Fly Form

First Stage: Body and Hackle

Chenilles of many colors, several thicknesses, and different fibers are available from companies that furnish fly-tying materials. There are other sources as well: tag sales, yard sales, and antique shops, and these should not be overlooked. They often prove to be treasure troves of handcraft materials that have been stored away in attics and forgotten for many years. A veritable gold mine awaits the fly tyer who chances upon such a hoard, for chenille was once a very popular household material used for crocheted caps, hats, short jackets, and shawls, among other things. It is no wonder that fishermen found it easily available and appropriated it as an attractive and useful material for their tying. Its very nature suggested to them the soft bodies of insects and worms!

Steaming chenille restores its fluffiness. Chenille-bodied flies that have been flattened in a crowded fly box can be restored to their original shapes by this simple method.

Chenilles made of cotton have a firm, velvety texture, while others, made of a synthetic, may have a deeper pile and a looser appearance. Some chenilles have metallic-like strands intermingling with silk-like strands, and there is one made entirely of a reflective tinsel-like material.

If the plain colors available are not suitable for your needs, white chenille can be dyed quite easily.

The technique of tying the flies in this stage is the same for all. By tying several of each pattern you will soon have a very impressive store of flies on hand. As you progress from one fly to the next you will find that each successive one seems to be mastered more easily.

Choose a strand of ginger-colored chenille for the first pattern in this first stage. Select a strand in good proportion to the size of your hook. Remove a bit of the chenille at the end of the strand to reveal the thread core.

With a tying thread of light brown or ginger to match the chenille, bind the thread core onto the hook above the barb. Wind the thread along the hook toward the eye to have it ready for tying off the chenille after the body is wound. Wind the body with close turns of the chenille, covering the tying thread and making the body nicely compact.

When the body has been wound and the chenille has been caught with the tying thread, clip off the chenille a short distance beyond and remove the

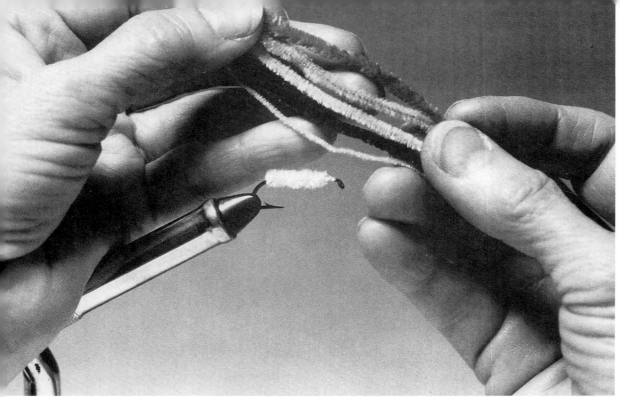

Select a strand of chenille that is best for the size of the hook on which it is to be used. On a hook like this, a fine strand would make a very thin body. It would be a waste of precious material to use that fine strand to build up a fatter body. The use of a heavier or thicker chenille on a hook this size would make the body both bulky and ungainly.

In order to tie a chenille body that tapers, a fine strand tied in first would make a small end for the body. A second strand, larger in diameter, would be used to finish the body. However, when a single strand of chenille suitable for a hook this size is used, the body will have a blunt end. This contour can be altered by trimming the chenille.

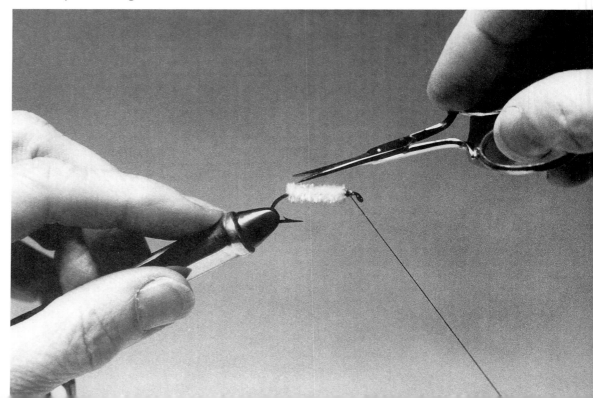

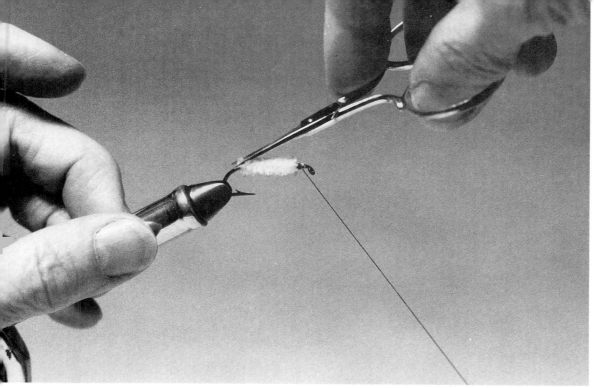

Clip away the chenille, a little at a time, from the tip of the body. Be careful not to nick the central core of twisted threads that hold the chenille together.

Bracing the scissors against your thumb gives you better control as you clip away the chenille above the barb. The rounded tip now gives the fly a tapered end, and a very different appearance.

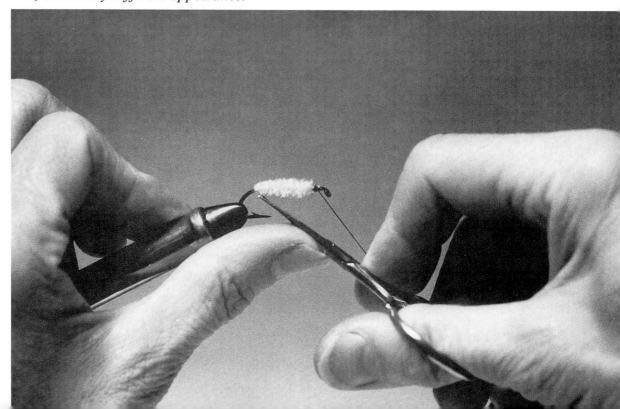

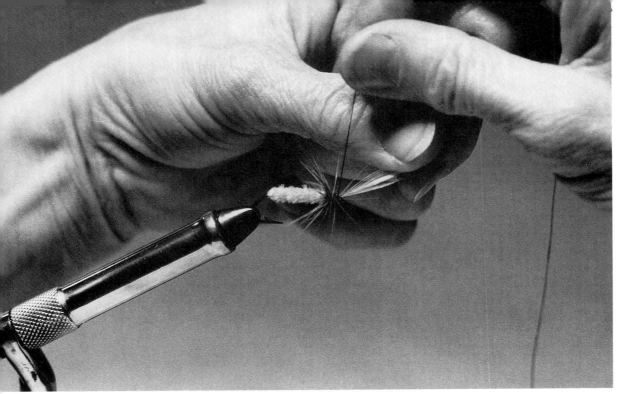

Chenille body and hackle complete the first stage in the second fly form.

fibers, again exposing the core of threads. Bind the core to the hook with two or three close turns of thread.

Select a light ginger-colored hackle of medium length and wind it on sparsely, to turn back over the fly body. Carefully clip off the hackle quill and complete the fly with a light brown head made with the tying thread. Your first fly in this first stage of the chenille-bodied flies is a Brown Wren.

Following the same procedure, select a strand of white chenille and a gray hackle. Although the body is white, you may use black tying thread. Just make sure the black thread is completely covered by the chenille and hackle except for the head of the fly. Your second pattern is a Gray Hackle, named only for the color of its hackle.

Use a ginger-colored tying thread for the next pattern because it will have a ginger-colored head. Make the body of the Green Grub with olive green chenille and use a list, or badger, hackle. At a quick glance, the dark centers of these hackles make it appear that the hackles are short, dark ones, but then the glint of the pale barbs is noticed. Perhaps this is the way a fish observes them, with the transitory sheen of light on the flues (or barbs) suggesting a natural lifelike movement.

Case Worm is the name of the next wet-fly pattern, and it might also be called a "Furnace and Yellow," after the materials with which it is made. Choose yellow chenille for this fly. Add a furnace hackle with flues a trifle longer than the hackles on the first three patterns. (A furnace hackle is the brown version of the badger hackle, having reddish brown flues and a very dark center.) Although the body is yellow, black tying thread may be used. Wind the hackle on sparsely two or three turns of it, and finish the fly with a neat black wrap-knot head.

For the Brown Sandy, use the same color thread you did for the Green Grub, since it, too, will have a ginger-colored head. Select dark brown chenille for the body and wind it on as closely as possible, overlapping a bit in the middle to make the body swell somewhat in the center of the hook. A small grouse feather will make a beautiful hackle for this pattern. Choose one that has flues about the length of the fly body and tie it on with the dull side away from the eye of the hook. Use one more turn around the hook with this feather than you used on the first four patterns.

Your sixth fly is very dark: a dark bluish black chenille body with a dyed-black hackle. The flues of this hackle should be no longer than that for the Brown Sandy, and it should be just as full. This is your None Such, an excellent fly that can be tied on all the smaller hooks.

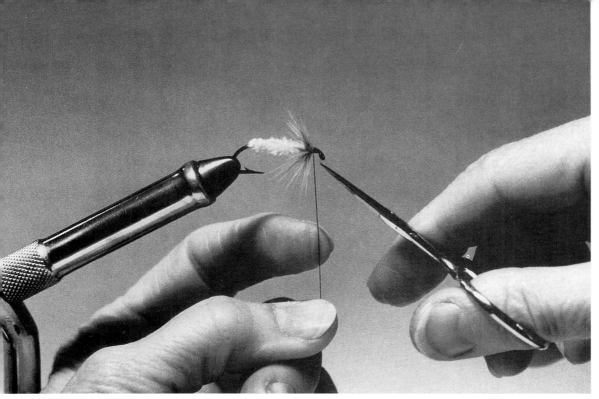

The choice of color for body or hackle often constitutes the only difference between one pattern and another.

Name of Pattern	Body	Hackle	Head
Brown Wren	Ginger Chenille	Light Ginger	Ginger (or Light Brown)
Gray Hackle	White Chenille	Gray	Black
Green Grub	Olive Green Chenille	List or Badger	Ginger
Case Worm	Yellow Chenille	Furnace	Black
Brown Sandy	Brown Chenille	Grouse	Ginger
None Such	Blue-Black Chenille	Black	Black
Additional Patterns			
Early Stone	Yellow Chenille	Straw (with Gray Center)	Dark Gray
Grouse and Orange	Orange Chenille	Grouse	Orange
Black Midge	Fine Black Chenille	Black	Black (very small hooks)
Black Sandy	Black Chenille	Brown	Dark Orange
Gray Gnat	Greenish Gray Chenille	Guinea	Dark Green
Brown Midge	Brown Chenille	Dark Brown	Red (very small hooks)

Second Stage: With Wings

A pattern dating from 1893 is the Thacher, a very useful fly today. Its white chenille body, black hackle, and wing of black-dyed goose make a dramatic color combination. However, the black hackle is not dyed and its dull underside has a brownish tinge. Tied on with the dull side away from the hook eye, it almost has the effect of two hackles mixed together. Since the body is white and the tying thread is black, the chenille should be wound on very carefully to make sure the thread does not show anywhere along the body.

The same attention is important for the second pattern, which also has a white chenille body. The hackle for the Cardinal is white, but the wing is bright red, of dyed goose.

Our third pattern is claret: claret chenille, claret hackle, and claret wing. And the name, appropriately, is the Claret Gnat. If you are dyeing the material for this pattern, dye it all in the same session so that it will all match as nearly as the

difference in materials will permit. For tying the Claret Gnat, use a claret-colored tying thread.

The Fosnot is tied with light gray tying thread, a yellow chenille body, light blue hackle, and a light gray wing. The gray wing may be made of light slate goose or duck. A gray wrap-knot head will complete this pattern.

The next pattern is the House Fly. Tie this one with a red-brown thread in order to give the fly a head of the same color. Use greenish gray chenille for the body. Select a greenish tan hackle with fairly short flues, and wind on two or three turns of it. To obtain this color for the hackle use a light brown one that has been tinted light green—the result is excellent for this pattern. When you are dyeing hackles, try to dye some for all sizes of hooks so that you will have them ready when you may need them.

The gray wings of the House Fly are a pair of very small hackles or hackle tips. Tie them on so that they will lie back over the fly body with their

Name of Pattern	Body	Hackle	Wing	Head
Thacher	White Chenille	Natural Black	Dyed Black Goose	Black
Cardinal	White Chenille	White	Bright Red Goose	Black
Claret Gnat	Claret Chenille	Claret	Claret-dyed Goose	Claret
Fosnot	Yellow Chenille	Light Blue	Light Slate Gray Goose	Light Gray
House Fly	Greenish Gray Chenille	Greenish Tan	Gray Hackles	Reddish Brown
Forest Fly	Gray Chenille	Brown Grizzly	Brown Grizzly Hackles	Claret Ostrich and Black Thread
Additional Patterns				
Nonpareil	Black Chenille	Dyed Black	White Goose	Black
Yellow and Black	Yellow Chenille	Dyed Black	Yellow Goose	Black
Lady Bird	Light Yellow Chenille	Badger Dyed Yellow	Mottled Gray Turkey	Black
Light Polka	White Chenille	White	Guinea Fowl	Black
Grass Green Dun	Bright Green Chenille	Light Grayish Tan	Dark Gray Goose	Brown
Yellow Robin	Yellow Chenille	Yellow	Slate Goose	Black

dull sides downward, and with their tips about even with the end of the hook. As you tie them on, separate them slightly with the tying thread and finish the fly with a neat red-brown head.

The Forest Fly has a body of gray chenille. The flues of its brown grizzly hackle should reach to the hook's barb. Tie on the narrow brown grizzly-hackle wings so that they will lie back over the body, and separate them slightly as you did for the House Fly.

After the wings are in place, but before you finish tying the head of the Forest Fly, make a tiny collar immediately in front of the base of the wings with a very short and fine strand of ostrich herl that has been dyed claret. You will find that two or three turns of the ostrich herl will be ample. This herl collar will cover some of the tying thread binding the wing. Tie the herl securely using a wrap knot, which will complete the head of the fly at the same time. The collar thus becomes part of the head, and very little of the wrap knot will show behind the eye of the hook. For this detail, refer to the black-and-white photos of the Waters (an additional pattern of the fourth stage in the first fly form), which also has a herl collar forming part of the head.

Compare the Nonpareil with the Thacher. The body and wing colors are simply reversed.

Third Stage: With Tag

The Black Imp is our first pattern in this third stage of the chenille-bodied flies. It is also the first to have a colored tag. Make the tag for this fly with red tinsel and the body with black chenille. Add a bright red hackle and a wing of black-dyed goose to make a striking pattern that is both dark and bright.

The second pattern is a Beeman. It has a silver tag and a body of light green chenille. Make its medium-length hackle a brown one, and tie on a wing of gray turkey or gray goose.

The next two Moth patterns have bodies, hackles, and wings of one color, as their names indicate. For the Yellow Moth use yellow tying thread. Give it a gold tag and a body of yellow chenille. Make the wing for this pattern with white goose

To a yellow chenille body and a badger hackle that has been tinted yellow, add a wing of mottled gray turkey. Measure the wings for length, their tips to extend beyond the hook no more than the length of the hook gape. Hold the wings in place with the left hand and bind them on.

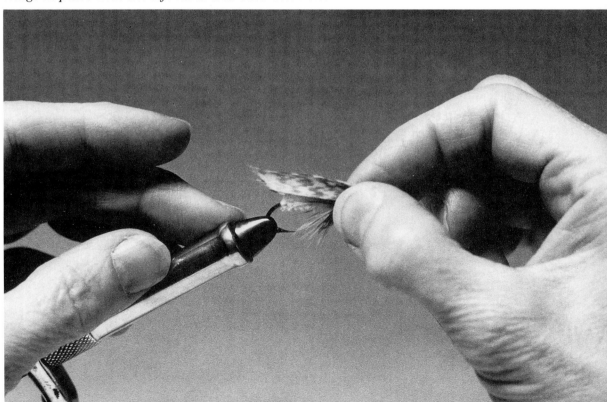

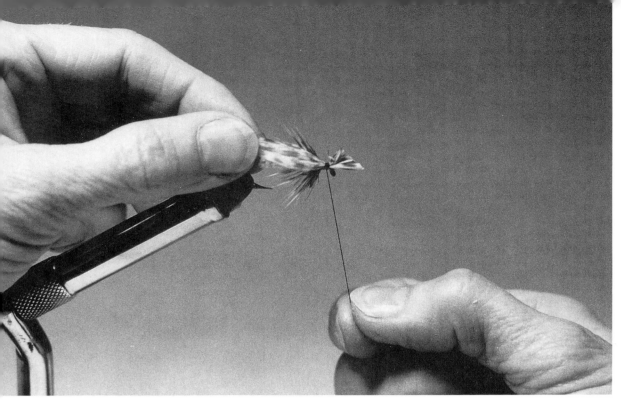

These hopper-like wings cover the shoulders of the fly, an additional pattern called Lady Bird.

Trim and taper the rough stub ends of the wing feathers. Leave as little of the material as possible . . .

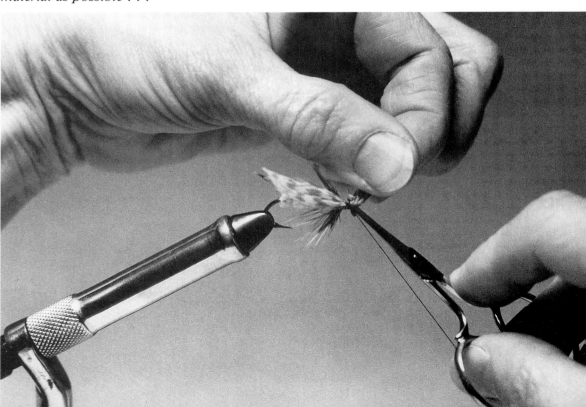

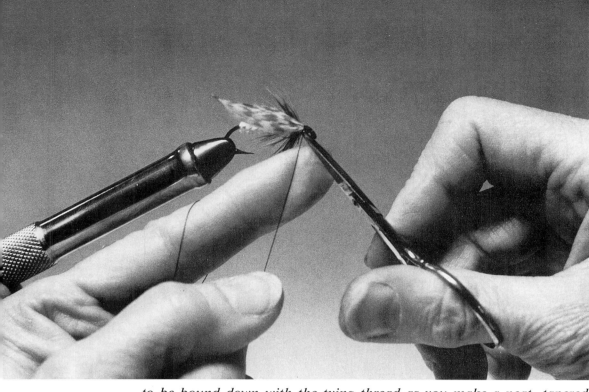

. . . to be bound down with the tying thread as you make a neat, tapered head. The hackles of this fly protrude above, from between the wings, and show below the body also.

Name of Pattern	Tag	Body	Hackle	Wing	Head
Black Imp	Red	Black Chenille	Bright Red	Black Goose	Black
Beeman	Silver	Light Green Chenille	Brown	Gray Turkey or Goose	Black
Yellow Moth	Gold	Yellow Chenille	Yellow	Yellow Goose	Yellow
White Moth	Silver	White Chenille	White	White Goose	Light
Red Oak Fly	Silver	Red Chenille	Grouse	Light Mottled Turkey	Black
Black Cap	Silver	Light Blue Chenille	Partridge	Black Goose	Peacock-Herl Collar and Black Head
Additional Patterns					
Brown Moth	Gold	Brown Chenille	Brown	Brown Hen	Brown
Wasp	Gold	Yellow and White Chenille Alternating	Brown	Black Goose	Brown
Red Drake	Silver	Red and White Chenille Alternating	Scarlet and White	Mallard with White Strips	Black
Strawberry	Gold	Scarlet Chenille	White	Grass Green Goose	Black
Brown Deer	Gold	Brown Chenille	Honey Dun	Gray Goose Tinted Brown	Brown
Winnie's Hopper	Gold	Yellow Chenille	Brown	Mottled Turkey	Black

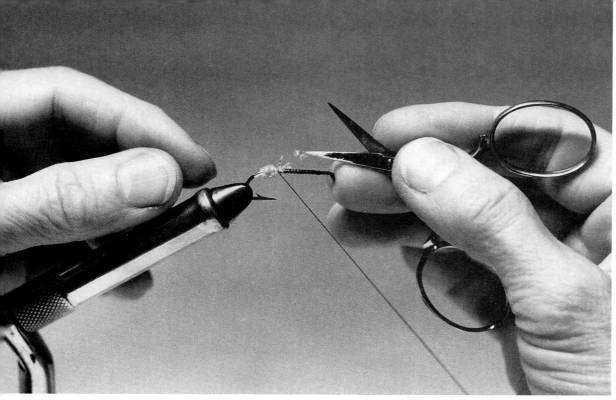

When chenille is used to make a tip, remove the fluff from the core of threads at the cut end before you bind these threads down completely. This will minimize any bulkiness beneath whatever additional body material you may use.

that has been dyed yellow to match both body and hackle.

The White Moth has a silver tag, and for this fly use a pale gray or white tying thread. Although the body, hackle, and wing are white, the head will turn out to be a little darker than pure white, even though a white tying thread is used. Waxing the thread will darken it a little.

Our fifth pattern is called the Red Oak Fly. It, too, has a silver tag. Make the body with red chenille. Use a small grouse feather for the hackle. Because the individual flues of the grouse feather are heavier than those of most wet-fly hackles, two or three turns of it around the hook will give the appearance of a rather full hackle.

Make the wing for this pattern with light mottled-oak turkey. (See the black-and-white photos for the Lady Bird, second stage.) Finish the Red Oak Fly with a neat black wrap-knot head and you will add another good fly to your growing supply of wet flies.

For the Black Cap make another silver tag. This time, use light blue chenille for the body. Select a partridge feather with its delicate marking to use

for the hackle. Partridge hackles appeared on lists of English fly patterns as early as 1496. The black cap here is the feather wing made from the glossy black-dyed goose feather that furnished the wings for the Thacher and the Black Imp. Forming part of the head immediately in front of the wing, make a little collar as you did for the Forest Fly, using short peacock herl this time instead of ostrich herl.

Fourth Stage: With Tip

We are ready now to add tips to our chenille-bodied flies. The application of the chenille to the hook should go smoothly. Make sure that, as you wind the Chenille on, it covers the tying thread completely.

The black silhouette in the color plate for this stage is shown with a floss tip in order to emphasize it as this particular stage in tying the second fly form. However, the tips of the following six patterns are made of chenille. The additional patterns listed below will have the floss tips.

Our first pattern, the Perry, has a silver tag and a tip of palest pink chenille. Against its black che-

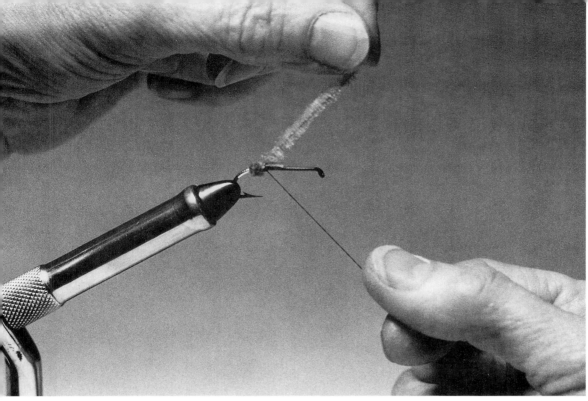

Here we find a tinsel tag in place, and a tip of dark cotton chenille. The rest of the body will be made of the light synthetic chenille that has been tied in, its thread core still showing. The core will be covered by tying thread and chenille.

nille body the tip appears to be almost white. Choose a dyed-black hackle of medium length and use two turns of it. The wing, also of medium length (to the bend of the hook), is white-tipped turkey.

Some of the broad dark turkey feathers end with a rather wide band of white. From this the wing strips must be carefully selected in order to have a small tip of white in proportion to the size of the fly being tied. Occasionally you will discover mottled-oak turkey feathers that are edged in white or very light cream. Set these feathers aside and use them as substitutes for the white-tipped turkey on patterns such as the Perry.

The next pattern is the Nez Perce. Make it with a gold tag and a black chenille tip on a white chenille body. Select a reddish brown wet-fly hackle and make the wing from gray turkey, plain or lightly mottled.

A Proctor, our third pattern in this fourth stage of the second fly form, has no tag. Its olive brown chenille tip occupies about one-third of its body length. The body itself is made with pink chenille—light, but not as pale as the tip on the Perry.

Add to this a light brown hackle and a speckled mallard wing. Although the main part of the body is light, the whole fly can be tied with black tying thread.

The White Miller pattern has no tag, although a silver one could be optional. Tie this fly with black tying thread, because the head is black. Make a small orange chenille tip and use white chenille for the rest of the body. Its hackle and wing are also white. Compare this fly with the fourth pattern in the third stage and you will find that it is a White Moth with an orange tip added.

Our fifth pattern in this stage is the Riley Fly. Here again a tag could be optional, but this pattern omits it. The tip is red chenille. The main part of the body is white. Add to this a brown wet-fly hackle of medium length, sparsely tied. Make the wing from gray speckled mallard, letting its tip extend only a very short way behind the bend of the hook.

The Grannom Gray is our sixth pattern. It has a yellowish green chenille tip. Tie the rest of the body with gray chenille. To these, add a smoky gray hackle and a light brown mottled turkey

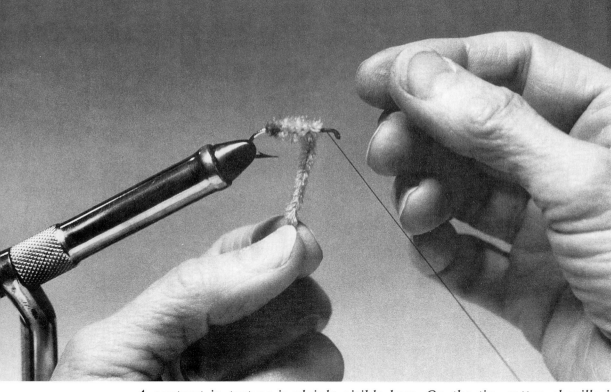

A contrast in texture is plainly visible here. On the tip, cotton chenille is compact, while the light-colored synthetic chenille, loosely bound by its core of twisted threads, is rough in appearance. This demonstrates how different results can be obtained by combining materials made of varying fibers.

Name of Pattern	Tag	Tip	Body	Hackle	Wing	Head
Perry	Silver	Pale Pink Chenille	Black Chenille	Black	White-tipped Turkey	Black
Nez Perce	Gold	Black Chenille	White Chenille	Red-Brown	Gray Turkey	Black
Proctor	——	Olive Brown Chenille	Pink Chenille	Brown	Speckled Mallard	Black
White Miller	——	Orange Chenille	White Chenille	White	White Goose	Black
Riley Fly	——	Red Chenille	White Chenille	Red-Brown	Speckled Mallard	Black
Grannom Gray	——	Yellow-Green Chenille	Gray Chenille	Smoky Gray	Light Brown Mottled Turkey	Black
Additional Patterns						
Yellow Tip	Gold	Yellow Floss	Gray Chenille	Straw Dun	Light Slate Gray	Dark Red
Yellow Spinner	——	Yellow Floss	Yellow Chenille	Light Yellow Grizzly	Light Slate Gray	Black
Riley	——	Black Chenille	White Chenille	Red-Brown	Speckled Mallard	Black
Hackstaff Hackle	——	Orange Floss	White Chenille	Light Gray	White Goose	Black
Yellow Tipped Dun	——	Yellow Chenille	Light Gray Chenille	Light Brown-Gray	Pale Gray Goose	Gray
Fancy Gnat	Gold	Small Bright Orange Floss	Dark Gray Chenille	Greenish Gray, Short	Greenish Gray Hackle Wings Tied Flat	Orange

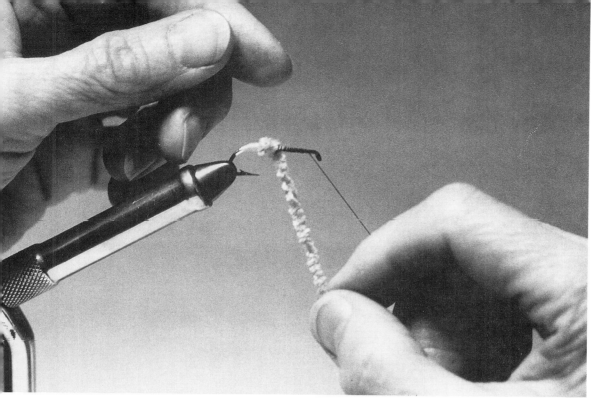

Although the black silhouette for the fourth stage is shown with a floss tip in order to emphasize it, the patterns shown in the color plates have chenille tips. Floss tips will be found among the additional patterns in this stage. Here a tinsel tag and floss tip are in place. The body chenille has been tied on and is covering the bound end of floss that forms the tip.

The square end of the chenille may be trimmed down to meet the floss tip or may be left as it is, making the body appear to be of two parts.

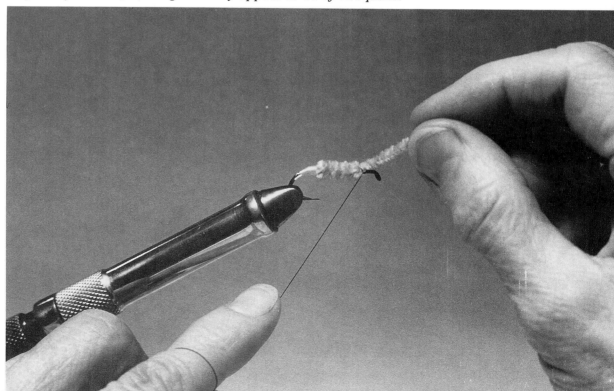

wing. A silver tag on this pattern is optional.

All Gnats can be tied in very small sizes. Whether they are intended to imitate small insects or not, they make very good wet flies in other sizes as well.

You will notice that the Hackstaff Hackle, among the additional patterns above, is the White Miller with a gray hackle instead of a white one, and the Riley differs from the Riley Fly only in the color of its chenille tip.

Fifth Stage: With Tail

In this fifth stage of the second fly form, tails will be added to our chenille-bodied flies. Some will have tags and some will have both tags and tips like those that were added to the preceeding stages in this form.

The first pattern, then, will be a Gray Moth. Unlike its predecessors, the Yellow Moth and the White Moth, this one will have not only a gold tag but a tail as well. Make the tail of a few wisps of grizzly hackle and the body with a medium gray chenille. The grizzly hackle from which the wisps for the tail were taken can now be tied on. For the wing, select gray goose that is a little darker than the gray chenille you chose for the body. Tie it on, over the body and hackle. Complete your Gray Moth with a black wrap-knot head.

The Yellowstone is a cheerful pattern with a gold tag. It can be tied with black tying thread since it, too, will be completed with a black head. The tail for this pattern is made with a few strands of yellow goose, about the length of the hook. It has a body of yellow chenille and an orange hackle with a short-to-medium length of flue that will reach the point of the hook. The wing is black-dyed goose.

Our Blue Miller has a gold tag, and the blue wisps for its tail can be taken from the dyed blue feather you will use for the hackle. An extra turn of the hackle around the hook will make it just a trifle heavier than the sparsely tied hackles you have been using. The chenille body and wing are intensely blue. Try to match the dyed goose for the wing to the blue of the chenille. Dyeing white chenille, white goose, and white hackles in the same dyeing session is always a good idea. Use black tying thread for this fly.

With a tip as well as a tag, the Rio Grande Queen is our next pattern. Using black tying thread, tie on a short gold tag. Use strands of goose dyed yellow for the tail, which should be no longer than the overall length of the hook. Use red floss for the tip, and make it short and tapered. The body itself is black chenille. Complete this pattern with a black hackle and a white goose wing. And, of course, a neat, tapered wrap-knot head.

A Rube Wood also has a gold tip. Make the tail with a few wisps of teal or speckled mallard. More fragile in texture and in handling are the teal and mallard flank and breast feathers, which resemble each other somewhat in appearance, but with practice they too can be used for beautiful fly wings. This famous pattern has a scarlet chenille tip on a white chenille body. Use a brown hackle of medium length on this fly. When you tie on the wing of teal or speckled mallard, measure carefully so that the tip will reach slightly beyond the bend of the hook but not to the end of the tail. The wing should arch over the body.

The sober pattern for the Ben Bent is very like that for the Gray Moth. It has a gold tip, but the hackle wisps for this tail are gray rather than grizzly. It also has a small tip of orange chenille on the gray chenille body. A honey dun hackle with a gray center, or a rusty dun hackle, is ideal for this pattern. Make the wing for this fly with gray goose, as you did for your Gray Moth.

Compare the Rio Grande Queen with the Nonpareil of the additional patterns in the second stage. Also compare the Nonpareil with the None Such of the first stage. A white wing added to the None Such has made the Nonpareil. A tail and a red floss tip added to the Nonpareil becomes the pattern for the Rio Grande Queen. The Rio Grande King without a tip has a brown hackle instead of the Queen's black one.

Sixth Stage: With Ribs

The pattern selected for our first ribbed chenille-bodied fly is called an Ingersoll. It has a fine gold-tinsel tag. When the tag is in place, do not cut the tinsel off. Just hold it out of the way while you tie on a few flues of pheasant tail feather for the tail of the fly. Make the tail no longer than

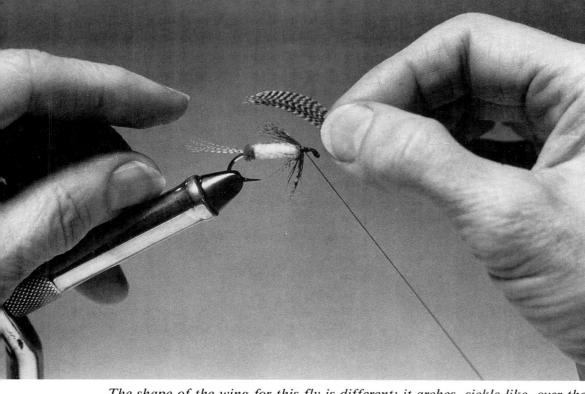

The shape of the wing for this fly is different; it arches, sickle-like, over the fly body. When you hold a barred feather of mallard or teal with its quill upward, the natural curve of its flues is apparent immediately. This curve is used in the wings shown here. Select feathers that match in size as well as in design in order to make a pair that will look the same on both sides of the fly.

The tip of the arched wing is lined up with the bend of the hook. Grasp the wings with your left hand and hold them in place, freeing the right hand to tie them on.

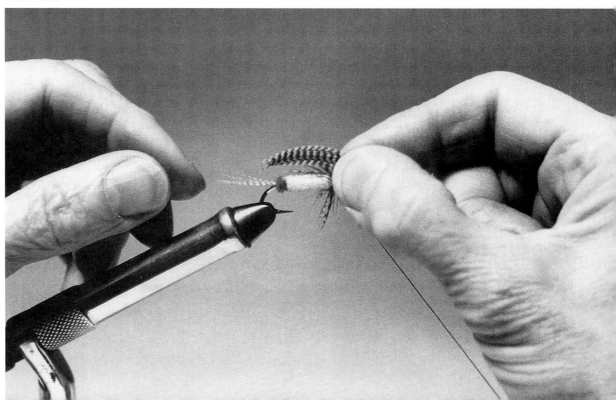

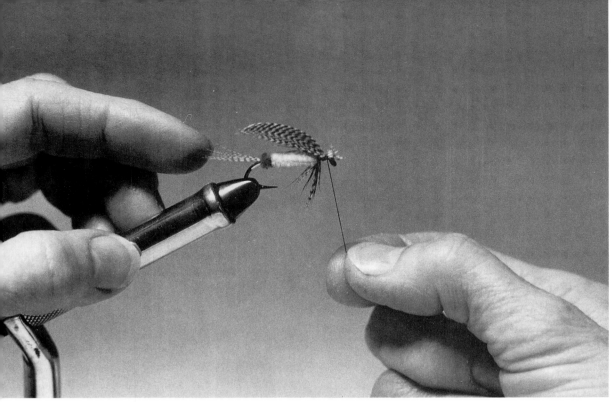

When you have trimmed the stub ends, tapering them away from the hook eye, finish this fly with a wrap-knot head. The wing may retain the sickle shape, or the flues at the wing tip may be permitted to spread, as they do on the Rube Wood shown in the color plate.

When in doubt about the snugness of the wrap knot, it can be made more compact by pinching the threads away from behind the eye as the tying thread is being pulled tight. The loops of the wrap knot will tighten as the pull on the tying thread takes up the small amount of slack.

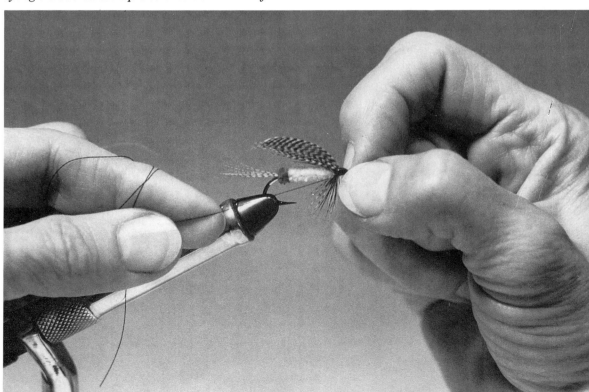

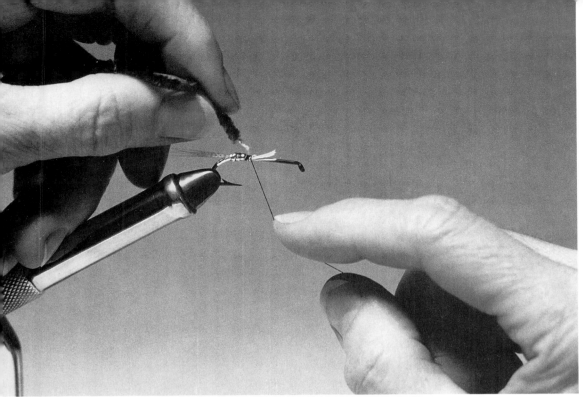

A long tinsel tag and a tail have been tied on. A tip of oval tinsel covers both the ends of the tag and of the tail. Threads of the oval-tinsel core extend beyond the place where the tinsel was nipped off. The core of the chenille is exposed also, and the chenille will be tied as close to the tinsel tip as possible.

The thread cores of both the tinsel and the chenille are bound down smoothly by the tying thread . . .

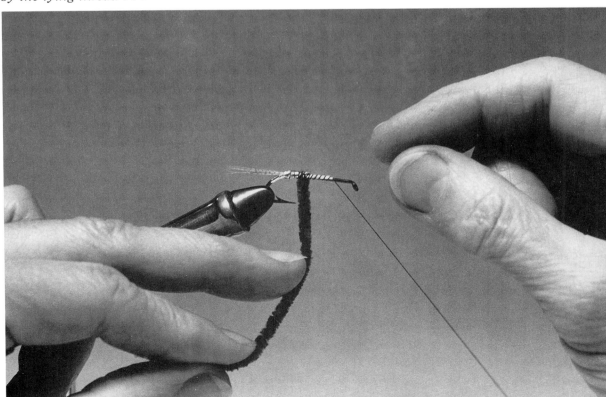

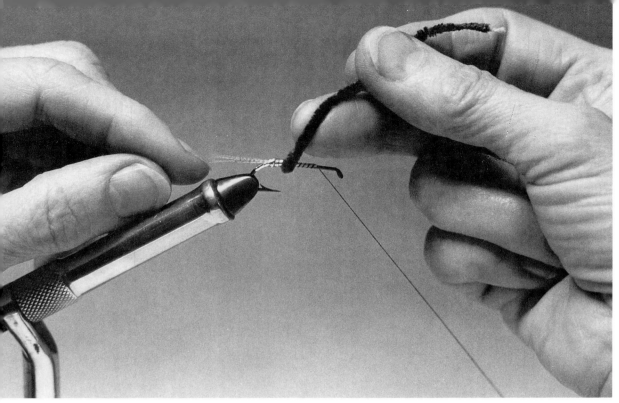

. . . and the first turn of the chenille around the hook meets the tinsel tag, covering the place where they are joined . . .

. . . and as it progresses along the hook the chenille will cover the thread cores entirely to form the rest of the fly body.

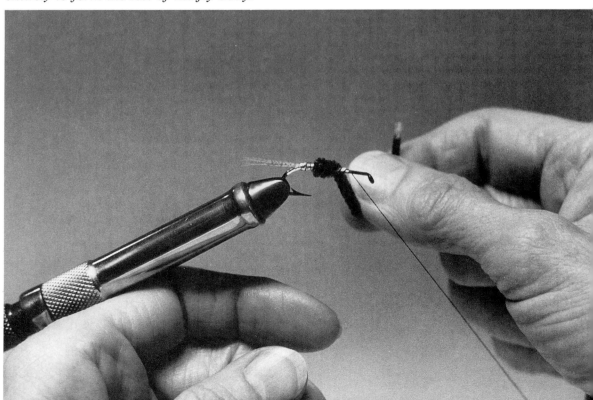

Name of Pattern	Tag	Tail	Tip	Body	Hackle	Wing	Head
Gray Moth	Gold	Grizzly Hackle Wisps	———	Gray Chenille	Grizzly	Gray	Black
Yellowstone	Gold	Yellow Goose	———	Yellow Chenille	Orange	Black	Black
Blue Miller	Gold	Blue Hackle Wisps	———	Blue Chenille	Blue	Blue	Black
Rio Grande Queen	Gold	Yellow Goose	Red Floss	Black Chenille	Black	White	Black
Rube Wood	Gold	Teal or Mallard	Scarlet Chenille	White Chenille	Brown	Teal or Mallard	Black
Ben Bent	Gold	Pale Gray Hackle Wisps	Orange Chenille	Gray Chenille	Honey Dun	Gray	Black
Additional Patterns							
Colorado Willow	Gold	Brown Hackle Wisps	———	Gray Chenille	Brown	Gray	Black
Orange and Blue	Gold	Tippet	Blue Floss	Orange Chenille	Claret	Light Brown Turkey	Black
Cheever	Silver	Lemon Wood Duck	Oval Silver	Bright Red Chenille	White	Black Goose	Black
Dusky Miller	Gold	Blue-Gray Wisps	———	Blue-Gray Chenille	Blue-Gray	Blue-Gray	Black
Rio Grande King	Gold	Yellow Goose	———	Black Chenille	Brown	White Goose	Black
Catbird	Gold	Dark Gray Goose	Dark Red Chenille	Black Chenille	Black	Dark Gray Goose	Black

the body of the fly. Now, fold that strand of gold tinsel back so that it will be in place to become the rib of this pattern.

Carefully tie in a strand of orange chenille over the cut ends of the tail flues and the fold of tinsel, making sure that the tinsel will emerge just between the juncture of the tail and body material. Using this continuous tinsel technique saves a few steps—in cutting the tinsel off after making the tag and in having to tie it on again when you need it for the rib. When both tag and rib are made with tinsel of the same width and color, and when you are tying several flies of the same pattern, this becomes a real time-saver. Wind the tinsel rib over the chenille body. The number of ribs you will be able to make on any chenille body depends on the width of the tinsel you have chosen.

Select a brown hackle for the Ingersoll and use two or three turns of it. Make its wing with strips taken from carefully matched feathers of dark brown mottled turkey. The Ingersoll is a very good pattern to use when hoppers are being fished.

Use a fine silver tinsel for the tag on the Florence. Use a few flues of brown mallard for the tail. Tie on a fine strand of silver tinsel for the rib, over the ends of tinsel tag and mallard tail. In turn, all of the stub ends of these materials will be completely covered by the body material.

For the body of the Florence use pink chenille. Even though the body material is light in color, black tying thread may be used because of the density of the chenille. Spiral the tinsel strand along the chenille body. Select a black hackle. Use two or three turns of it and then, with another rich, dark chocolate brown mottled turkey wing, you will have completed another beautiful fly. The continuous tinsel technique can also be used here very well.

The Orange Miller is exactly the same in construction, beginning with a tag of gold tinsel. About three flues of scarlet goose, the length of the body, will be enough for the tail of this fly. Use a fine gold tinsel for the rib, over a body of orange chenille. The Orange Miller is fashioned with a white hackle that has flues just long enough to reach to the bend of the hook. A wing made of white goose completes this pattern.

The name of the Green Turkey, our next chenille-bodied pattern to have a rib, refers to the color of the body and to the material from which the wing is made. For this pattern, start with a silver tinsel tag.

Since the tag and rib are made with two different colors of tinsel, the continuous tinsel method cannot be used here. Bind off the strand of silver that makes the tag with as few turns of thread as

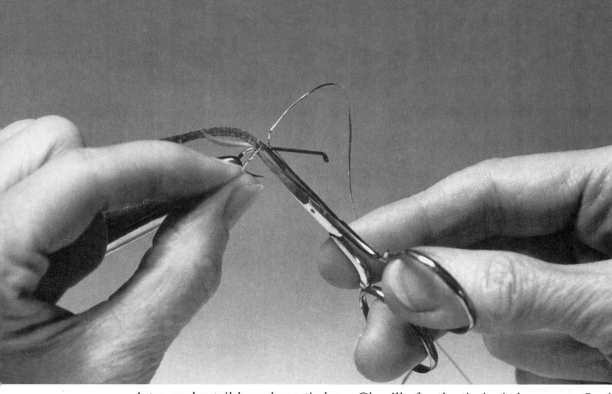

A tag and a tail have been tied on. Chenille for the tip is tied on next. Oval tinsel for the rib is tied on over the stub end of the chenille, and the excess is trimmed away.

possible, and tie on a few brown flues of pheasant for the tail. The central tail feather is excellent for this purpose. Its flues are evenly matched on both sides of the central shaft, and they do not cling together as do the flues of turkey, goose, or duck. Each flue is edged with minute brown herl. These flues are very useful as tails for a pattern such as this one, and for many others.

Next we will tie in a strand of narrow gold for the rib. Hold it out of the way while you make the body with a strand of yellowish green chenille. For the hackle, choose a brown one with flues that will reach to the barb of the hook. Wind it on sparsely after the rib has been wound on and secured. Make the wing of the Green Turkey with strips of mottled gray turkey and finish the fly with a neat black head.

The Blue Turkey pattern is similar to the previous one, but not the same. It has a fine, flat, silver tag. It has a tail made of scarlet goose, but this time the rib is made with a fine oval or round silver tinsel. The body, as the name indicates, is blue. Use a hackle of guinea feather, sparsely tied. The same gray mottled turkey feathers that furnished wing material for the Green Turkey can be

used for winging your Blue Turkey as well.

Now, for a fancier pattern, try a P.J. It has a gold tag and a tail of yellow goose. This pattern calls for a tip and a rib. The rib should be tied on after the tip has been made and should spiral only over the body of the fly—not over the tip. The tip for the P.J. is red chenille. The rib is fine gold wire. Use white chenille for the body itself, and wind the gold wire over it.

If the white chenille you are using is made of a synthetic fiber, its "pile" may be somewhat longer and looser than it would be if it were made of cotton. The result may be a somewhat fuzzy body into which the wire rib will become embedded, there to sparkle intermittently along the body of the fly. Oval tinsel, being wider, would bind down the loose pile, making the ribs more visible.

The wing for a P.J. is a little more elaborate than for any of the foregoing patterns. Make a regular wet-fly wing as you have been doing, with strips of scarlet goose. After the wing is in place, but before you make the wrap-knot head, cut two slender strips of white goose from matching feathers. Lay one strip on each side of the scarlet wing to bisect it. These strips should match the contour

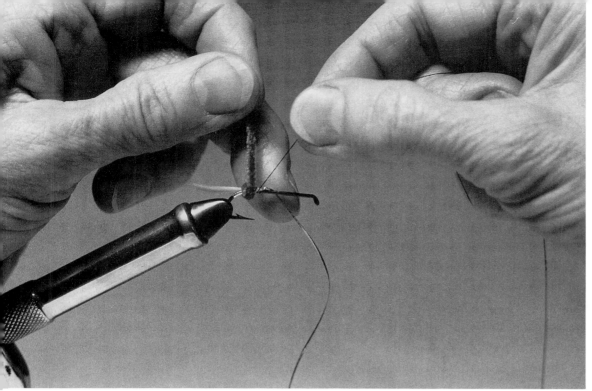

The chenille tip will cover the stub end of the oval tinsel. Here, the tip material is ready to be tied off. The tinsel will be used as a rib over the body only, not over the tip.

Now, with the tip in place, chenille for the body is tied in. The oval tinsel has been laid back out of the way because it will not be needed until the chenille body has been wound on and secured.

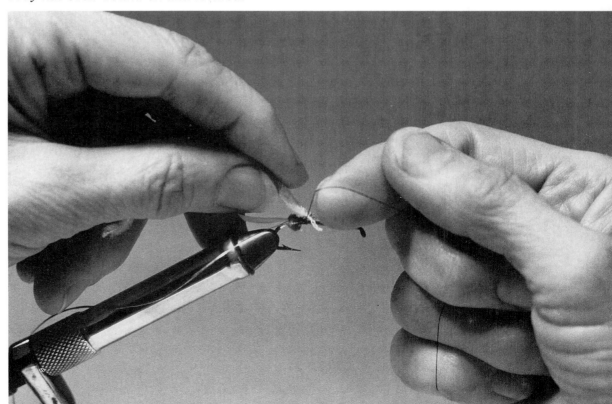

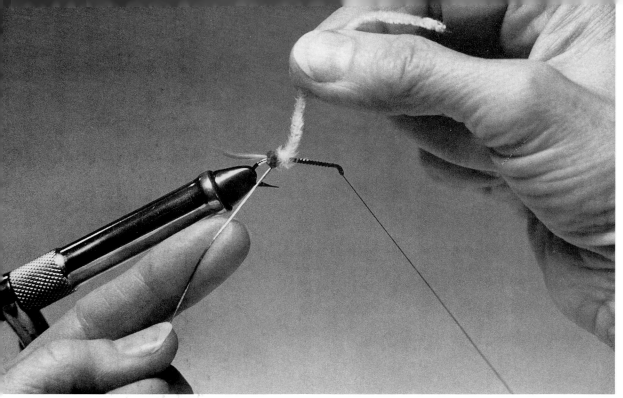

The strand of tinsel can be held out of the way each time the body chenille is transferred to the right hand as it is wound on. Note how the fluffy chenille of the body strand contrasts with the firm fiber of the chenille that makes the tip.

The width of the oval tinsel being used here will permit about five evenly spaced ribs on this chenille body. If a fine, flat, or round tinsel, or wire, were used instead, more ribs would be possible on a body of this size but would be less visible over the chenille.

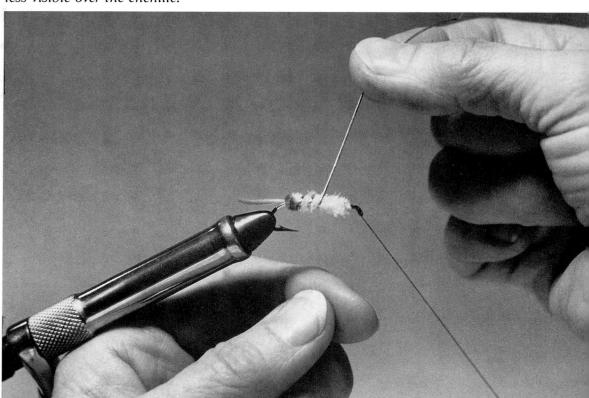

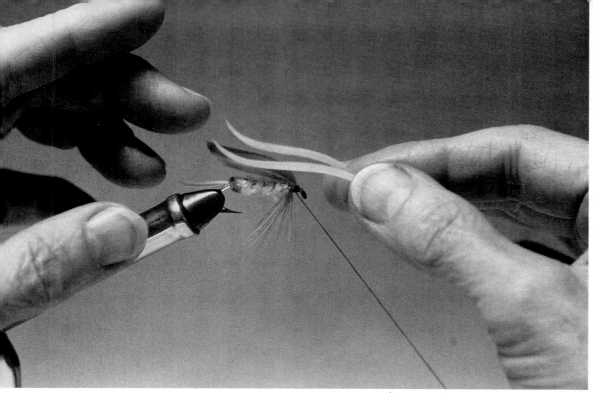

After the primary wing is in place, and before the head has been finished, narrow strips of a contrasting color can be laid on each side. These white strips of goose are being measured against the wing to make sure they are the same length. Grasped by the fingers of the left hand and held in place, they can be tied on.

This simple and decorative touch gives the fly the appearance of having a built *or* married *feather wing. The excess material of the extra strips will be trimmed away.*

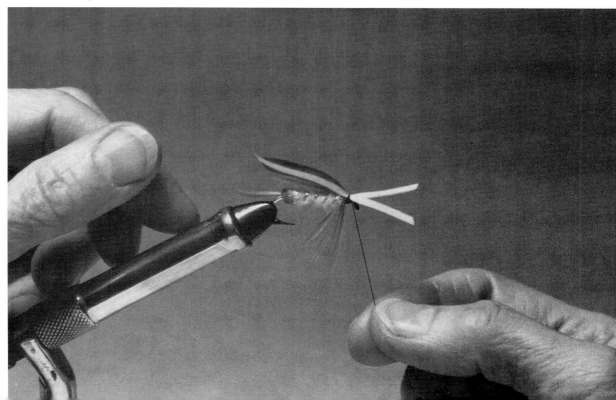

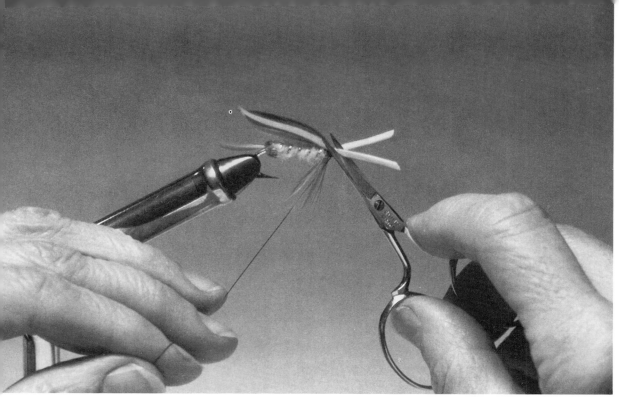

With your scissors held at an angle, clip away each strip separately, making sure that the stub is tapered close to the stubs of the main wing.

Carefully trim the stubs of the additional strips as well as those of the main wing. This will reduce the amount of material over which the tying thread must be wound in order to make the wing secure. When this is done and the wrap knot is tied, the result will be a neatly tapered head—and a very showy fly.

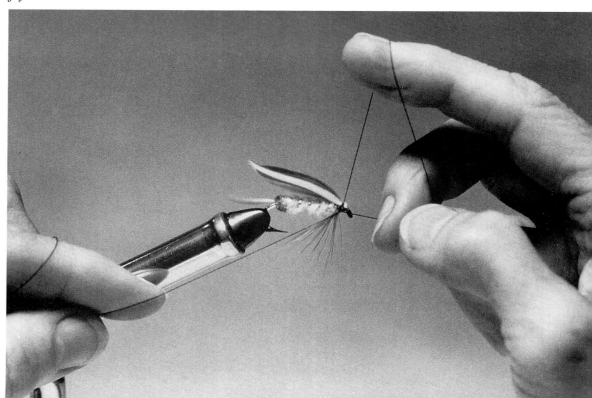

of the scarlet wing. Carefully tie them on against the wing. Trim the cut ends away neatly and complete the pattern with a black head. When you have finished, the result will be a wing that will have the appearance of a built-wing.

The pattern for the Ambrose Bucktail is a departure from the feather-wing and feather-tail flies, but only in the substitution of hair for wing and tail. Feathers are still in use as hackles. It is an excellent pattern for trout, and tied in larger sizes it is a good fly for bass fishing as well. The proportion of hair for the tail and wing, in length, should be about the same as for a feather tail or wing. The amount of hair should be carefully estimated in order to avoid bulkiness.

The Red Drake and Elliott have wings similar to those of the P.J. In construction they are the same; only the colors are different.

Name of Pattern	Tag	Tail	Rib	Tip	Body	Hackle	Wing
Ingersoll	Gold	Pheasant Tail Wisps	Gold	———	Orange Chenille	Brown	Brown Mottled Turkey
Florence	Silver	Brown Mallard	Silver	———	Pink Chenille	Black	Brown Turkey
Orange Miller	Gold	Scarlet Goose	Gold	———	Orange Chenille	White	White Goose
Green Turkey	Silver	Pheasant Wisps	Gold	———	Yellow-Green Chenille	Brown	Gray Mottled Turkey
Blue Turkey	Silver	Scarlet Goose	Silver	———	Blue Chenille	Guinea	Gray Mottled Turkey
P.J.	Gold	Yellow Goose	Gold	Red Chenille	White Chenille	Orange	Scarlet with White Strip on Each Side
Additional Patterns							
Gray Turkey	Silver	Scarlet Goose	Silver	———	Blue Chenille with Red Chenille Shoulder	Guinea	Gray Turkey
Ambrose Bucktail	Oval Gold	Red and White Deer-tail Hair Mixed	Oval Gold	———	Yellow Chenille	Red and Black Mixed	Natural Deer-tail Hair over White
Kendall	Silver	Maroon Hackle Wisps	Flat Silver	———	Maroon Chenille	Dark Maroon	Dark Brown Turkey
Red Quail	Gold	Scarlet Goose	Flat Gold	Gray Chenille	Red Chenille	Scarlet	Light Brown Turkey or Quail
Red Drake	Silver	3 Mallard Wisps	Flat Silver	Red Chenille	Red and White Chenille	Scarlet and White Hackle	Mallard with Scarlet Strips
Elliott	Silver	Pheasant and Scarlet-Hackle Wisps	Silver Wire	———	White Chenille	Green Hackle	Mallard with Scarlet Strips

	Partridge and Green	Grouse and Yellow	Grouse and Orange	Black Hackle Blue	Guinea and Yellow	Little Ginger Wren
	Little Sand Fly	Oak Fly	Field Fly	Orange Sedge	Firefly	Green Bottle Fly
	Fern Fly	Pink Fern Fly	Brown Sedge	Cinnamon Fly	Bunting	Light Olive Dun
	Female Field Fly	Wetzel Grannom	Polka Dot Moth	Golden Spinner	Golden-Eyed Gauze Wing	Olive Spinner
	Gosling	Apple Green	Bright Fox	Watersmeet	Baldwin	Martin
	March Brown	Dark Montreal	Grizzly King	Professor	Fin Fly	Good Evening Fly

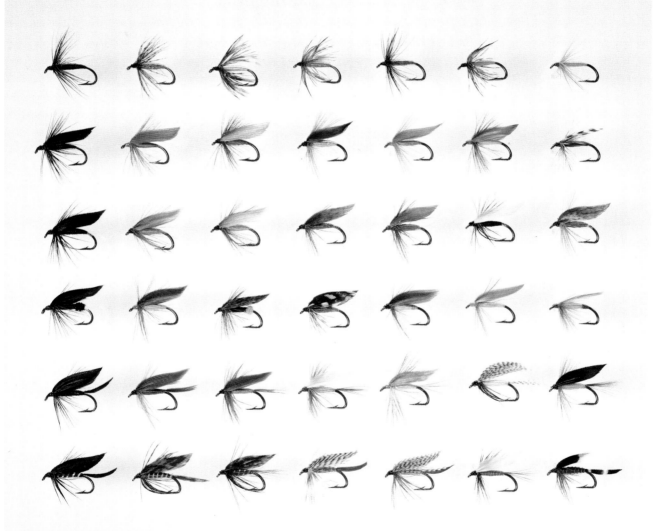

But the time has come when the ice cakes break
And the freshets flood the fields
Then your heart beats quick and you feel the thrill
That comes as a cure for many an ill
with the lure of your rod and reel.

A.F. Brewer, "Song of the Rod and Reel"

Floss Body
The Third Fly Form

First Stage: Body and Hackle

Floss, a material readily available for use in fly tying, may be obtained in many different colors. It is made from both natural and synthetic fibers. Synthetic-fiber flosses tend to be more slick and slippery to handle than silk, but will make beautiful bodies for flies. Floss is found in skeins, twisted loosely or closely, and in several weights. It may also be found on spools, in smooth, untwisted strands. Floss is an indispensable addition to the fly-tyer's stock of materials.

Floss is vulnerable to soilage, and a convenient, inexpensive, and practical way to protect and store the skeins is to wind the strands onto cards cut to fit a covered box. The cards may then be filed by color. In this way, the amount necessary for a particular pattern can be removed and the remainder left undisturbed in the box. In this way, too, excessive handling of an entire skein will be avoided, and the reserve will remain fresh and ready for use. Excessive handling of a skein of floss will soil and roughen it, because it will absorb oil from the fingers. The minute filaments that make up a strand of floss will catch rough fingers, and its smooth and shiny appearance will be dulled and coarsened.

Most of the following simple patterns in this first stage of the third fly form take their names from the colors and feathers from which they are made. All are tied in exactly the same manner— only their colors constitute the differences between them. Whether you tie in the floss at the wing position or the tail position, make the body a slim oval for all of the patterns in this stage.

The first pattern, then, is the Partridge and Green. To make the body, choose a moss green floss from your floss file. Tie a slim oval body, neatly tapered above the barb and swelling slightly in the center of the shank. Keep the floss strand snug and smooth between your fingers as you wind it on. Remember its tendency to slip if all of the filaments are not given the same tension. Use a dark green tying thread.

When the body is tied, touch the tapered end with the tiniest drop of a thin, clear lacquer to hold the fine filaments of floss in place and to prevent them from slipping backward down the bend of the hook (just as you did for the floss tips

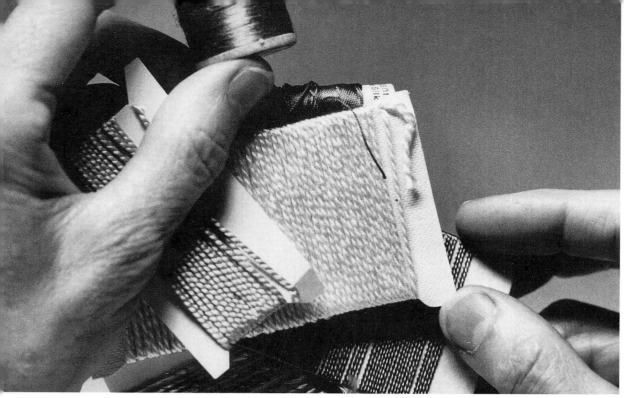

Floss is available in several weights and twists, as well as in smooth strands.

on the herl-bodied flies in the fourth stage of the first fly form).

Choose a partridge hackle of medium length and tie it on, binding the quill end of it to the hook. Grip the tip with your hackle pliers if the feather is too small to be held securely by the tip with your fingers. Wind it on, catch it with the tying thread, and clip off the excess. Complete the fly with a wrap-knot head coated with several applications of very thin head varnish or lacquer, permitting each coat to dry thoroughly before the next one is applied.

Our second pattern is the Grouse and Yellow, with a body of yellow floss. For the hackle, choose a grouse feather, which is a darker brown than the partridge. Make sure the flues of both partridge and grouse hackles curve back over the fly bodies as you wind them on. Make the body with orange floss, and you will have a Grouse and Orange to add to your growing collection.

The next pattern is called a Black Hackle Blue. The hackle is jet black, an intense color best obtained by dyeing the feather. The body is made with a strand of bright blue floss; the color is sometimes called an "electric" blue. Use the brightest blue floss you have for this pattern.

For the Guinea and Yellow choose a warmer yellow floss for the body than you used for the Grouse and Yellow. "Warmer" refers to a yellow floss that has orange, not greenish, overtones. Use a guinea fowl hackle for this pattern and tie the materials on as you did for the first four patterns in this stage.

For a Little Ginger Wren use a ginger-colored tying thread. The entire fly, including the head, is the color of ginger and its ginger-colored hackle is a bright yellowish light brown. It is an attractive and effective wet fly. Tie it as you did the others in this stage.

Second Stage: With Wings

Our first winged floss-bodied fly is the Little Sand Fly. Choose copper-colored floss for the body. Use a ginger-colored hackle and make the wing by using strips of goose feathers that have been dyed a yellow brown. In essence, this is a Little Ginger Wren with an added wing. The copper-colored floss is only a little different in tone from the ginger-colored floss. The tying thread for the Little Sand Fly can be light brown, ginger, copper, or orange in color, and makes an attractive head, whichever one you choose. After using head varnish over heads in these colors, you will find they alter only slightly.

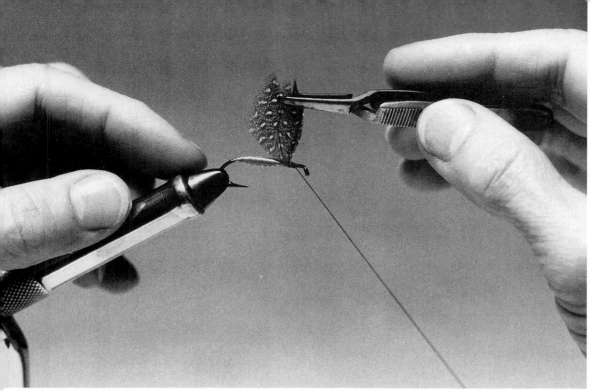

A spotted feather of guinea fowl makes an excellent hackle. Bind it to the hook by its stem, or quill, with its dull side toward the fly body. Hold by the tip with fly-tying pliers and wind it around the hook. Short feathers, such as guinea, partridge, or grouse, can be easily managed in this way.

Hold the flues back with the left hand while the hackle is being wound on. In this way, each turn of the hackle can be placed precisely and none of the flues will be bound down unnecessarily.

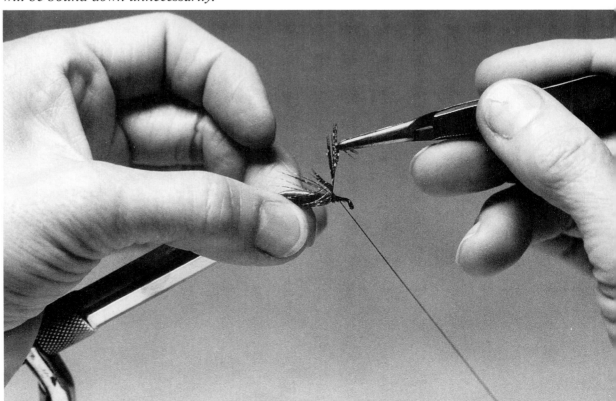

Name of Pattern	Body	Hackle	Head
Partridge and Green	Moss Green Floss	Partridge	Very Dark Green or Black
Grouse and Yellow	Yellow Floss	Grouse	Black
Grouse and Orange	Orange Floss	Grouse	Black
Black Hackle Blue	Bright Blue Floss	Black	Black
Guinea and Yellow	Warm Yellow Floss	Guinea	Black
Little Ginger Wren	Ginger Floss	Ginger	Ginger
Additional Patterns			
Brown Hackle Green	Light Green	Bright Red-Brown	Green
Partridge and Orange	Bright Orange	Partridge	Dark Orange
Partridge and Red	Clear Red	Partridge	Black
Partridge and Gray	Gray Floss	Partridge	Black
Claret and Grouse	Claret Floss	Grouse	Brown
Ashey	Silver Gray Floss	Dark Grizzly Tinted Light Brown	Gray

Use a black tying thread to make a black head for the next pattern. The Oak Fly has an orange floss body, so make sure the tying thread is covered entirely with the floss. With a brown hackle and a wing of goose dyed light brown, the Oak Fly is very close in appearance to the Little Ginger Wren and the Little Sand Fly. The light brown goose used here is almost tan. A very pale gray goose wing feather tinted a very light brown makes a beautiful wing for this pattern.

Our Field Fly is quite different in color from these first two patterns, having a light gray floss body, a bluish gray hackle, and a wing of goose that has been dyed a dark blue-gray. The method of tying is the same you have been using. The slate gray goose feathers take dye very well, and the natural slate color mutes the harshness of many intense dye colors.

The Orange Sedge is related to the first two patterns in this stage. It has a light orange floss body, a light ginger hackle, a light ginger brown wing, and a light-colored head. Primrose-colored

tying thread may be used. Only the varying shades of color separate these three patterns. They are beautiful variations on the same theme.

A Firefly is made with a luminescent yellowish green floss body. Tie it on with a light green or light gray thread. It has a smoky gray hackle and a wing of light slate goose that has been tinted light green. It is tied in exactly the same way as the foregoing floss-bodied flies, and differs from them only in the colors of the materials.

For the Green Bottle Fly use black tying thread. The body is of dark green floss with a grizzly hackle. Make its wings with a pair of small and slender grizzly hackles or of grizzly hackle tips that have short flues. Tie them on to lie flat above the body of the fly, as you did for the last two patterns in the second stage of the chenille-bodied flies.

Third Stage: With Tag

We come now to the third stage of this fly form. Here a tag is added to the floss body. The con-

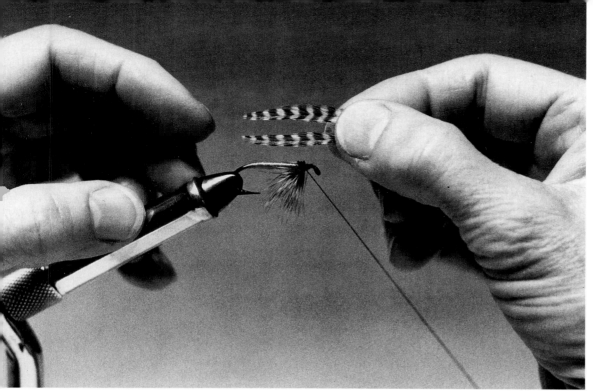

For this pattern, the hackle is divided on top of the hook, then drawn down and anchored below the hook with the tying thread to make a "throat." The feathers used for the wings are carefully chosen to be counterparts of each other. With their dull sides downward and the quill stems together, transfer the wings to your left hand. Tie them to the hook, keeping them flat and parallel on top of the fly body.

Bind the quills securely and finish the fly with a wrap-knot head.

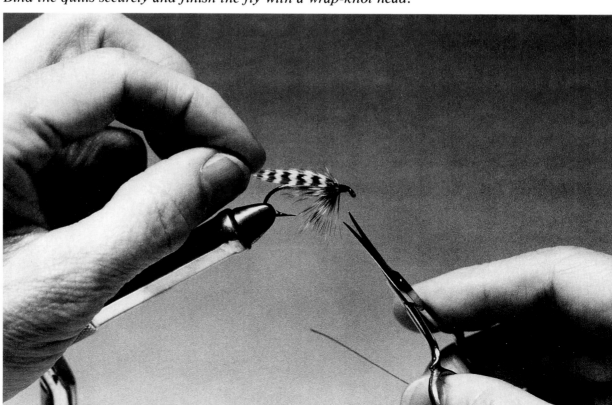

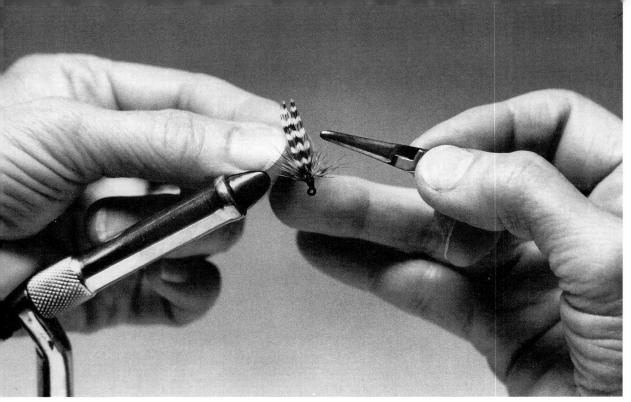

Seen from directly on top, the wings are together. The matching pattern of the feathers makes a beautiful design for this fly.

Name of Pattern	Body	Hackle	Wing	Head
Little Sand Fly	Copper-Colored Floss	Ginger	Yellow-Brown Goose	Copper (Orange)
Oak Fly	Orange Floss	Dark Brown	Light Brown or Tan	Black
Field Fly	Light Gray Floss	Blue-Gray	Dark Blue-Gray Goose	Black
Orange Sedge	Light Orange Floss	Light Ginger	Ginger-Brown Goose	Primrose
Firefly	Luminescent Green Floss	Smoky Gray	Gray-Green Goose	Light Gray or Green
Green Bottle Fly	Dark Green Floss	Grizzly	Grizzly Hackles Tied Flat	Black
Additional Patterns				
Baigent's Brown	Yellow Floss	Furnace	Hen Pheasant	Black
Trout Fin	Red Floss	White	White Goose	Black
Emerald Dun	Green Floss	Smoky Gray	Slate Goose	Green
White Caddis	Green Floss	Short White	White Goose	Black
Cooper's Dun	Orange Floss	Black	Brown Turkey	Dark Orange
Tailless Golden Dun	Orange Floss	Gray	Slate Goose	Black

struction of the patterns to follow is the same for all of them. As with the tags on the herl-bodied and chenille-bodied patterns, the tinsel tag for the floss-bodied flies is tied on above the barb and point before the body material and it is secured with as few turns of tying thread as possible. Make a smooth foundation for the thin edge of the floss strand because it must cover the bound ends of tinsel and the tying thread completely. The tying thread makes tiny ridges that must be covered smoothly.

Whether the tying thread is closely matched to the color of the body floss or not, no single turn of it should be apparent at the very end of the body. The floss strand has, by its very nature, a more transparent quality than do the heavier, more dense herl and chenille. With practice, you can taper the floss over the area where the tinsel of the tag has been bound on, leaving no indication of it where tag and body are joined. This is the area where increasing care must be observed as tails and ribs are added on in the successive stages to follow. Your ability to master this detail will increase with each fly you tie in this third stage, and in the following stages.

The first four patterns in this stage of the third fly form have tags of fine, flat gold tinsel. The remaining two have tags of fine, flat silver tinsel. Our first pattern is a Fern Fly, with a narrow (fine) gold-tinsel tag. For this pattern, choose a lighter orange floss than you did for the Oak Fly (second stage). The hackle for the Fern Fly is brown like that of the Oak Fly, but its wing is made of medium slate-colored goose (neither light nor dark gray).

The Pink Fern Fly, as its name implies, has a pale pink floss body. Its tag is gold, although a silver tag makes a beautiful addition. The only discernable difference between this pattern and the preceding one is the color of the floss body. The hackle is brown, and the same pair of goose feathers that provided the wing material for the Fern Fly may be used for the Pink Fern Fly. Both are lovely additions to your collection of wet flies.

For a Brown Sedge, select a strand of medium brown floss from your color file. After you have made a gold-tinsel tag, make a slim oval body with the brown floss. Add a brown wet-fly hackle of medium length. Over these, tie a wing made of strips taken from a matched pair of mottled brown turkey feathers. The earth tones of this fly are very effective when the pattern is tied in smaller hook sizes.

The Cinnamon Fly, our fourth pattern in this third stage, is very much like the Brown Sedge. With its gold tag and body of cinnamon-colored floss, it is sometimes called a Cinnamon Sedge. It has a reddish brown, or fiery brown, hackle. The wing is made from cinnamon-colored turkey feathers. These feathers naturally are a plain golden brown instead of the mottled brown used for the Brown Sedge. The head of the Cinnamon Fly is brown, therefore, you will use brown tying thread throughout.

A Bunting has a silver tag. Its black floss body and black hackle are capped with a wing of white goose. Compare this pattern with the None Such (first stage of the second fly form). Body, hackle, and wing are the same color; the only difference is in the material from which the body is made and the addition of a tag. Compare also with the Rio Grande Queen. The colors of the body, hackle, and wing are identical. Only minute variations and additions separate many patterns from one another.

For a Light Olive Dun, make another silver-tinsel tag. Choose a rather light, slightly grayed olive-colored floss for the body of this fly. Use a light olive hackle, and for the wing select a pair of mottled-oak turkey feathers from which you can take matching sections that are grayish (rather than brown), to give the wing a subdued appearance. Mottled-oak turkey feathers, as described earlier, have a great range, both in design and in color.

Fourth Stage: With Tip

Floss tips on floss-bodied flies should rise gradually from the hook shank to meet the main part of the floss body, with no break in the overall smooth oval body contour. This can be accomplished with practice. When the floss for the tip has been wound on, tie it off as smoothly as possible by tapering the stub end in order to have an even surface over which to wind the body floss. Wind the tying thread forward to the place where

Name of Pattern	Tag	Body	Hackle	Wing	Head
Fern Fly	Gold	Light Orange Floss	Brown	Medium Slate Goose	Black
Pink Fern Fly	Gold	Pale Pink Floss	Brown	Medium Slate Goose	Black
Brown Sedge	Gold	Medium Brown Floss	Medium Brown	Mottled Brown Turkey	Black
Cinnamon Fly	Gold	Cinnamon Floss	Fiery Brown	Cinnamon Turkey	Brown
Bunting	Silver	Black Floss	Black	White Goose	Black
Light Olive Dun	Silver	Light Gray Olive Floss	Light Olive	Mottled Gray-Brown Turkey	Black
Additional Patterns					
Raven	Silver	Dark Green Floss	Black	Black Goose	Black
Orange Fern Fly	Gold	Light Orange Floss	Brown	Dark Slate Goose	Black
Silver Fern Fly	Silver	White Floss	Light Gray	Light Slate Goose	Black
Red Ash Fly	Gold	Red Floss	Blue Dun	Brown Mallard	Black
Hawthorne	Silver	Black Floss	Black and Claret, Mixed	Black-dyed Goose	Black
Dew Fly	Silver	Primrose Floss	Light Reddish Brown	Dark Gray Goose	Black

the wing will be tied on later.

Tie the strand of body floss in at the wing position. Wind it back over the tying thread to where you tied off the tip material. By allowing the strand of floss to spread a little as you wind it on you can fill in underlying irregularities, joining the floss body smoothly to the tip, and covering its cut and bound ends entirely. Your final winding of the body floss toward the eye will give the body an even, lustrous surface.

Although tags on all patterns are optional, unless definitely specified we will omit them on some of the following patterns.

Our first floss-bodied pattern to have a tip is the Female Field Fly. It differs in three respects from the pattern of the Field Fly (second stage). It has a small yellow floss tip on the gray floss body and a brown hackle instead of a gray one. The wing is a dark slate gray, instead of the dark blue-gray you used for the Field Fly pattern. These two flies are related only by name and body color. With the exception of the added tip, the basic construction of both is the same.

A tip for the Wetzel Grannom is made with a fine greenish yellow chenille, instead of floss. The body itself is made with black floss. The hackle is

a dark grayish brown, with flues a trifle shorter than medium length. Its slightly narrower wet-fly wing is made with matched strips of pheasant tail feathers. Choose flues that do not separate at the ends as those of the central tail feather do. The brown of pheasant tail feathers is a different brown from that of brown turkey wing or tail feathers.

Our third pattern in this fourth stage is strikingly different in color from the foregoing ones. A bright orange floss tip is indicated, on a steely blue body. Tie on a guinea-feather hackle of medium length, and wind it on sparingly. Also, make the wing of guinea fowl. Tie the whole pattern with a dark blue tying thread in order to give it a dark blue head, and you will have tied a Polka Dot Moth. Several of these flies, graduated in smaller sizes, will make a beautiful display in your fly collection.

The fourth pattern is a Golden Spinner. For this fly, make a small green tip of floss on a pale yellow floss body. Black tying thread may be used, for the head is black, but make sure the thread does not show through the light colors of the tip and the body. Now select a brown hackle, tie it on sparingly, and over it tie a wing of light slate goose.

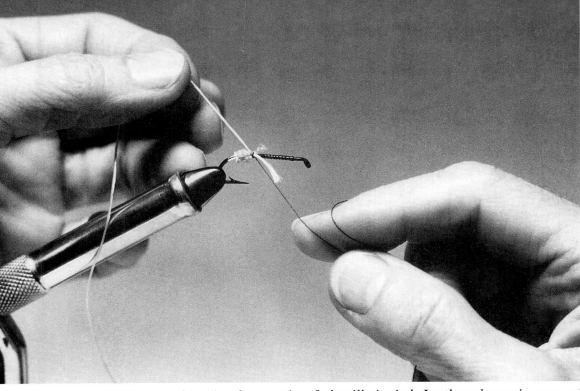

With a tinsel tag in place, a tip of chenille is tied. Its thread core is exposed and a strand of floss is attached as closely as possible to the tip. The stub ends of both the floss and the thread core of the chenille will be bound down together as the tying thread is wound toward the hook eye. These in turn will be covered as the floss body is wound smoothly over them.

With a tinsel tag and floss tip in place, the darker floss body is a smooth continuation of the lighter tip. A hackle of spotted guinea feather has been tied on, and a wing of guinea feather is being measured for length against the body before being transferred to the left hand to be tied on. Notice the different effects that can be obtained with these versatile feathers.

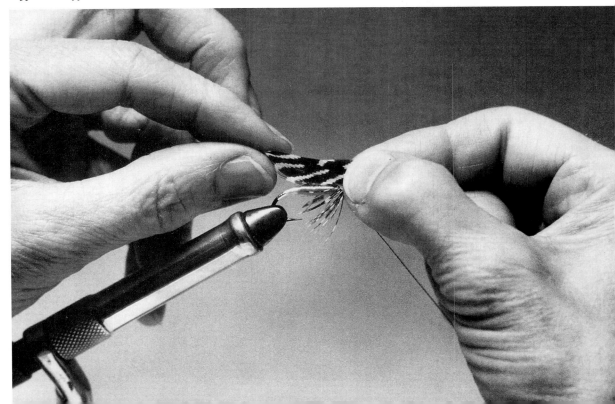

Name of Pattern	Tip	Body	Hackle	Wing	Head
Female Field Fly	Yellow Floss	Gray Floss	Brown	Dark Slate	Black
Wetzel Grannom	Greenish Yellow Chenille	Black Floss	Dark Gray-Brown	Pheasant	Black
Polka Dot Moth	Bright Orange Floss	Bright Blue Floss	Guinea	Guinea	Dark Blue
Golden Spinner	Green Floss	Pale Yellow Floss	Brown	Light Slate	Black
Golden-Eyed Gauze Wing	Luminescent Green Floss	Light Green Floss	Light Green	Light Green	Yellow
Olive Spinner	Rich Brown Floss	Silver-Gray Floss	Light Gray	Dun Hackles	Brown
Additional Patterns					
Red Hackle	Fine Yellow Ostrich Herl	Dark Green Floss	Red-Brown	Slate	Black
Captain Scott	Red Floss	Dark Brown Floss	Black	Speckled Light Gray Turkey	Black
Canada	Scarlet Floss	Red Floss	Light Brown	Gray Turkey	Black
Red Fly	Brownish Claret Chenille	Brown Floss	Claret-dyed Goose	Pale Gadwall or Teal	Brown
Scorpion	Gray Thread	Orange Floss	Furnace	Woodcock	Black
Gauzy-Winged Night Fly	³⁄₅ Dark Brilliant Green Floss	¹⁄₅ Dark Blue Floss ¹⁄₅ Black Floss	Very Short and Sparse Black	Light Gray Hackle Tips Flat over Body	Black

Make the tip for the Golden-Eyed Gauze Wing from the luminescent yellowish green floss that was indicated for the body of the Firefly (second stage). Make the rest of the body with light green floss, and tie on a light green hackle. For the wing, use duck or goose that has been dyed a light green. With a tying thread of warm yellow, you will give this fly a yellow head.

Tie the Olive Spinner, our sixth pattern, with brown tying thread. Make its tip with a rich brown floss. Tie the remainder of the body with a light silvery gray floss. Use a light gray hackle, with flues of medium length, and tie it sparsely. The wings for this pattern are grayish brown (or dun-colored) narrow hackles tied flat and slightly spread. The brown head makes this a very handsome fly indeed.

Fifth Stage: With Tail

For the six patterns in this fifth stage, you will be introducing tails to the floss-bodied flies. You will concentrate on those without tips. Although tags can be optional on patterns that do not specify them, only our fourth pattern requires one.

Our first pattern is a Gosling, with a tail of slate gray goose. About three strands of it is enough to make a tail of good proportion for a #10 hook; make it no longer than the length of the body. Use a medium shade of green for the floss body. Select a light gray hackle—not a grizzly—and wind it on sparingly. Over this, tie a wing of slate gray goose, and complete the fly with a neat wrap-knot head of black tying thread. Checking back to the additional patterns in the second stage of the form, you will find this pattern is the Emerald Dun with a tail.

Our next pattern is similar to the first. In place of the gray tail and hackle of the Gosling we will use flues of dyed brown goose for the tail, and a brown hackle. Make the body with green floss, but this time a little lighter than the green you used for the Gosling. Make the wing the same slate gray goose. This pattern is called an Apple Green, distinguished from the Gosling only by the difference in the color of tail and hackle.

The Bright Fox has a tail of brown hackle flues, which can be taken from the wet-fly hackle you have selected. This time the body is made with yellow floss. After the brown hackle is in place, tie on a white goose wing. Use brown tying thread for this fly, for the head is brown also.

Use primrose tying thread for a light-colored head and make a gold tag for the Watersmeet. A few wisps taken from a honey furnace hackle will make the tail. This feather is a ginger hackle with a white center. The familiar red-brown furnace hackle has a dark center, and a straw hackle is pale ginger with a gray center. When a honey furnace hackle is used on a fly it gives the illusion of color detached from the fly. (When these hackles are found among other hackles, they should be sorted out immediately and kept for the special patterns that specify them.)

Use a pale yellow floss for the body of the Watersmeet. Its hackle is the honey furnace from which the tail was made. For the wing, select slate-colored goose that shows a slightly mottled pattern. When pairs of these mottled feathers appear among others, they too should be set aside for special use.

Wisps of gray mallard feather make the body-length tail for a Baldwin. Although the pattern specifies a body of white floss, use a fine black tying thread in order to give the fly a black head. A claret hackle, with flues that reach only to the barb of the hook, should be used sparingly. Over the body and hackle, arch a wing of gray speckled mallard—the gray equivalent to lemon wood duck.

An 1896 pattern called the Martin specifies a tail made of scarlet ibis and black hackle fibers. The tips of a red breast feather from the more plentiful source of golden pheasant is a good substitute for the scarlet ibis, which is not available today. The black hackle should be one that has been dyed to a glossy black. Use a few wisps of each color for the tail. No trout would reject this fly because of the absence of a few strands of scarlet ibis in the tail. This handsome pattern has a body of warm yellow floss and an orange hackle. A wing of black goose is in striking contrast to these bright colors, and a neat black head completes the tying of another very attractive fly.

Sixth Stage: With Ribs

A floss body, with its smooth surface, is par-ticularly lovely when ribbed. Although tinsel ribbing is specified for many floss-bodied patterns, a contrasting strand of twisted floss can also be used, making a raised rib and adding texture. For our first pattern we will use a strand of twisted floss for the rib on a March Brown. Since a tag is optional, we will omit it here.

Tie on a tail of dark brown mottled turkey. Separate a strand of yellow floss and use part of it for the rib. A full strand of floss would make a rib too heavy for a small fly body. Tie in the partial strand of yellow floss and hold it out of the way while you tie on a strand of brown floss for the body. Keep the yellow floss strand out of the way while you wind on the body floss. When the body has been shaped into an oval and the excess material has been trimmed away, twist the yellow floss into a firm cord. Carefully wind it around the brown body. Maintain its tight twist as you spiral it along toward the eye of the hook, spacing the ribs evenly along the fly body.

When you have secured the floss rib and trimmed the excess away, tie on a dark grouse hackle. Two turns of the hackle is sufficient. Over this, tie on a wing of dark brown mottled turkey. Finish with a wrap-knot head, and your March Brown is complete—another well-known and effective pattern to add to your collection.

The Dark Montreal is our second ribbed pattern. This time make a short tag of fine, flat gold tinsel. Make the tail of a few flues of scarlet hackle. The rib, too, is a fine, flat gold tinsel. Since the tag and rib are made with the same kind of tinsel, this is a pattern on which you can use the continuous tinsel technique (see the first fly form, sixth stage).

Use a dark red or magenta floss for the body. Over it, wind the narrow gold rib. Use a hackle that matches the color of the body as closely as possible, and for the wing use dark brown mottled turkey, the same as you did for the March Brown.

For our third ribbed pattern in this form, we have the famous Grizzly King. Tag and rib are the same as for the Dark Montreal. Scarlet hackle flues, or flues of scarlet goose, can be used for the tail. Tie the body with a green floss, and after you have wound on the gold rib, select a grizzly hackle with flues that reach only to the bend of the hook.

Name of Pattern	Tag	Tail	Body	Hackle	Wing	Head
Gosling	————	Slate Gray Goose	Green Floss	Light Gray	Gray Goose	Black
Apple Green	————	Brown Goose	Light Green Floss	Brown	Gray Goose	Black
Bright Fox	————	Brown Hackle Flues	Yellow Floss	Brown	White Goose	Brown
Watersmeet	Gold	Honey Furnace Flues	Pale Yellow Floss	Honey Furnace	Mottled Gray Goose	Primrose
Baldwin	————	Gray Mallard	White Floss	Claret	Speckled Mallard	Black
Martin	————	Red from Pheasant Breast	Warm Yellow Floss	Orange	Black Goose	Black

Patterns with both tags and tips are included in the following additional patterns.

Additional Patterns							
Name of Pattern	Tag	Tail	Tip	Body	Hackle	Wing	Head
Dorset	————	Furnace Hackle Wisps	————	Green Floss	Furnace	Barred Teal	Black
Captain	Gold	Scarlet and Yellow Wisps	Peacock Herl	Red Floss	Brown	Slate Goose	Black
Calder	Gold	Barred Wood Duck	Peacock Herl	Red Floss	Brown	Light Brown Turkey with Peacock Sword Over	Black
Bouncer	————	Short Orange Hackle Wisps	Orange Floss	Black Floss	Orange	Yellow Goose	Black
Widow	Silver	Short Black Hackle Wisps	White Floss	Black Floss	Black	Black with White Top	Black
Lady Beaverkill (Wet)	————	Long Pintail Flues	Lemon Yellow Chenille	Gray Floss	Dark Ginger	Gray Duck or Light Slate Goose	Black

A tail of dark turkey, without a tag, has been tied on, and the dark floss body is ribbed with a light strand of tightly twisted floss.

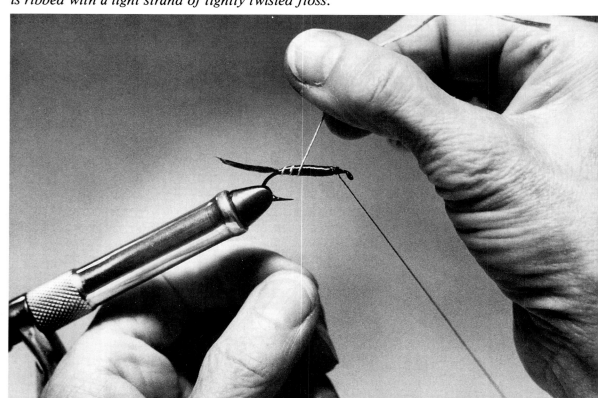

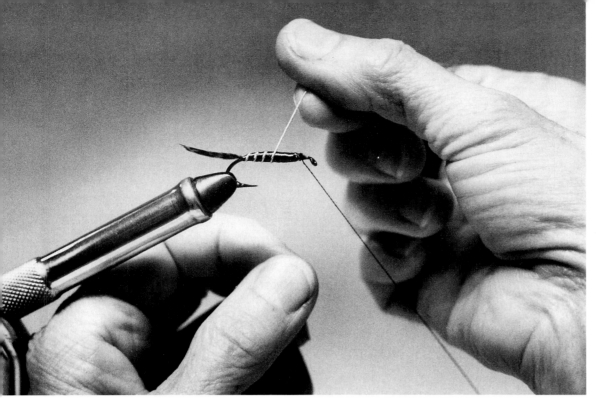

With a fine strand of floss tightly twisted into a slim cord, it is possible to place six or seven evenly spaced ribs along this floss body.

With the tag, tail, and body in place, you are ready to wind on the tinsel rib as though it were a continuation of the tinsel tag.

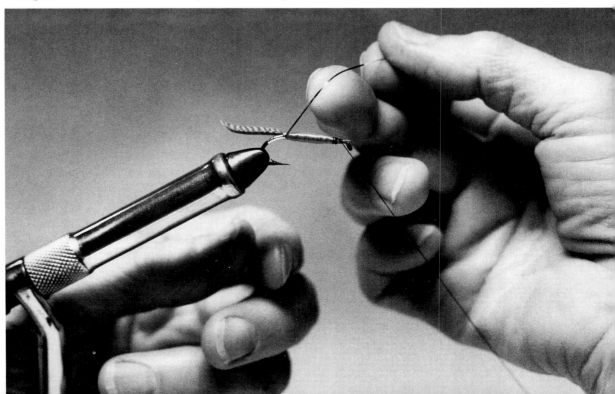

Tie it on with the flues turning back over the body. Use a wet-fly wing made of gray speckled mallard for this excellent pattern.

To change this pattern to a Hairwing Grizzly King, use a small bunch of frosty squirrel hair for the wing. Choose hair with short white tips in good proportion to the size of your hook. Remove all of the undercoat from it before tying it on with its even tips just reaching to the end of the tail.

Another very famous pattern is the Professor, which is a color phase of the Grizzly King. The only difference in tying between these two feather-wing patterns is the way in which the tails are made. The tag and rib are made with fine, flat gold tinsel. Make the tail of the Professor with a narrow strip of barred teal above a narrow strip of red goose. Together, the strips should be about six flues wide for a fly on a #10 hook. Keeping it in proportion to the hook, the tail should be the length of the body. This time, make the body with yellow floss. After ribbing it with gold tinsel, select a red-brown wet-fly hackle and wind on a few turns of it. For the wing, used barred teal or speckled mallard. The markings and color of these two are very similar.

I once witnessed an interesting experiment done with these two feather-wing patterns. Both were used on the same leader over excellent trout water to determine if the fish could detect any difference in the color of the flies. For this purpose, the Professor was tied without the strip of barred teal in the tail. One pattern was used at the leader tip and one as the dropper fly. On successive casts, and over a period of several days with changing weather and light conditions, when the fish were interested in a yellow-bodied fly they would take the Professor, no matter where it was tied on the leader. When they were interested in a green-bodied fly they struck the Grizzly King, even when the placement of the two flies was reversed. The silhouette and size of both patterns was identical—only the hackle and body color differed. Was the choice made by color? So it seemed.

The next pattern does not require a tag, although a silver one may be optional. Make the tail for the Fin Fly from a few wisps of brown hackle flues. Keep the tips of the flues even, and make the tail a trifle shorter than the length of the hook

shank. Use a silver wire for the rib. Make a neat oval body of red floss. You will find that with the silver wire the ribs can be spaced more closely together as you wind it along the body. Select a furnace hackle with a small, dark center, and with flues that will reach to the barb when you wind it on. Measure the white goose wing against the body for the correct length and tie it on. Finish with the neat wrap-knot head and give it several coats of thin, clear lacquer, permitting each coat to dry thoroughly before the next is applied.

The name of our sixth pattern tells you what the fly is, rather than naming the materials from which it is made. It is a good-for-evening fly—the Good Evening Fly—to use at the end of the day, toward dusk.

For the tail, use a few strands of barred wood duck that has rather narrow bars of both black and white. Tie in a round gold tinsel for the rib, carefully stripping away some of the tinsel to expose the thread core and making sure to catch some of the tinsel, as well as the thread core, with your tying thread. Make the body for this fly with red floss, a darker red than the floss you used for the Fin Fly. (Here is a situation where your floss file will save you the time and trouble of searching for the right shade.) Use a few turns of brown hackle with flues reaching only to the barb of the hook. Select a pair of white-tipped mallard feathers, and from them take strips that will make a dark wing with a white tip. This attractive pattern is also a very effective one.

Among the additional patterns at the end of this stage, the one called Fortune's Favorite specifies the use of a pair of small jungle cock "eyed" feathers as shoulders of the fly. Jungle cock eyed cape fathers, once so plentiful, are in extremely short supply. The enamel-like tips of these unique feathers, made by a progressive widening of the central quill at its tip, have been used lavishly as shoulders and wings on classic salmon-fly patters, and as wings on the other patterns as well. Their being banned from importation gave rise to the manufacturing of plastic imitations as substitutes. The photographed copies are good likenesses in color, but the texture cannot be duplicated.

Fortunately for fly tyers, at this writing a serious project is under way to raise these beautiful

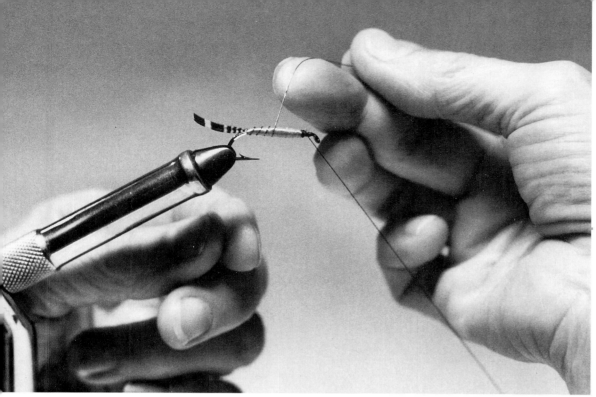

For the Good Evening Fly or the Silver Gray, a flat tinsel tag and a tail of barred wood duck are in place on a floss body. A rib of round tinsel is wound on. With this fine tinsel, as many as eight ribs can be nicely spaced along a body of this size.

birds in the United States, and for the first time in many years the capes and skins are being offered for sale legally. This is an enormous undertaking, because the enamel-like spots do not develop until the birds are three or four years old.

There are other breeds of domestic fowl that have feathers somewhat similar in appearance, though not in texture, to those of the Gray Jungle Fowl cape feathers with which we are familiar. Feathers from the fancier breeds of domestic show

"Eyed" jungle-cock feathers have been used lavishly for wings, cheeks, and shoulders on many fly patterns.

These golden brown feathers with their white tips cupped in dark brown or black can substitute for jungle fowl as decorative cheeks on many patterns.

birds, such as the Mille Fleur or the Speckled Sussex, might become useful to fly tyers for decorative use on fly patterns if a plentiful source were to be developed by a breeder of these lovely birds.

While lacking the enameled quality of the cape feathers of the gray jungle fowl, these other attractive birds do have spotted feathers, and one in particular has golden brown feathers that end with a white spot cupped in a thin sickle of black or dark brown. Or the tip of a guinea fowl feather

can be used. Another obvious substitute for the eyed jungle fowl feathers is a dark hackle on which two spots of enamel, one below the other, have been carefully painted.

For a light-colored fly like the White Mayfly, it is always a good idea to use a very light-colored tying thread. If a thread is to be used for a rib, it should be heavier than the tying thread. Buttonhole twist can be used this way and is available in many colors.

Here, a single spot on a guinea-fowl feather can be used as a substitute for jungle fowl.

An ornithologist friend might be willing to part with a pair of spotted feathers from the exotic Tragopan Pheasant.

Name of Pattern	Tag	Tail	Rib	Body	Hackle	Wing
March Brown	———	Dark Mottled Turkey	Twisted Yellow Floss	Brown Floss	Dark Grouse	Dark Brown Mottled Turkey
Dark Montreal	Gold	Scarlet Wisps	Fine Flat Gold	Magenta Floss	Magenta	Dark Brown Mottled Turkey
Grizzly King	Gold	Scarlet Wisps	Fine Flat Gold	Green Floss	Grizzly	Speckled Mallard
Professor	Gold	Teal and Red Goose	Fine Flat Gold	Yellow Floss	Brown	Speckled Teal or Mallard
Fin Fly	———	Brown Wisps	Silver Wire	Red Floss	Furnace	White Goose
Good Evening Fly	———	Barred Wood Duck	Fine Round Gold	Dark Red Floss	Brown	White-tipped Mallard
Additional Patterns						
Silver Gray	Silver	Barred Wood Duck	Round Silver Tinsel	Light Gray Floss	Light Gray	Light Duck
Frosty Roux	Silver	Frosty Squirrel Sulphur Hackle Wisps	Fine Flat Silver	Pale Yellow Floss	Sulphur	Frosty Squirrel
Hairwing Grizzly King	Silver	Scarlet Hackle Wisps	Fine Flat Gold	Green Floss	Grizzly	Frosty Squirrel
Fortune's Favorite	Silver	Cinnamon Turkey	Black Floss	Yellow Floss	Green	Mallard or Teal Tinted Green
Catskill	———	Gray Mallard Dyed Orange	Fine Flat Gold	Orange Floss	Brown	Mallard Dyed Orange
Voedisch Polar	———	Red Hackle Wisps	Silver Tinsel	Black Floss	Black	Polar Bear

Additional Patterns						
Name of Pattern	Tag	Tail	Tip	Rib	Body	Hackle	Wing
White Mayfly	Silver	Teal or Mallard	Pink Chenille	Pink Thread	White Floss	White	White Goose with a Strip of Pink Goose Over

Yellow Stone Fly	Grizzly and Yellow	Crane Fly	Claret and Partridge	Gray Hackle Orange	Gauze Wing
Fiery Brown	Deer Fly	Dark Alder	Claret and Gray	Orange Dun	Golick Green
Utah	Gray Dun	Blue Bottle Fly	Walla Walla	Brown Drake	Scarlet Gnat
Brown Grannom	Tree Hopper	March Dun	Early Evening Dun	Little March Brown	Leaper
Olive Dun	Golden Dun	Great Dun	Sulphur Dun	Shad Fly	Little Fox
Dark Gray Dun	Late Evening Dun	Green Mantle	White Tip Montreal	Armstrong Fontinalis Fin	Bergman Fontinalis Fin

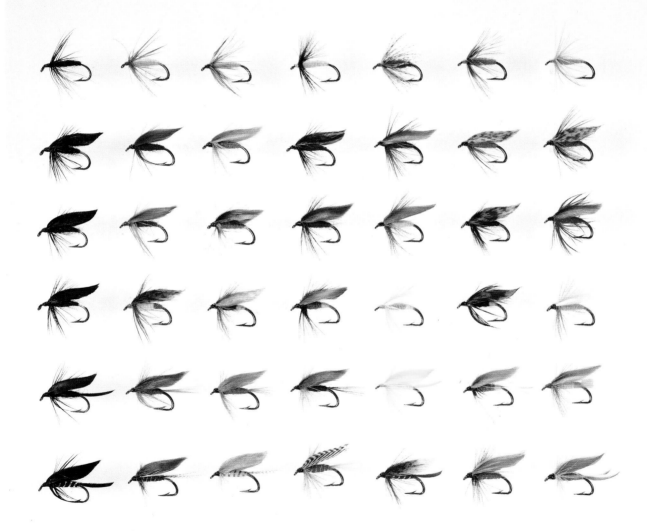

Yes, the sun is up and the fly is out
That will tempt the eye of the golden trout.
Let thy skill be good, and thy line be strong
And the prey shall be thine, ere the morn be long.

Henry Phillips, "Good Fishing"

Yarn Body
The Fourth Fly Form

First Stage: Body and Hackle

Yarns of various weights and fibers, both natural and synthetic and of many colors, are in ample supply. Excellent sources are yarn and handcraft shops, as well as fishing-tackle catalogues that offer fly-tying materials.

This material comes ready for fly-tying use as is. Many diameters and textures are available, and you may choose those most appropriate for the size hook you intend to use.

Heavy yarn would be unnecessarily bulky on a small hook. But the strands may be unwound, separated, and twisted into finer strands. It would be a waste of material to use a fine yarn for a fly body on a large hook. Care in the selection of materials is always sound economics.

Yarn color may be used as it is found commercially, or you can alter it when necessary by judicious dyeing.

To protect your supply of yarn, a "file" such as the one used for floss can be developed and maintained. By using boxes of uniform size for this purpose, you will have your materials neatly arranged, handy, and dust- and tangle-free.

In this fourth fly form, wings for all of the patterns are standard wet-fly wings, and need not

be illustrated again until we come to a special detail in the sixth stage. The winding of tags, also, has been covered in the first three fly forms.

For the first fly with a yarn body, choose a strand of yellow yarn of a size suitable for the hook you are using. Now, select a brown hackle with flues that reach to the bend of the hook. Tie this pattern with brown tying thread. The shape of the body may be oval or tapered from tip to hackle. Practice tying both of these shapes. Your first pattern is a Yellow Stone Fly. Make oval bodies for all of the flies in this first stage. Select good wet-fly hackles with flues long enough to reach to the bend of the hook you are using, and you will have an enviable set of very handsome patterns. The practice you have in tying each successive pattern will make the next one easier.

For the Grizzly and Yellow, select yellow yarn that is a bit deeper in color than for the Yellow Stone Fly — a warmer yellow. For the grizzly hackle, use one on which the black and white bars are not too definitely marked, but are a bit blurred, giving the hackle a grayish appearance. This pattern can be tied with black tying thread.

The Crane Fly should be tied with yellow tying thread. Its body is yellow also, although a brighter

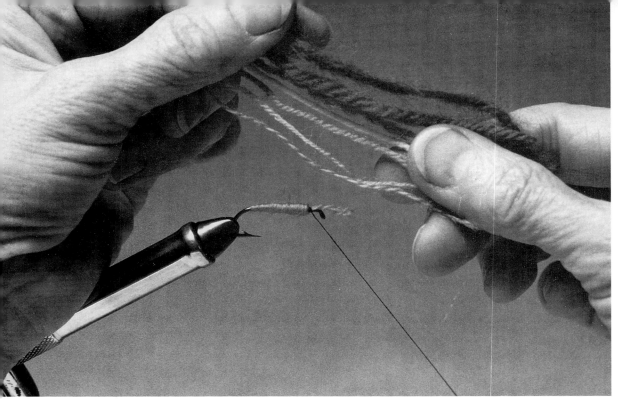

These are yarns of various weights, fibers, and textures. A tapered body, prepared with a yarn suitable for the size of the hook, waits to be completed.

An oval-shaped body has been tied with yarn of the correct weight. To use a finer yarn would be wasteful, and a heavier yarn would be too bulky.

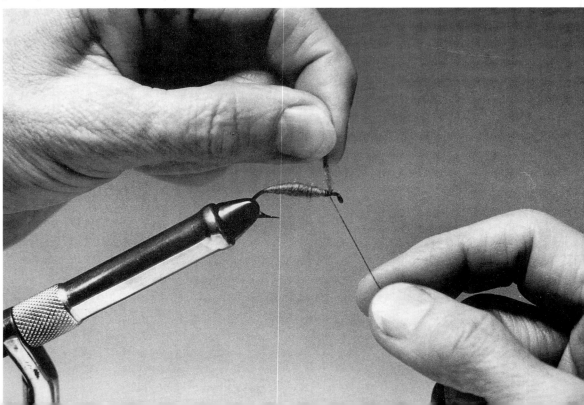

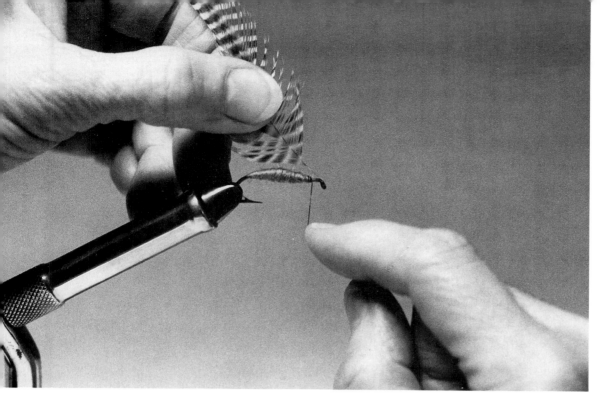

When you add a hackle to a yarn body what results is a very useful fly. This finely barred grizzly hackle will create a dark overall effect.

Carefully hold back the flues while the hackle is being wound on . . .

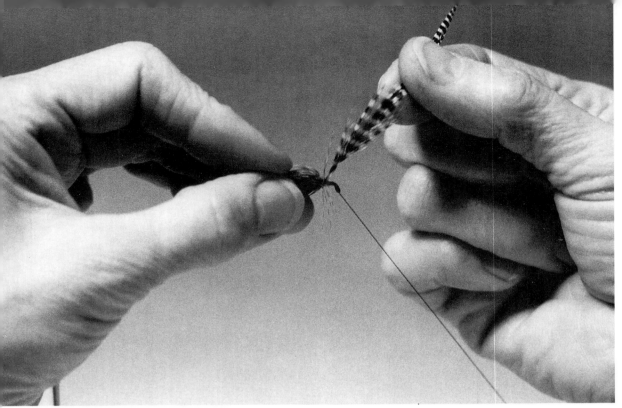

. . . this will enable you to place the turns of hackle as close together as possible without binding down any of the flues that are already in place.

Although three turns of this hackle make the fly appear fairly heavy, the hackle itself is very fine and soft, which will permit the fly to sink rapidly.

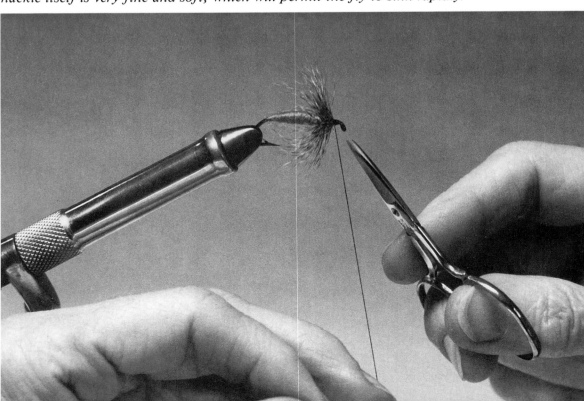

yellow than you used on either of the first two patterns in this fly form. The hackle is black. Although the tying thread is yellow, the head should be very bright, and this you do with a carefully applied coating of yellow lacquer. (Very small quantities of colored lacquer can be obtained in hobby shops that sell miniatures kits.) It makes a beautiful head for this fly, but coat very carefully to prevent any of the lacquer from spreading into the hackle.

Tie the Claret and Partridge with an orange tying thread. The name of this pattern identifies the materials from which it is made. Select a strand of claret-colored yarn for the body, and fashion it into an oval. When you have secured it and clipped away the excess yarn, use a small partridge feather for the hackle. The waxed orange tying thread will make a dark orange head.

Find among your supply of hackles another grizzly with indistinct, rather dark, marking for your Gray Hackle Orange. After you have tied the body with a strand of orange yarn, using a tying thread of a light color such as primrose or light yellow, wind on a few turns of the hackle. Finish

with a neatly tied wrap-knot head. Because the light-colored thread is waxed it will darken a little with use, but the wrap-knot head will still be comparatively light in color. This pattern, and the one to follow, do not require dark or black heads.

The primrose or light yellow tying thread can also be used for the Gauze Wing, our sixth pattern in this stage of the yarn-bodied flies. This fly has a light green yarn body, and its sparsely tied hackle is a light, bright blue.

Second Stage: With Wings

Our yarn-bodied wet flies began with just a body and a hackle. To these we will now add wings. As with the dubbing-bodied flies in the next chapter, the yarn has expanded the use of color for the bodies of our next patterns.

A "fiery" brown is a bright reddish brown, whether the reference is to a hackle, yarn, floss, or other material. It is also the name of the next pattern. The Fiery Brown has, as you might expect, a yarn body of the color for which it is named. Both the hackle and the wet-fly wing of

Name of Pattern	Body	Hackle	Head
Yellow Stone Fly	Yellow Yarn	Brown	Brown
Grizzly and Yellow	Warm Yellow Yarn	Grizzly	Black
Crane Fly	Bright Yellow Yarn	Black	Yellow
Claret and Partridge	Claret Yarn	Partridge	Orange
Gray Hackle Orange	Orange Yarn	Dark Grizzly	Primrose
Gauze Wing	Light Green Yarn	Light Bright Blue	Primrose
Additional Patterns			
Brown and Black	Brown Yarn	Black	Black
Yellow Sally	Light Yellow-Green Yarn	White Dyed to Match	Black
Gray Marlow	Gray Yarn	Grizzly	Black
Wood Duck and Orange	Orange Yarn	Lemon Wood Duck (Small)	Black
Freak	Yellow Yarn	Guinea Fowl	Black
Ginger Ash	Gray Yarn	Grizzly Tinted Ginger	Black

dyed goose are reddish brown. The wing may also be made with dark cinnamon turkey feather strips, but pick out your most fiery brown hackle for this fly. The tying thread should be black because this pattern has a black head, as do all of the patterns to follow in this stage.

Our Deer Fly has a gray wool body. If you do not have wool yarn, use any plain gray yarn available. Use a light gray hackle with flues that will reach to the bend of the hook. The strips of gray goose for the wing should match the hackle in tone. The Deer Fly is a beautiful neutral-colored fly pattern, excellent to use under many fishing conditions.

The body of the Dark Alder is a deep, purplish dark red. Choose a glossy black hackle that has been dyed for this pattern. (A natural, undyed black hackle has a tendency to be brownish on its underside.) The yarn for the body of this dark pattern should be neither dark red nor purple, but a good blending of both colors. Tie on a wing of dark brown turkey and give the wrap-knot head

several thin coats of clear fly varnish or lacquer to make it as glossy as the hackle.

Yarn for the body of the Claret and Gray is reddish brown and the hackle should match this color as closely as possible. Hackles should be dyed with other body materials in order to have the color conform between two or more dissimilar materials. Make the wing for this pattern with gray goose, and complete the tying of the Claret and Gray with a shiny black wrap-knot head.

Our next pattern, the Orange Dun, is an uncomplicated fly, with its body made of orange-colored yarn. Its medium brown wet-fly hackle will have flues that just touch the point of the hook, not quite as long as what was used for the Deer Fly. Make the wing for this fly with a light mottled turkey that has a speckling of tan and brown on a creamy background. Keep paired feathers together to have them ready for use when a pattern specifies a particular color or marking.

Make the next pattern with a strand of green yarn that is slightly more olive than clear green.

Name of Pattern	Body	Hackle	Wing	Head
Fiery Brown	Red-Brown Yarn	Fiery Brown	Dark Cinnamon Turkey	Black
Deer Fly	Gray Wool Yarn	Gray (Long)	Light Slate Goose	Black
Dark Alder	Deep Purple-Red Yarn	Glossy Black	Brown Turkey	Black
Claret and Gray	Claret Yarn	Claret	Gray Goose	Black
Orange Dun	Orange Yarn	Brown	Mottled Turkey	Black
Golick Green	Olive Green Yarn	Brown-Green	Mottled Turkey	Black
Additional Patterns				
Whitchurch Dun	Yellow Wool Yarn	Ginger	Gray Goose	Black
Sunset	Yellow Yarn	Yellow	White Goose	Black
Herb Howard	Black Yarn	Badger	White Bucktail Tied Flat	Black
Grizzly Grannom	Brown Yarn	Grizzly	Dark Brown Mottled Turkey	Black
Brown Gnat	Brown Yarn	Brown	Gray Mottled Turkey	Black
Flagger	Yellow Yarn	Grizzly	Cinnamon Turkey or Goose Dyed Cinnamon	Black

The hackle for our Golick Green is a brown one that has been tinted green. The wing for this pattern is the same as the one you used for the Orange Dun, a light speckled or mottled Turkey.

Wings for all of these patterns are uniform for the same-size hooks, with their tips extending beyond the hook no more than the width of the gape. The hackles are of uniform length also, except for the second pattern, the Deer Fly, which specifies one that is a trifle longer.

Compare the Sunset with the Yellow Sally (in the additional patterns of the first stage in this fly form). It is a color phase of the Yellow Sally with a wing added.

Third Stage: With Tag

Tie the Utah with cinnamon-colored or light brown tying thread. Make a small, flat gold-tinsel tag before tying the body with a cinnamon-colored yarn. The oval-shaped body should cover all evidence of the tying thread and cut ends of the tinsel tag. Select a light ginger-colored hackle with flues the length of the hook for this pattern. Make the wing with cinnamon turkey. With a cinnamon-colored head, this pattern is a light version of the Fiery Brown, with a tag added. Although tags can be optional, sometimes in the recording of two fly patterns just the addition of a tag is the only discernable difference between them.

Our Gray Dun is a good example of this. For its tag you will use a fine, flat silver tinsel. Make the body with a medium gray yarn, and use a light grizzly for the hackle. The tying thread is black. The wing for this fly is dark slate gray goose. When you have tied the wrap-knot head and put on a final coating of clear lacquer, compare this fly with your Deer Fly (second stage). Only a silver tag, a hackle with a break in the tone of gray, and a slightly darker wing make the subtle difference between these patterns. Place them side by side and you will see how slight the difference really is.

These are very minute details with which to designate a separate and distinct pattern. No doubt, one was developed without knowledge of the other but, interestingly enough, on a day when one pattern appeals to the fish, the other pattern may not. It is worthwhile to make several of both

for your growing stock of wet flies. (Note: This is an example of how tenuous the claim of "originating" a pattern can be.)

The Blue Bottle Fly has a fine, flat gold-tinsel tag. Use black tying thread for this pattern, for although the blue yarn for this body is a bright, intense blue, the hackle and head are black. Use the same shade of gray goose for the wing as you did for the Gray Dun.

For a Walla Walla, use black tying thread. Make a small gold-tinsel tag and use yellow yarn for the body. Select a brown hackle with flues that reach to the bend of the hook. Make the wing with strips of cinnamon turkey. Finish the tying with a shiny black wrap-knot head. If you had used a brown tying thread instead of the black, your Walla Walla would be based on a Yellow Stone Fly of the first stage, with a tag and a wing added.

The Brown Drake also has a fine, flat gold tag. For the body of this fly, choose a dark brown yarn and tie another oval body. Among your badger hackles you should find some that vary in color—some with tips that are white, cream, light ginger, or even light brown with dark edges. These are still not the rich brown of the furnace hackles. From these darker badger hackles, select one of the darkest for your Brown Drake. The wing for this handsome dark pattern is dark brown mottled turkey, and the head is black.

Body and hackle for the Scarlet Gnat are both bright red. Its tag is gold. After you have tied the tag and wound on the red yarn, making the oval body, select a hackle with flues that are a little longer than those in the foregoing patterns. The flues on this pattern should extend to the tip of the wing. You can estimate the length of the hackle flues by comparing them to flies you have already tied. Make the wing for the Scarlet Gnat with slightly narrower strips of slate goose than you have been using—one or two fewer flues in each strip. They are matched and tied on in the same way as the others. The hackle will show both above and below the wing.

Compare the Black Bunting with the Nonpareil of the second stage of the second fly form. The only difference is the addition of a silver tag and the use of yarn instead of chenille for the body material.

Name of Pattern	Tag	Body	Hackle	Wing	Head
Utah	Gold	Cinnamon Yarn	Ginger	Cinnamon Turkey	Light Brown
Gray Dun	Silver	Gray Wool Yarn	Light Grizzly	Dark Slate Goose	Black
Blue Bottle Fly	Gold	Blue Yarn	Black	Gray Goose	Black
Walla Walla	Gold	Yellow Yarn	Brown	Cinnamon Turkey	Black
Brown Drake	Gold	Brown Yarn	Dark Badger	Dark Brown Mottled Turkey	Black
Scarlet Gnat	Gold	Scarlet Yarn	Scarlet	Slate Goose	Black
Additional Patterns					
Gray Owl	Gold	Cream Yarn	Grizzly	Tan Goose	Black
Gravel Bed	Gold	Dark Gray Yarn	Black	Dark Slate Goose	Black
Black May	Gold	Black Yarn	Black	Light Slate Goose	Black
Black Bunting	Silver	Black Yarn	Black	White Goose	Black
Gray Miller	Silver	Bluish Gray Yarn	Light Gray	Light Slate Goose	Black
Brown Turkey	Silver	Dark Brown Yarn	Dark Brown	Dark Brown Turkey	Black

Fourth Stage: With Tip

Tips are easily constructed on the yarn bodies by using a finer yarn for the tip than for the body. However, if the yarn you have is heavy enough to be separated into strands, do so, and use one less strand for the tip than for the body. Make sure the tip and body meet smoothly. Although floss, chenille, and herl can be used for tips on certain patterns, we will concentrate here on tips of the same material as the body.

The Brown Grannom pattern does not specify a tag, but the rest of the patterns in this fourth stage do. The small tip on this fly is made with bright green yarn. Use a primrose-colored tying thread or a very pale gray to make the head light. Choose a pale yellow or cream-colored yarn for the main part of the body; a few turns of brown hackle will suffice. Tie on a wing of mottled dark brown turkey.

The Tree Hopper is tied with black tying thread. Fashion a short gold tag and a light bluish green tip, being careful to cover the black tying thread securing them. The main part of this body is a dark green yarn, and the hackle is ginger grizzly. The barring on a ginger grizzly is often slight, and a light brown hackle can be substituted for it with-

out changing the pattern. Use gray mottled goose for the wing.

For our third pattern, the March Dun, choose a yellow yarn for the tip, and make it cover the ends of the gold tag and the black tying thread. The main part of this body is an olive green yarn. Select a furnace hackle with a small, dark center so that the fiery brown tips will reach just to the bend of the hook and the dark center will appear to be a short hackle beneath the hook. Using a pair of light gray goose feathers that have been tinted green, make the wing for the March Dun. Finish the pattern with a smoothly tapered black wrap-knot head.

A gold tag and a pale yellow wool tip tied with primrose thread is the beginning of the Early Evening Dun. The rest of the body is a light blue yarn. Select a light yellow hackle with flues that extend just a trifle beyond the end of the hook, and for this fly make the wing with matched strips of white goose. As with all of the flies tied with pale-colored tying threads, the head of the Early Evening Dun will be light.

Our Little March Brown is similar in appearance to the Brown Drake in the previous stage. However, this one has a gold tag and a yellow yarn

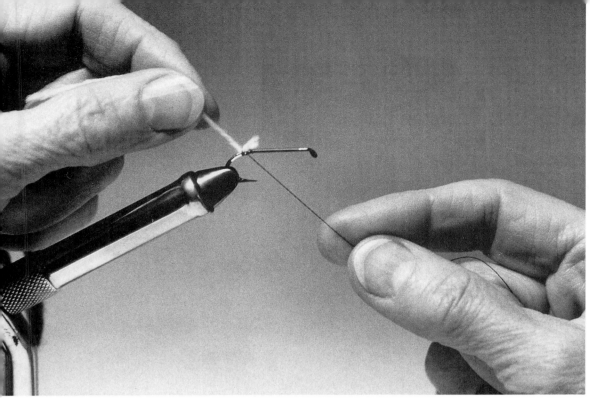

A tinsel tag is in place. A fine strand of yarn for the tip is tied on over the stub end of tinsel. Its own stub end will be bound down with two turns of tying thread and covered completely as the tip is fashioned.

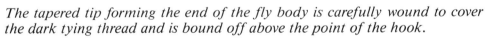

The tapered tip forming the end of the fly body is carefully wound to cover the dark tying thread and is bound off above the point of the hook.

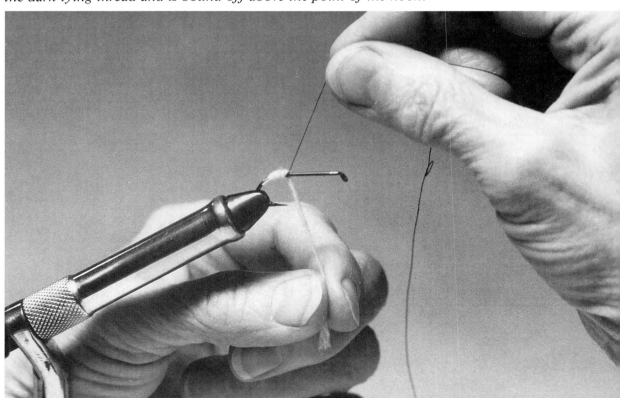

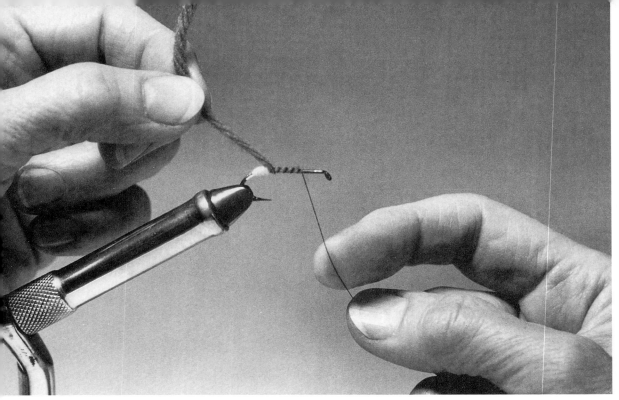

A strand of yarn, slightly heavier than the one used for the light-colored tip, is bound by the tying thread over the cut ends of the tip and along the hook. This will make a slight padding for the body as the yarn is wound forward and over it.

As the yarn for the body is wound on, its first turn around the hook will join the tip smoothly.

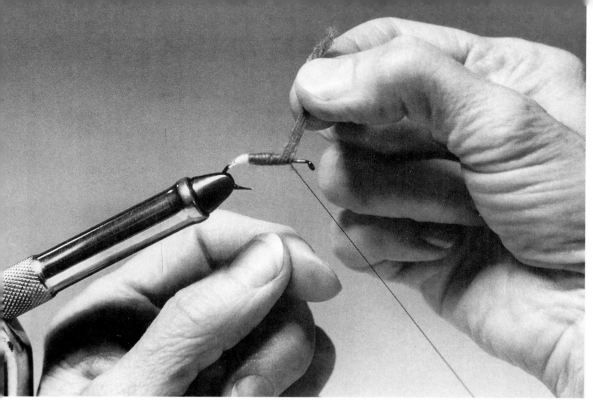

By allowing the strand of yarn to spread and overlap slightly in the center as it is wound on, an oval-shaped body appears over the slight padding thus created.

When the end of the dark yarn has been trimmed away, the body is ready for a hackle and a wing.

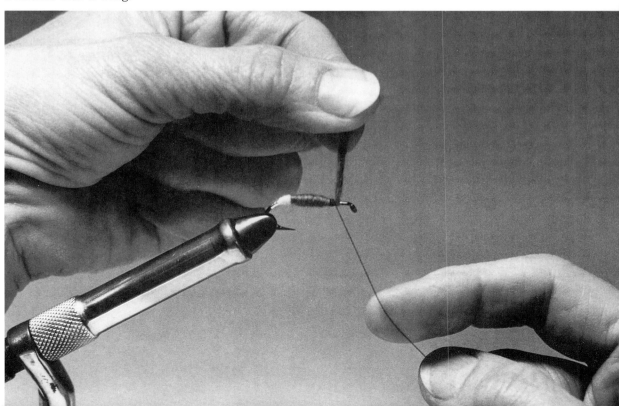

Name of Pattern	Tag	Tip	Body	Hackle	Wing	Head
Brown Grannom	———	Green Yarn	Pale Yellow Yarn	Brown	Dark Brown Turkey	Light
Tree Hopper	Gold	Light Green Yarn	Dark Green Yarn	Ginger Grizzly	Gray Mottled Goose	Black
March Dun	Gold	Yellow Yarn	Olive Green Yarn	Furnace	Gray-Dyed-Green Goose	Black
Early Evening Dun	Gold	Light Yellow Yarn	Light Blue Yarn	Light Yellow	White Goose	Light
Little March Brown	Gold	Yellow Yarn	Red Brown Yarn	Grouse	Dark Brown Turkey	Black
Leaper	Gold	Warm Yellow Yarn	Bluish Gray Yarn	Orange	White Goose	Black
Additional Patterns						
Adirondack	Gold	Yellow Yarn	Light Brown Yarn	Orange	White Goose	Black
Green-Tipped August Dun	Gold	Small Green Yarn	Orange Yarn	Orange	Slate Goose	Black
Explorer	Gold	Small Green Ostrich Herl	Orange Yarn	Partridge and Ginger	Light Slate Goose	Black
Piker	Gold	Orange Floss	Orange Yarn	Brown	White Goose	Black
Cooper	Gold	Small Yellow Chenille	Orange Yarn	Black	Mottled-Oak Turkey	Black
Challenger	Silver	Small Red Chenille	Brown Yarn	Furnace	Black Goose	Black

tip, and the brown yarn of the body is a richer, reddish, brown. Instead of a dark badger hackle, choose a grouse hackle with flues that reach just to the bend of the hook. You will complete this pattern with a wing of dark brown mottled turkey and a black head.

The sixth pattern is called a Leaper. It too is made with a gold tag and a yellow tip, but this time you will make the tip with yarn that is a warm yellow—almost a light orange in color. Use a bluish gray yarn for the rest of the body. This should be a fairly light blue-gray, not dark. Your pattern for the Leaper is completed with a bright orange hackle, sparsely tied, a wing of white goose, and a black head. It is a color phase of the Early Evening Dun, as you will see when the two flies are laid side by side. It has a darker tip, a brighter hackle, and a darker head to identify it.

Fifth Stage: With Tail

Our first pattern in the fifth stage of the fourth fly form is an Olive Dun. Not all of the patterns in this stage will have tags or tips, but all will have tails.

The tail for an Olive Dun is made with a few wisps of olive hackle flues, and black tying thread is used throughout in order to make a black head. Use olive-colored yarn for the body, tapering it over the area where the stub ends of the tail are secured and making sure the tying thread is completely covered. Use the rest of the feather from which the tail was made for the hackle. Tail, body, and hackle should all be the same shade of olive. Make the wing for this pattern from slate gray goose.

The second pattern is a Golden Dun. Its gray wisp tail can be made from a few flues taken from the all-gray hackle you will carefully match to the color of the slate gray goose wing. For the body, choose an orange yarn, and after fashioning an oval-shaped body wind on two turns of the gray hackle. Tie on the gray goose wing and complete the fly with a neatly tapered wrap-knot head.

For our next pattern, make a short gold tag before tying on a divided tail of brown mallard, and use dark brown yarn for the body. Choose a light blue-gray hackle (lighter than the hackle for the Golden Dun) and wind on a turn or two more than you have been using. The flues for this hackle should reach only to the hook barb. The wing of slate gray goose will be a little darker than the hackle. You now have another handsome dark fly with a black head—this one called a Great Dun.

The next pattern is quite different in color, although the method of tying is the same. This fly should be tied with a light yellow or primrose tying thread because the entire fly is a pale sulphur yellow. No tag for this pattern is required, although a short silver one may be added with good effect. The tail for a #10 hook is three or four flues wide and is taken this time from the same pale sulphur yellow goose feathers from which you will also take strips for the wing.

The tail may be made in either of two ways: a single strip of the goose feather is adequate; or a divided tail, made with two strips of matching feathers, can be used for this pattern. When two strips are used, tie them on to curve outward, away from each other. Whichever tail you choose, make it the same length as the body.

After the tail has been tied on and the body has been wound, use a sparsely tied sulphur hackle with flues that will reach to the point of the hook. Tie the wing strips on with their dull sides together so they will curve toward each other, neatly and firmly, over the pale oval of the body and the pale hackle. Finish the light head with several coats of

clear lacquer. The name of this lovely pattern is Sulphur Dun.

The pattern for a Shad Fly has a silver tag. Since this fly will have a badger hackle, select one that has a fairly small dark center. (The width of the dark centers can vary.) Use a few of the light tips of the flues for the tail. Make a small tip of yellow yarn before you tie the rest of the body with a medium gray yarn. Wind on a few turns of the hackle and tie on the wet-fly wing of medium-to-light gray goose. Finish this fly with a neat wrap-knot head, as you have done for all your other patterns.

For the Little Fox, tie on a small gold tag using a copper-colored or golden brown tying thread. The tail for this fly is a short tuft of yellow yarn. Tie the strand of yarn on above the point and barb. Clip it off even with the bend of the hook. Fray the short yarn tail into a tuft with the point of your scissors. Make a tip for the Little Fox with pale orange yarn, just slightly darker than the tuft tail. Use light tan or cream-colored yarn for the main part of the body. Select a ginger grizzly for the hackle (or a plain dark ginger) and wind it on sparingly. Make the wing from strips of light gray goose. With your tying thread you will make a copper-colored wrap-knot head as you finish this

Name of Pattern	Tag	Tail	Tip	Body	Hackle	Wing	Head
Olive Dun	———	Olive Hackle Wisps	———	Olive Yarn	Olive	Slate Goose	Black
Golden Dun	———	Gray Hackle Wisps	———	Orange Yarn	Gray	Slate Goose	Black
Great Dun	Gold	Brown Mallard Wisps	———	Brown Yarn	Blue-Gray	Slate Goose	Black
Sulphur Dun	Silver	Sulphur Yellow Wisps	———	Sulphur Yellow Yarn	Sulphur Yellow	Sulphur Yellow Goose	Primrose
Shad Fly	Silver	Badger Hackle Wisps	Yellow Yarn	Gray Yarn	Badger	Light Slate Goose	Black
Little Fox	Gold	Yellow Yarn Tuft	Light Orange Yarn	Tan or Cream Yarn	Ginger Grizzly	Light Slate Goose	Brown
Additional Patterns							
Romaine	———	Barred Wood Duck	———	Dark Green Yarn	Black	Barred Wood Duck	Black
Will's Fiery	Gold	Yellow Goose	Yellow Yarn	Black Yarn	Black	Gray Mallard	Black
Belgrade	Gold	Scarlet and White Hackle Wisps	Small Brown-Blue Peacock Herl	Yellow Yarn	Claret	Slate Goose Dyed Claret	Black
Wilson's Fly	Gold	Tippet	———	Orange Yarn	Orange	Gray Mallard	Black
Flambeau	Silver	Black Goose (Short)	Bright Orange	Bright Yellow Yarn	List Dyed Yellow	Black Goose	Black
Stebbins	Gold	Widgeon	———	Green Yarn	Furnace	Dark Slate Goose	Black

attractive fly. Be as economical as possible with the bindings of tying thread because you will be tying on several materials that must be secured but not overburdened with too much thread.

Sixth Stage: With Ribs

For the first ribbed pattern in this stage, we will tie a Dark Gray Dun. The tag will be made of a narrow, flat silver tinsel, which will also become the rib when you use the continuous tinsel technique. Make the tail with a few flues of lemon wood duck, and make the oval body with a strand of dark gray yarn. On a #10 hook, the fine silver tinsel can be wound on in five or six evenly spaced ribs, and the first turn of tinsel will be at the end of the oval body, where it meets the tail. Select a badger or list hackle with flues that extend to the bend of the hook. Use dark gray goose for the wing, and complete the fly with a black wrap-knot head.

A Late Evening Dun has a gold tag, a tail made from a few flues of gray mallard, and a rib of fine, flat gold tinsel over a light yellow yarn body. Choose a light bluish gray hackle for this fly, and make its wing from a medium-to-light gray goose. Black tying thread will make the black head. In fact, all of the following patterns have black heads.

A Green Mantle is all green except for the tag, rib, and wing. The tag is made with a fine, flat gold tinsel. When the tag is in place, tie on a few flues of green hackle for the tail. Round gold tinsel will make the rib, so the thread core must be exposed before you tie it in to make as little bulk as possible when you bind it on the hook over the stub ends of the hackle tail. Use a strand of green yarn for the oval body. You will find that you are able to make one or two more ribs on the fly body with the round tinsel than you did with the flat tinsel. The round tinsel will make a raised rib, changing the textural appearance of the fly body. Use about three turns of the green hackle from which you took the flues for the tail. Make a wet-fly wing with speckled gray mallard or teal, and with a shiny black wrap-knot head this pattern is complete.

For a White Tip Montreal the tag is flat gold. Use the same strand of tinsel for the rib, also.

Make the tail for this fly with flues of goose dyed red. Wind the rib over a body of claret-colored wool yarn, or yarn of another fiber if you do not have the wool. Use a hackle that has been dyed claret to match the yarn body. White-tipped turkey feathers are dark with a white edge at their tip ends. If you do not have them with short white ends (some may be out of proportion for the size hook you are using), then a brown turkey feather that has a very light edge can be used in its place. Finish the fly with a neat tapered wrap-knot head, coated several times with clear head lacquer.

Many patterns have been designed to represent the fins of the brook trout during spawning season, when its color is most brilliant. A few of these patterns require wings of more than one color. We will use two patterns as examples of building these multicolored wings for fly patterns, the Armstrong Fontinalis Fin and the Bergman Fontinalis Fin.

In order to understand how these wings are made and why the strips of feathers from different birds combine so well, we should know what is involved. Webster's says:

A series of somewhat obliquely directed processes on each side of the stem, or central shaft (of a feather), are called barbs. Barbs bear in like manner barbules, and these in turn, barbicels. The barbicels end, in many cases, in small hooks or hamuli, which hook on to the barbules of the next barb, uniting the whole series of processes into a vane or web. Absence of hamuli causes a feather to be soft and fluffy.

This ability of the barbs (flues, fibers) to cling to one another by the minute hooks on the tips of their barbicels is used by fly tyers to create multicolored combinations of feather fibers. The method of building these combinations in fly-tying parlance is often referred to as "marrying" the various fibers, or flues, to one another. It is also a process of building a homogeneous unit from strips or strands taken from the feathers of unrelated birds.

Multicolored "married" feather-fibers copy nature's own way of making an apparently "solid" feather out of many tiny strands. These strands, or flues, of different colors, and not necessarily from

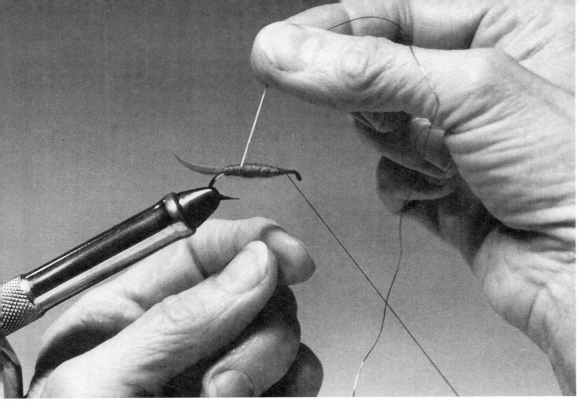

A strand of fine tinsel may appear to bury itself here and there in a yarn body as it is wound parallel with the winding of the yarn.

This can be overcome to a great extent by holding the tinsel vertically as successive turns of it are wound on.

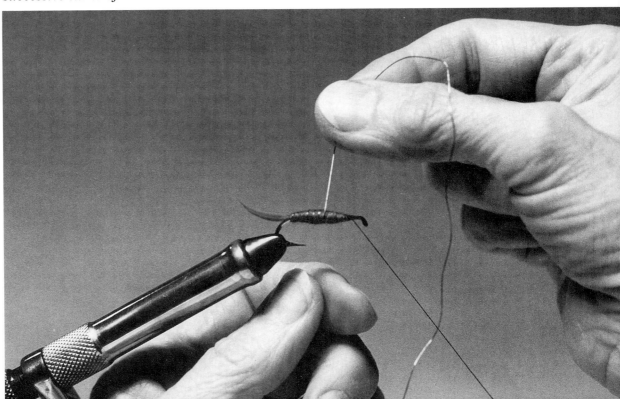

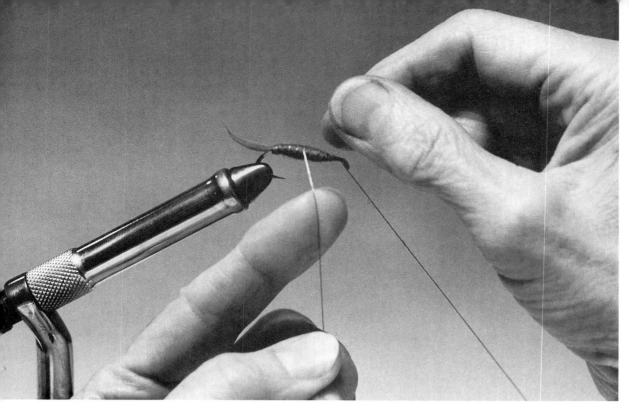

In order to wind a rib that is counter to the direction in which the body material was wound, bring it down on the side nearest to you. Carry it beneath the body . . .

. . . and bring it up from underneath the body, on the side away from you. Repeat this action, spacing each turn carefully. A tinsel rib wound in this manner will cross over the body material instead of biting into it.

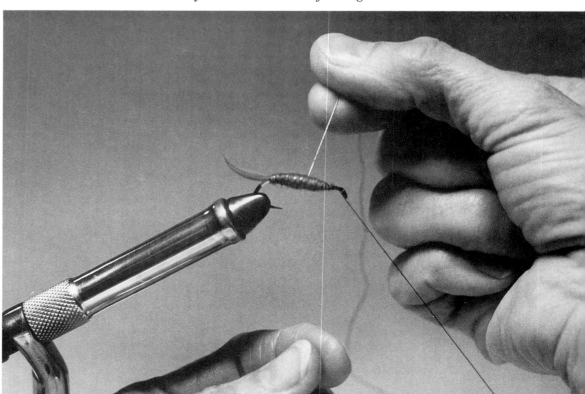

A turkey feather is slowly being pulled apart, showing a marked distortion of its pattern. The outer tips are still held firmly together by the tiny hooks on each barbule that edge the flue, or barb.

Flues of a piece of swan feather being pulled to separate them. They cling tenaciously. Note that the fly-tying vise can be seen through the translucent barbules.

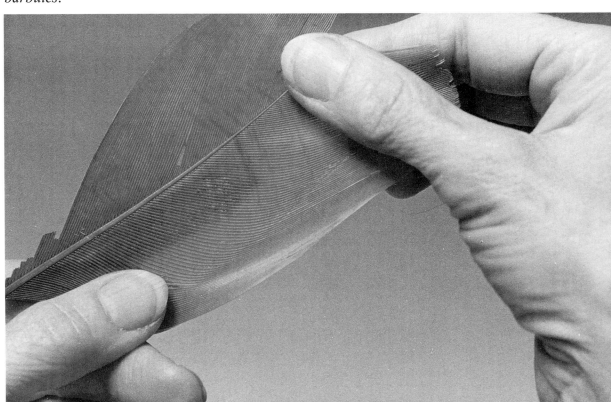

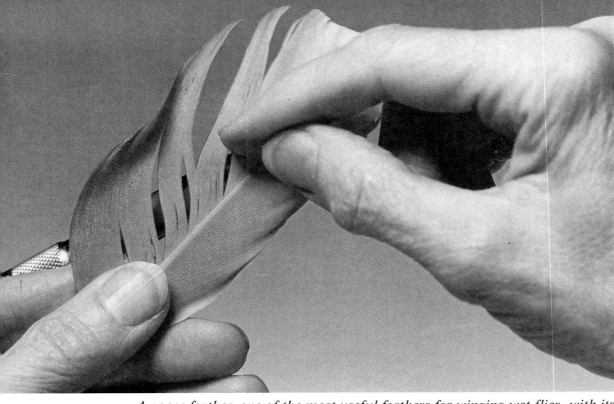

A goose feather, one of the most useful feathers for winging wet flies, with its flues pulled apart. These may be reunited . . .

. . . by stroking the feather gently between thumb and fingers several times from the central shaft toward the outer tips.

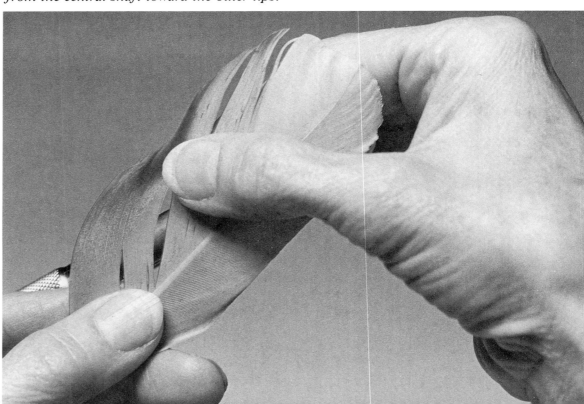

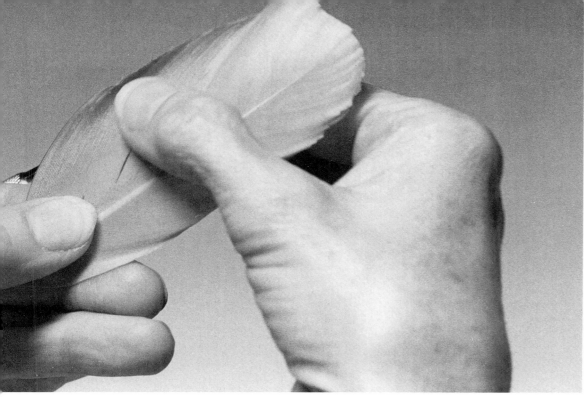

The splits gradually disappear as the flues below are joined again to the ones above.

the same kind of bird, can be joined, and a fly wing built. Swan can be attached to turkey, duck, goose, and so on. The flues must be chosen from comparable sides of the feathers—right side must be used with right, left side with left. Beautiful wings for flies are the result.

This method, here in its simplest form of two or three colors combined for wet-fly wings, is also used for the traditional, classic salmon-fly patterns that incorporate many different-colored strips from the feathers of many different birds.

The number of flues in each colored strip to be used is gauged by, or dependent upon, the width to which the wing may be built for the size of the fly on which it will be tied. When you are tying several flies of the same pattern, which requires pairs of wings made with more than one color, it is a time-saver to build the wings first in order to have the wing strips uniform, matching left and right, and proportionately the same. You can also make them in several different sizes, for smaller or larger flies, in order to have them ready when you need them.

The depth of each flue may vary with the different feathers available. However, it is not difficult to maintain the correct proportions by adding a flue to a very fine feather strip, or removing one if

necessary, in order to obtain visual uniformity.

The next two patterns have identical wings. The tails, ribs, and hackles are different, but the wings for both patterns can be made at the same time.

Although the Armstrong Fontinalis Fin precedes that of the Bergman Fontinalis Fin on the color plate, we will consider the Bergman pattern next, because the tails for it are built like the wings, and can be made at the same time.

Orange goose furnishes the main strip of feather for the wings of both patterns. A narrow strip of gray goose is immediately above the orange, and a narrow strip of white goose makes the top edge. The entire wing, of course, is in proportion to the hook you are using: two-thirds orange, one-sixth gray, one-sixth white. Make sure that the feathers match right and left before you cut the segments for the wings. Make sure, also, that the completed built-wing is no wider than if it were made of a single strip of one color.

The tails are made the same way. They are much narrower, however, and the combined width of the three strips for the tail should be no wider than if the tail were made with a single strip of goose flues. Build the strips for the tail using the same proportion of flues as for the wings—just use fewer flues of each color.

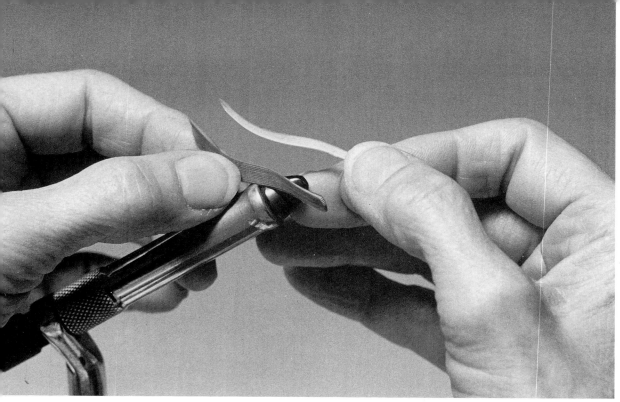

A segment of slate-colored goose for the lower part of a wing, with a narrow strip of white goose for the top.

Held one above the other so that the tips match, the separate strips are placed together. The minute hooks on the barbicels cause the lower strip to cling almost immediately to the barbs above.

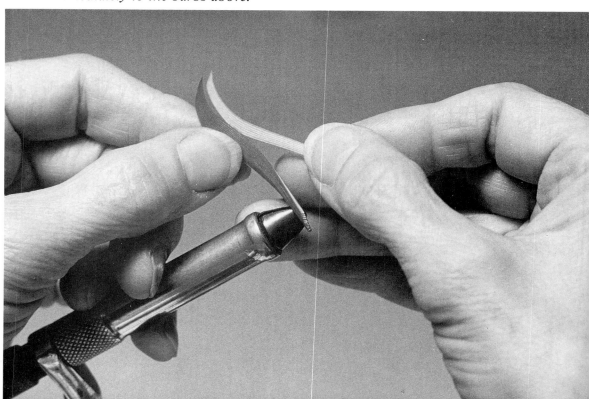

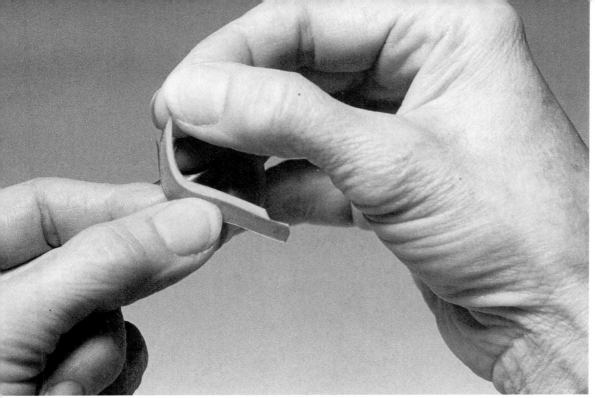

A gentle stroke between thumb and fingers from the cut edge toward the outer tips will help the feather strips to mesh.

Pull the tip of the top feather away from the lower strip, and the part still attached will cling so well that it will not fall away.

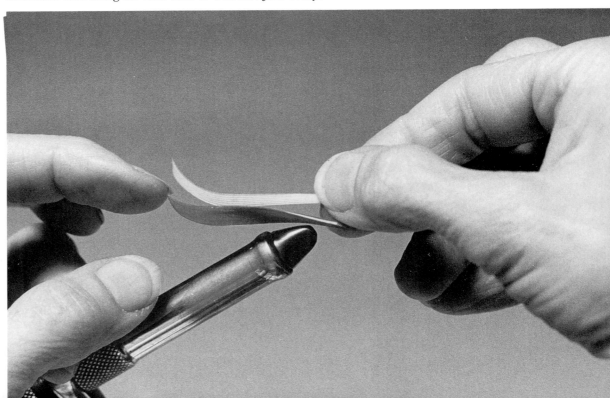

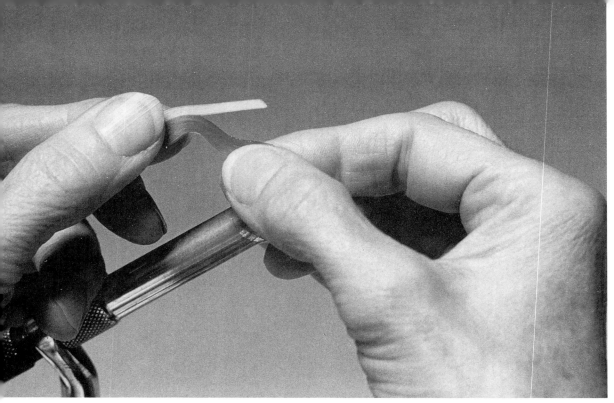

Pull apart from the cut edge and you can observe Nature's zipper at work.

Another stroke, and the two separate strips from feathers of different birds have formed a single, bicolored segment of feather. Many narrow strips of different colors can be built into a wing in this way. Flues from the opposite sides of matched feathers will form the mate to this one.

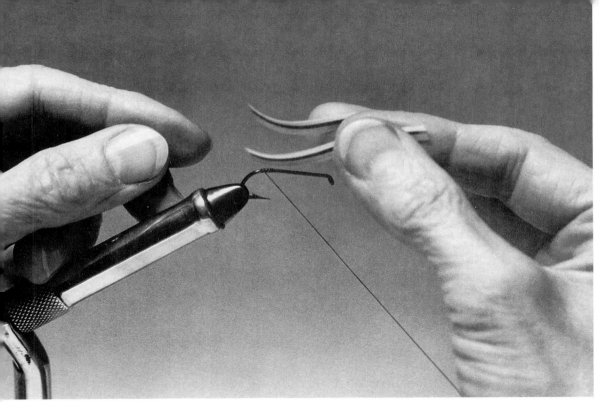

For the Bergman pattern of the Fontinalis Fin, tails and wings are made with three strips of goose feathers, two of which are dyed. The tails are narrow— no wider than if they were made of a single strip of one color.

Tied on above the barb of the hook, the tails flare outward, away from each other, making a divided tail.

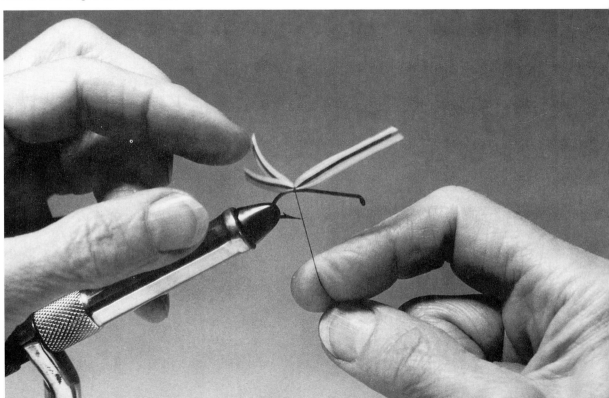

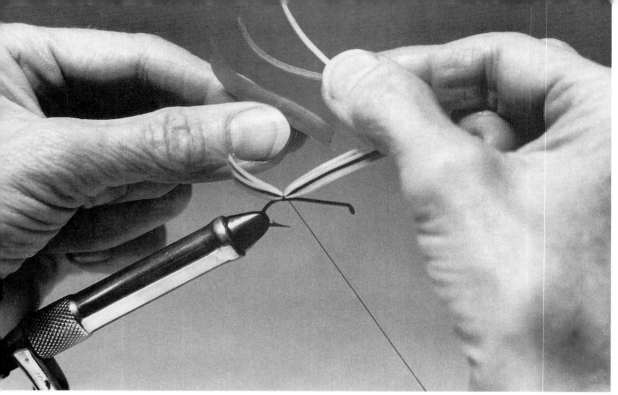

The wings for both Bergman's and Armstrong's Fontinalis Fin pattern are made with feather strips of three different colors, also. The three strips of feathers for the wings are held here, one above the other, in their correct order. The main strip of the wing is the lowest, widest one.

Gentle stroking with the fingers from the cut edges outward to the tips will "zip" the two narrow strips together. These are then lowered to rest against the widest strip . . .

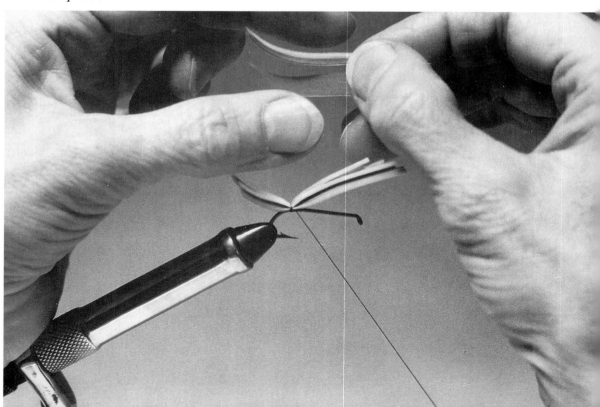

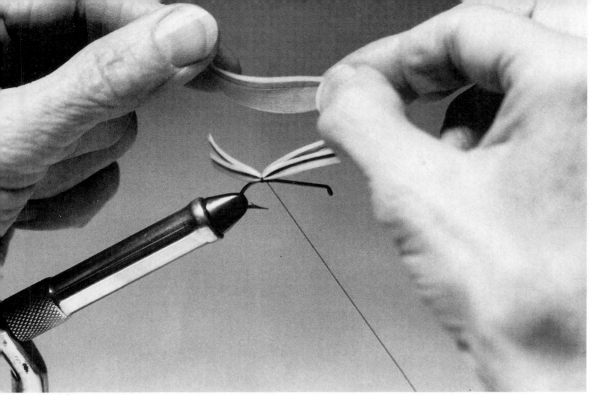

. . . and the stroking action is repeated, uniting the widest strip with the two above and creating a single wing strip of three different colors. Repeat the process with strips from matching feathers to make a pair.

For the body of the Bergman pattern, a strand each of orange and gray yarn of the same weight are tied on together, side by side, as a single strand. They are wound on as a single strand, as well.

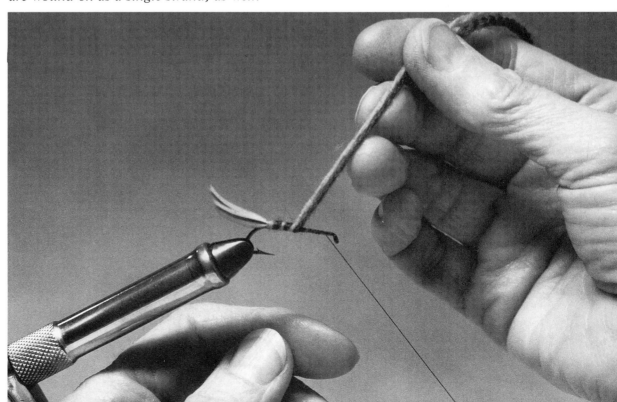

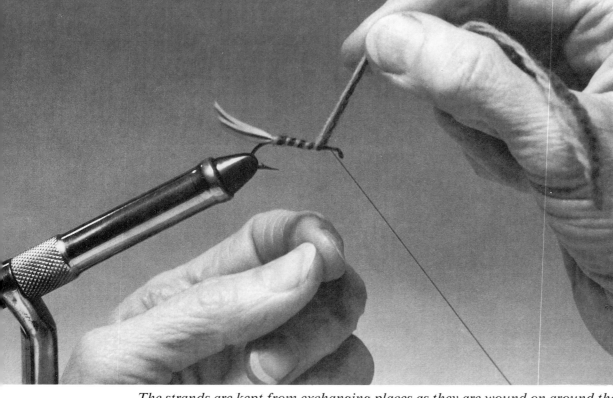

The strands are kept from exchanging places as they are wound on around the hook to form the body. When the relationship of each strand to the other is maintained like this, the slim body will be ribbed evenly.

Tie the tails on to curve away from each other by placing their dull sides on the outside of the pair. The natural curve of the goose feathers from which they were made will be evident, and the result will be a divided tail. Make the tail no longer than the length of the body of the fly.

The body of the Bergman pattern is orange yarn ribbed with a strand of gray yarn. This effect can be achieved in either of two ways when the yarns are of the same size and weight. One way is to tie in the strand of gray yarn as you would if the rib were to be made of tinsel. Tie in the strand of orange yarn, fashion an oval body with it, and spiral the gray strand over it. The other way is to use the two strands of yarn as though they were one. Tie both strands on together, side by side, with the orange strand next to the tail, and wind them on together as a single wide strand, making sure that they do not exchange places as you wind them along the hook. Secure them when you reach the wing position. Clip the excess away carefully to leave as little bulk as possible. The body will appear to be ribbed. This is a good shortcut when limited time is a factor in your tying.

The hackle for Bergman's Fontinalis Fin is pale blue, with tips that reach just to the bend of the hook. Use it sparingly; two or three turns of it are ample. You are ready now to tie on the multi-colored wings. With their dull sides together, hold them against the fly body to judge their correct length. The tips should extend approximately the width of the gape beyond the body, not quite to the end of the tails. Transfer them to your left hand and tie them on. It should be no more difficult to control wings made of a combination of feather flues than it would if they were single strips of one color. Secure the wings. Trim the stub ends of wing material, tapering them to make a base for your wrap knot. Make the neatly tapered wrap-knot head and give it several thin coats of clear lacquer.

Armstrong's Fontinalis Fin has a tail of white hackle wisps, no longer than the body. Tie on a strand of fine, flat or round gold tinsel for a rib. A strand of orange yarn will make an oval body. When you have fashioned the body, spiral the rib of gold tinsel over it. Select a furnace hackle this time, and choose one that has a dark center, small

114

in proportion to the hook you are using, its tips just reaching to the bend of the hook.

Match the wing strips right and left. You are now ready to tie the wing on as you did for the previous pattern. Judge their correct length against the hook, hold them in position, and carefully tie them on. Trim away the stub ends, making a nicely tapered base for your wrap knot, finish tying the head, and give it a coat of clear lacquer.

Name of Pattern	Tag	Tail	Rib	Body	Hackle	Wing
Dark Gray Dun	Silver	Lemon Wood Duck	Silver	Dark Gray	List	Dark Gray Goose
Late Evening Dun	Gold	Gray Mallard	Gold	Pale Yellow	Blue-Gray	Light Gray Goose
Green Mantle	Gold	Green Wisps	Gold	Green Yarn	Green	Gray Mallard
White Tip Montreal	Gold	Red Goose	Gold	Claret Yarn	Claret	White-Tipped Turkey
Bergman Fontinalis Fin	———	Orange/Gray/White Goose	Gray Yarn	Orange Yarn	Pale Blue	Orange/Gray/White*
Armstrong Fontinalis Fin	———	White Hackle Wisps	Gold	Orange Yarn	Furnace	Orange/Gray/White*

Additional Patterns							
Name of Pattern	Tag	Tail	Tip	Rib	Body	Hackle	Wing
Olive Wren	Silver	Gray Mallard	Yellow-Green Angora	Silver	Olive Brown	Furnace	Light Brown Turkey
Laramie	Silver	Claret or Deep Wine	Fine Oval Silver	Silver	Claret	Black	Dark Gray Goose
Schaefer	Gold	Tippet	———	Gold	Red-Brown	Grizzly	Green/Dark Blue/Red*
White River	Silver	Light Gray Wisps	———	Twisted Red Floss	White Yarn	Badger	White Goose
Langlade	Silver	Teal	———	Fine Silver	Pale Gray	Light Green	Light Gray Goose
Lake Edward	Gold	Yellow Goose	———	Fine Round Gold	Light Brown	Scarlet	Brown/Dark Blue/Yellow*
Black Creek	Gold	Lemon Wood Duck	———	Fine Flat Silver	Black Yarn	Honey Dun	Lemon Wood Duck
Nekoosa	Gold	Brown Mallard	———	Fine Flat Gold	Gray Yarn	Furnace	Black Goose with Orange Head

*Material for the built-wings is listed here from the bottom strip up, since it is the widest one for these patterns.

As a general rule, a rib is wound only over the main part of the body, not over the tip.

	Dark Sedge	Dark Blue Sedge	Lemon and Gray	Brown Hackle Orange	Furnace Brown	Colonel Goss
	Woodruff	Cowdung	Claret Dun	Light Gnat	Light Sand Fly	Square Tail
	Dubbed Olive Gnat	Grass Hopper	Evening Dun	Pale Evening Dun	March Dun	Light Sedge
	Small Dark Sedge	Bright Spec	Female Grannom	Blue Tip	Little Light Fox	Female Gray Gnat
	Namekagon	Lady Beaverkill	Green Sack	Female Hendrickson	Cahill	Dubbed Brown Stone
	Old Irish Iron Blue Dun	Gold-Ribbed Hare's Ear	Pale Sulphur Dun	Brown Mallard	Brown Miller	Larry St. John

The sweet breezes blow, the morning sun shines
The white clouds drift slow down the sky;
'Tis a day that is perfect for sport with the lines,
For artistic cast of the fly.

Isaac McLellan, "The Angler's Chant"

Dubbing Body
The Fifth Fly Form

Webster's says that *dubbing* is the body substance of an angler's fly. *Dub* means to dress, as a fly, hook, or line, and also to strike cloth with teasels to raise a nap.

Dubbed bodies for flies are sometimes referred to as *dubbin* bodies. The act of "dressing" the hook — of fraying or plucking the material and applying it to the hook — is called dubbing. The material itself is called "dubbing" and the process of spinning or twirling it onto a thread in order to wind it around a hook for a fly body is also called "dubbing."

Regardless of their color or whether they are made of yarns, furs, or combinations of these, all of the flies in this fly form have dubbed bodies. These bodies may be made from a variety of individual materials. Combinations of them in many colors may be made or purchased preblended. Any material that can be frayed or plucked and spun onto a thread can be used to create a dubbed fly body. Yarns of wool, mohair, cashmere, angora, or any of the synthetic yarns are useful, as well as almost any fur. The soft undercoats of fur spin well, and the guard hairs, when they are not too long, may be included to give a bristling, rough appearance to a fly body (a distinctly buggy look), or to catch the light occasionally. Traditionally, these materials are used separately or combined in whatever proportions and colors the tyer prefers, if not specified in a pattern.

Dubbed bodies may be slim and tapered, chunky and round, oval, or they may start slim and then swell behind the area of wing and hackle for an indication of wing case or thorax. Whether or not the fish are cognizant of these small differences in body shape is of no matter; if the end result is successful fishing performance, all is well.

Insect colors subtle, muted, and variable can be made from yarns available in myriad earth tones, tints, and textures. Furs of all kinds provide a wealth of grays and browns, creams and tans in their soft undercoats, which make beautiful dubbings alone or in combination with dubbings made from fraying yarns. By mixing furs with yarns or mohair with wool, for example, varying textures can be obtained to create a variety of effects. Textures can also be changed by including the short guard hairs from pieces of fur that have them, such as the masks and ears of hares and rabbits. Mohair has an interesting texture of its own, and can be mixed with the dubbings of other fibers besides wool.

Synthetic dubbings have been prepared in many colors and are available for the tyer who wishes to take shortcuts in his tying, but it is good to know how to blend the dubbings for one's own use, as well. Part of the fun of fly tying is in learning how to create your own blends and effects. Artificial fibers tend to be moisture-resistant and nonabsorbent, more suitable for dry than for wet flies, which should sink quickly after they have been cast upon the water of a lake or stream. Pre-blended dubbings can be incorporated with those of your own choosing, however, for the particular effect you desire.

The frayed or plucked materials can be spun directly onto a well-waxed tying thread, which is the simplest and most direct method. A fly body so made usually cannot be unwound. Or those materials can be spun onto well-waxed threads that have been cut to predetermined lengths suitable for winding onto hooks of various sizes later. These prepared dubbed threads are called *spindles*, and should be carefully stored away according to color for future use.

Still another method of preparing the dubbed threads requires the use of a double thread with the dubbing material caught between as the two threads are twisted together—a chenille-like result. Or they can be made with a loop of the tying thread, in between which the dubbing material is caught, and the loop tightly twisted.

The wax used on the thread should be slightly sticky, or tacky, in order to help the dubbing adhere to the thread. As the tacky wax dries out, or hardens, it forms an almost permanent bond and the resultant fly body is very durable.

A word about color: attempting to describe a color is like trying to explain a flavor to someone who has never experienced it. Color combinations used for dubbing fly bodies defy accurate description. Primary and secondary colors can be understood, but the fine gradation of their blending depends a great deal on "the eye of the beholder."

Color charts as used by printers vary depending on how their inks differ in density, quantity, and chemistry, and on the type of paper on which those inks are printed. Attempts at standardization of colors might be done by a numbering system of accepted basic chemical pigments, as in the systems devised by Munsell, Ostwald, and Lukeisch, but the introduction of synthetic color pigments brings about new problems. Light also must be taken into consideration. Daylight, incandescent, and fluorescent lights all have widely different effects on how color is perceived.

The fly tyer's colors are, to a great extent, approximations of the natural things with which he is familiar, and to which he can relate. Cinnamon, for example, is about the color of stick cinnamon, or of ground cinnamon, or as close to it as feathers, fur, floss, and yarn can come when they are dyed. Ginger is the color of the spice. White is not always a pure, pristine white; naturally white hackles vary a great deal in tint. Black has many tones and if it is shiny, or "steely," the sheen can be white! Blue feathers do not contain actual blue pigment—the color we see depends upon the arrangement of the black pigment and how it refracts the light prismatically.

Early fly tyers have left descriptions of the fly patterns they tied. Most often they dyed their own materials, but usually not with commercially produced dyes. Those they did use were identified by trade names that no longer exist today. More popular were the many natural materials they used for dyeing—woods, roots, and berries. The dyeing process required many hours of preparation of the dyes, and of the feathers to accept those dyes. Brazilwood, logwood, pearl ash, redwood, yellow wood, camwood, sumac, the bark of the alder tree, and the fresh outer coverings of walnuts are some of the substances that were used for dye making.

It might be fun to try some of those early recipes, but the exact amount of dye to use and the exact moment at which to remove the feathers from the dye are never precisely given. Thus the color considered to be correct then cannot be known with any certainty today. Additionally, antique flies, however carefully preserved, may have lost some of their original colors in some degree. But we can still admire what remains of their original beauty.

First Stage: Body and Hackle

The body material for the fifth fly form is the same for all of the six stages of the fly patterns to follow. Only the components and colors of the dubbing material will change. Be sure to prepare enough of each of the dubbings to have a reserve supply on hand for use later, when you want to repeat a favorite pattern. It is a good idea to label the different blends with the name of the pattern for which it was made.

Our first pattern is a Dark Sedge. Mix the dubbing, using equal amounts of a medium dark green yarn and a brown fur. The body will be dark, and in this blend of brown and green neither color should dominate. The resulting mixture will be more of a brownish green olive than anything else, and as you are dubbing it into a slim oval body you can adjust the mixture if either of its component colors tends to be more pronounced. Select a dark red-brown hackle and wind it on with its glossy side toward the hook eye.

For the body of the second pattern, use dyed seal's fur in equal amounts of dark blue and brown. A black hackle, tied on in the same manner as the first, will give you a Dark Blue Sedge.

Our third pattern will be a brighter one. Blend equal amounts of seal's fur, dyed a lemon yellow, with yellow yarn. You will notice the subtle differences in the texture of yarn combined with seal or other furs. The body for this fly is a pleasing oval one also. Add a medium gray grizzly hackle and you will have a Lemon and Gray. All three of these patterns have exactly the same construction using dubbed material. Only the color combinations make them different from one another.

For the body of the fourth pattern, use orange wool if you have it—if not, use whatever yarn you have in a bright, almost pure orange. For this pattern, build up the body into a slightly more rounded shape while you are dubbing it onto the thread and hook. Select a bright reddish brown furnace hackle that has a good dark center. Wind it on as you did the others and you will have a Brown Hackle Orange, a pattern that takes its name from the colors of the materials from which it is made, as did the previous pattern. It is an excellent wet fly.

The next pattern is a darker version of the same fly. Make the body of a bright brown dubbing of yarn and wind it on the hook so that it will be slightly more rounded than oval in shape. With

another furnace hackle in place you will have a Furnace Brown. (My records for this bright brown dubbing show it to be a mixture of one-quarter bright orange, one-quarter cinnamon, one-quarter cedar, and one-quarter brown.)

You have made the first five flies all in the same way, adding a trifle more dubbing for the last two than for the first three, thereby altering the overall shape of the bodies. These slight changes in shape, as well as in color, are found throughout fly tying. Individual preferences for slight alterations in body shape, hackle length, or type of wing are practically limitless. But the basic procedure remains constant.

For the sixth pattern we will make another very small change in the shape of the body. Starting as for an oval body, let the dubbing build slightly when it approaches the hook eye, before the hackle is tied on. Not quite as pronounced as the slim silhouette for this first stage, this shape nevertheless is a modification of it.

Use a red-orange dubbing for the body. To make the dubbing, use about one-quarter bright red yarn to three-quarters true orange yarn. Frayed and blended together, the red will somewhat mute the stridency of the orange. Select a badger, or list, hackle for this pattern, and you will have a Colonel Goss. Remember that a badger hackle has the dark center of a furnace hackle, but its flues are white or cream-colored instead of brown, while a list hackle is the same except that it has a dark edging on its light flues, just as a coch-y-bondhu is a furnace hackle with a darker edge.

Second Stage: With Wings
The first pattern in this second stage of the fifth fly form is a famous one: the Woodruff. Its olive green body is usually made of wool dubbing, but yarn of any fiber can be used. Dyed seal's fur may also be used, or a mixture of yarn with fur. A wet-fly hackle, brown and fairly long, should be chosen.

On many wet-fly patterns, especially those without tails, the slightly longer hackle is a distinct advantage. Sparsely tied, their longer flues give the illusion, when submerged, of trailing legs and will also give an appearance of movement when manipulated with the fly rod.

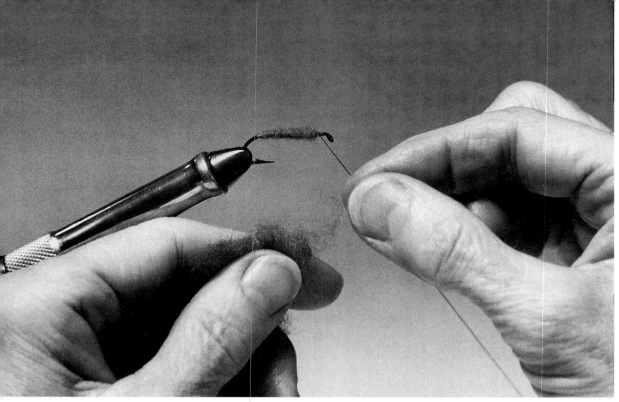

A slim tapered body is made with dubbing applied sparsely to the tying thread where it is wound on above the barb, gradually increasing as it is wound toward the hook eye.

For an oval body, increase the amount of dubbing toward the center of the hook and decrease it gradually as it nears the eye.

Name of Pattern	Body	Hackle
Dark Sedge	Green Yarn and Brown Fur Dubbing	Dark Red-Brown
Dark Blue Sedge	Dark Blue and Brown Seal Fur Dubbing	Black
Lemon and Gray	Yellow Yarn and Lemon Yellow Seal Fur Dubbing	Grizzly
Brown Hackle Orange	Orange Yarn Dubbing	Brown
Furnace Brown	Bright Brown Yarn Dubbing	Furnace
Colonel Goss	Red-Orange Yarn Dubbing	Badger or List
Additional Patterns		
Black Hackle Blue	Dark Blue-Dyed Fur or Yarn Dubbing	Black
Davidson Hackle	Dark Orange and Brown Yarn Dubbing Mixed	Light Brown and Yellow Hackles Together
Imp	Dark Muskrat Dubbing	Tiny Bright Red with Gray in Front
Trail Fly	Yellow Yarn and Gray Fur Dubbing	Grouse
Granger	Dark Brown Fur Dubbing	Partridge
Cream Partridge	Cream-Colored Fur Dubbing	Partridge

A speckled mallard-feather wing and a green head complete the pattern. Green tying thread may be used for tying the entire fly.

For the second pattern, use a dubbing made from dark olive green and cinnamon-colored yarn, frayed and blended together in even proportions. Since this fly will have a brown head, spin your dubbing on a brown tying thread. The wet-fly wing of medium gray (or slate) goose feather completes this pattern and you have the well-known Cowdung, an excellent pattern in sizes 10 and smaller.

Our third pattern is a Claret Dun. This fly also has a wing of slate goose, but slightly darker than that for the Cowdung. Gradations of gray tints and shades are to be found on all slate goose feathers. Careful selection and matching will give you quite a wide range of gray in only a few matched pairs of feathers.

The claret body material and hackle are dyed. A ginger hackle tinted red will usually yield a pass-able claret color. Remember that not all feathers are affected by dyes in the same way. This is also true of furs and hairs. If you do your own dyeing, be prepared to experiment.

The next pattern is all gray: light gray dubbing for the slender oval body, and a light grizzly for the hackle. Choose lighter slate goose strips for this fly than you used for either of the two foregoing patterns. This fly is called a Light Gnat, and the only dark spot on it will be its black head.

The Light Sand Fly will have, as its name suggests, a body of sand-colored dubbing, which usually turns out to be tan. Its hackle should be cinnamon brown, and make its wings of a medium shade of gray goose with a narrow strip of cinnamon turkey laid over its top edge — our second encounter with the built- (or married) wing technique. You will not find this difficult to master when you remember that both the turkey and goose feathers must match right side to right side and left side to left side. A strip from the left side

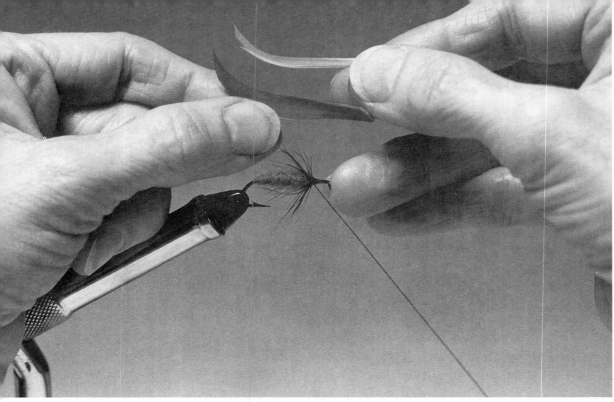

For patterns having feather wings of two or more colors, the wings must be built, *or* married. *Here, strips of different colors from the left side of two goose feathers make half of a pair of wings. To make a full pair, strips from both sides of matching feathers must be used.*

With the natural tips placed together, the narrow strip is eased down against the lower strip edge to edge. A single gentle stroke of the fingers should join the two into one interlocking strip of feather.

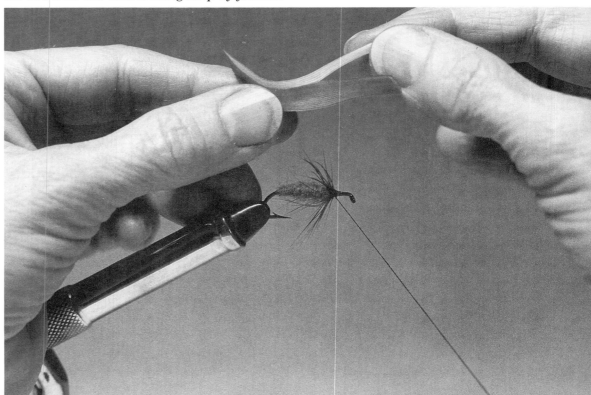

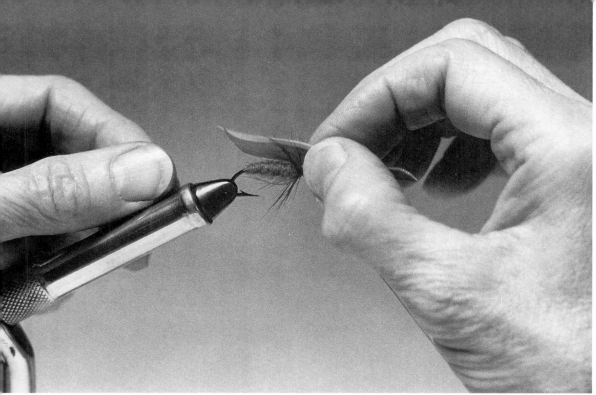

Pairs of these built- or married-feather wings should be prepared for use before the fly bodies are tied. Use them as you would if the wings were made of single strips of feather.

A beautiful hair wing of frosty squirrel tail, as for the Square Tail pattern, has been chosen for a pleasing proportion of black and white and gauged to the size of the fly being tied. This wing will lie back over the body in wet-fly manner.

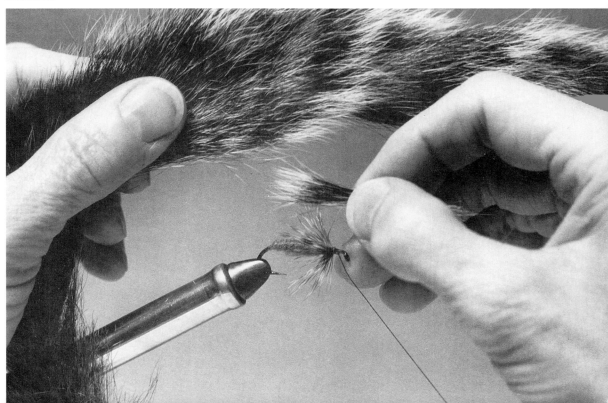

Name of Pattern	Body	Hackle	Wing	Head
Woodruff	Olive Green Dubbing	Brown	Speckled Mallard	Green
Cowdung	Dark Olive Green and Cinnamon Dubbing	Brown	Gray Goose	Brown
Claret Dun	Claret Seal Dubbing	Claret	Dark Goose	Black
Light Gnat	Light Gray Fur Dubbing	Light Grizzly	Light Goose	Black
Light Sand Fly	Sand-Colored Fur and Yarn Dubbing	Brown	Slate with Cinnamon Over	Black
Square Tail	Dark Muskrat Fur Dubbing	Grizzly	Frosty Squirrel	Black
Additional Patterns				
Dark-Dubbed Sand Fly	Sand-Colored Dubbing	Havanah Brown	Dark Slate with Brown Turkey Over	Black
Brown Sedge	Medium Gray Dubbing	Dark Brown	Medium Gray Goose	Black
Bard's Alder	Medium Gray Dubbing	Grizzly	Light Gray Goose	Black
Small Male Sedge	Dark Red-Brown Seal Dubbing	List	Grouse or Dark Turkey	Black
Dark Fox	Golden Brown Yarn Dubbing	Black (Short)	Cinnamon Goose	Black
Golden Midge	Bright Yellow Yarn Dubbing	Bright Brown	Light Slate Goose	Black

of one feather will not attach to a strip from the right side of another.

Most wings so far have been made of feathers. Hairwinged patterns are excellent wet flies also and have appeared among the additional patterns listed in the second, third, and fourth fly forms. Our next pattern has a wing made of hair, from the tail of a gray squirrel. Squirrel tails, both the gray (frosty) squirrel, with its hair ranging in color from light gray with a tannish base (brindle) to a broad band of black tipped with white, and the fox squirrel, whose tail hair is a golden brown with a band of black near the golden brown tips, have furnished fly tyers with beautiful excuses for winging their flies with hair in lieu of feathers. The fine, soft undercoats from the base of these tails make excellent dubbing—gray or ginger or a mixture of the two.

But for the gray body of our Square Tail, we will use gray dubbing from a piece of muskrat fur. The fur nearest to the hide is a dark bluish slate gray. With it, make a slender tapered body.

Choose a grizzly hackle with flues that will reach the bend of the hook. When it is tied on to lie back and around the fly body, select a small tuft of frosty squirrel for the wing.

For flies size #10 and smaller, try to choose hair that has a fairly short white tip so that the dark part of the hair will be over the body of the fly, with the white ends of the hair extending just beyond the bend of the hook. Make the natural white tips of the hair as even as possible in order to make the end of the hair wing "square," in keeping with the name of the pattern. Tie the tuft of hair on to lie back over the hackle and body. The angle of the wing can be adjusted with the tying thread around its base. After it has been secured to the hook and before the cut ends are trimmed away, anchor it once more. The cut ends of the hair wing should taper down from where the wing is tied on to the base of the hook eye, forming a foundation for the head of the fly as it is covered with a wrap knot.

Comparing the Square Tail with the Light Gnat, you will find three points of difference. The darker body, darker grizzly hackle, and hair wing on the Square Tail have made only a slight alteration in the pattern of the Light Gnat. It could rightfully be called a dark hairwing version of the Light Gnat.

Frosty squirrel can be used on many patterns specifying a white-tipped feather wing, and those patterns then become the hairwing versions of the feathered ones. Hair wings are very durable.

Third Stage: With Tag

Gold-tinsel tags are used on all of the next six patterns. Only the colors of body and hackle vary with the shades of the gray goose wing material, which is used for all except one. That one will have a whole-feather wing.

The first pattern is the Dubbed Olive Gnat. With the gold tag in place, make the dark olive dubbing for the body with yarn that you have dyed and frayed, or from yarn that you have found in this color. The hackle for this fly should be a rather dark and dull gray with a very slight brownish cast, sometimes called an "iron dun." For the wing, use strips of slate gray goose. This is an excellent and effective pattern.

Our second pattern is a Grass Hopper. Grasshoppers have been interpreted in several different ways by different tyers, so this pattern is one of many. Its body, made of a slightly greenish yellow yarn dubbing, is shaped into a neat oval. A furnace hackle and a wing of medium gray goose complete it. This is no attempt to imitate an actual hopper. It is, however, a very fine wet fly. Its gold-tinsel tag is very short, and its head is black.

Our third pattern is the Evening Dun. For this fly, use a light gray tying thread so that it will have a gray head. The gold-tinsel tag is short for this pattern. Make the body with a light yellow dubbing. For the hackle, choose one that is fairly long and pale gray. (A white hackle may be tinted a very light gray). With a wing of light gray goose, the pattern is complete.

The next pattern is a lighter version of the one just tied. The light yellow yarn dubbing you used for the Evening Dun may be mixed with a tiny amount of white angora or white yarn dubbing to lighten it. Spin this dubbing on a pale yellow or primrose-colored tying thread because the fly

should have a very light yellow head. The hackle is also a very light yellow. Make the wing with light gray goose. You now have a Pale Evening Dun. The difference between these two patterns is minute—only the pale color of the hackles and the heads separates them. Both are excellent flies with which to fish.

For our fifth pattern, use a tying thread of medium gray in order that the fly have the gray head required. Spin a tapered body with a dubbing of green yarn slightly on the blue-green side, rather than a bright kelly green. As you wind on the dubbing, make the body a bit fuller through the center and toward the head, for here you will "pick out" the dubbing beneath the hook to take the place of a hackle throat. Make the wings from strips as wide as the hook's gape of a medium-to-light gray goose, and you will have another useful pattern, the March Dun.

For your Light Sedge use a light tannish or cream-colored fur dubbing. Dubbing from some natural furs often varies from cream to pinkish cream to a light tan. Choose tan for the body of this fly. Select a ginger hackle of medium length; two or three turns of it will be ample. Separate it at the top to enable a single-feather wing to lie flat over the body after it is tied on. The wing is made with a breast or shoulder feather rather than a feather suitable for a hackle. Select a feather from a brown hen or widgeon.

Fourth Stage: With Tip

Tips on the following patterns are made of dubbing, chenille, and floss. Any of these tips could be made of any of the three materials without drastically altering the patterns. Only the difference in colors is important here. If a pattern specifies a particular material, that material should be used, of course, but if just the color of the tip is indicated in a pattern listing, it may be made of the dubbing, of chenille, of floss, or even of ostrich herl; the choice is left to you. All of the following patterns have tags.

A Small Dark Sedge is an excellent pattern when it is tied on #10 and smaller hooks. It has a gold tag. For this fly use primrose tying thread. Its small tip is made of light yellow-green dubbing to form the end of its dark brown dubbing body. Use

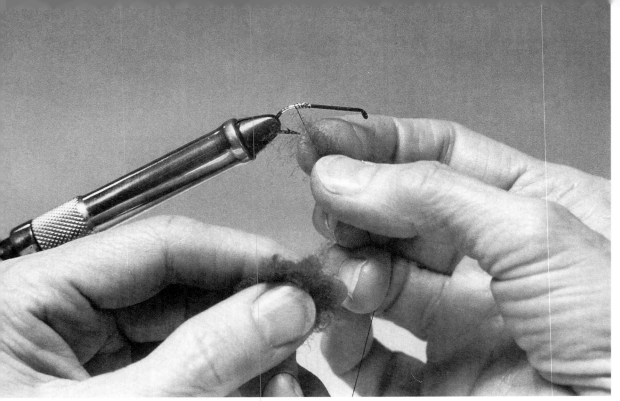

A tinsel tag has been tied on the hook. The cut and bound end of tinsel will be covered entirely by the dubbing as it is wound on.

Body dubbing may begin above the barb and wound toward the eye. It may also begin at the "wing position" and be wound back to cover the thread that binds the cut end of tinsel, then brought forward again. Use whatever way is easiest for you to form a tapered or oval body.

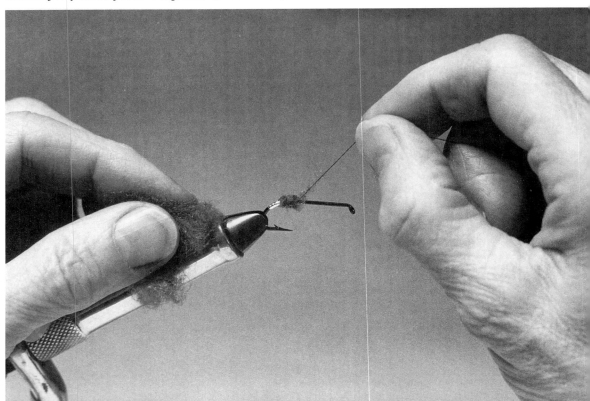

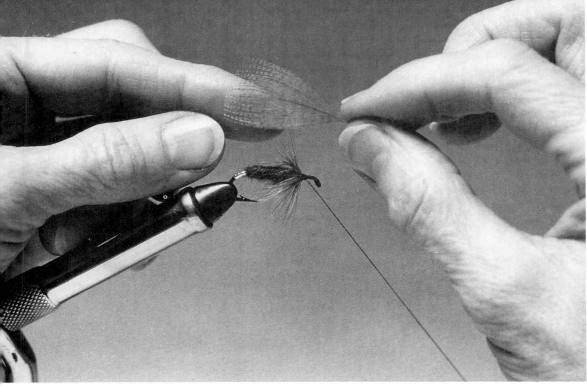

A single feather with an evenly distributed color pattern across its entire width. A small shoulder or breast feather, similarly marked, may also be used.

Here the single widgeon feather is being measured for length above the fly body. It may extend just the length of the hook or it may extend beyond the hook by the width of the gape. Although these are not mandatory measurements, they are pleasing and practical proportions for a tailless wet fly of any size.

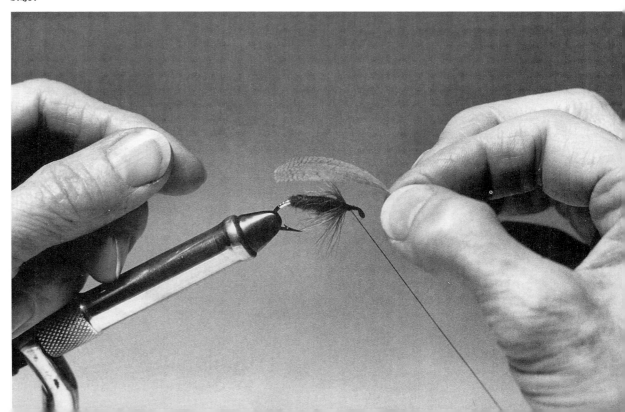

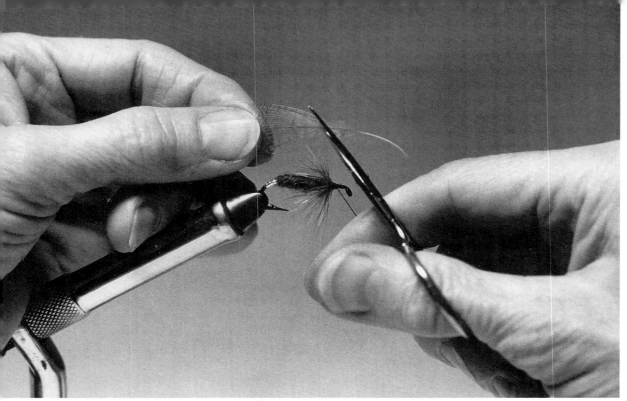

When the length of the wing has been determined, notch the feather flues at the place where the quill will be bound onto the hook.

The tiny stubs of flues remaining on the quill will aid in anchoring it firmly in place when it is bound by the tying thread. The natural curve of the feather will parallel that of the body. Make sure the wing is secure before clipping off the excess quill. A wrap-knot head will complete the tying.

Name of Pattern	Tag	Body	Hackle	Wing	Head
Dubbed Olive Gnat	Gold	Dark Olive Green Dubbing	Iron Dun	Slate Goose	Black
Grass Hopper	Gold	Greenish Yellow Dubbing	Furnace	Medium Slate Goose	Black
Evening Dun	Gold	Light Yellow Dubbing	Pale Gray	Light Gray Goose	Light Gray
Pale Evening Dun	Gold	Pale Yellow Dubbing	Light Yellow	Light Gray Goose	Primrose
March Dun	Gold	Bluish Green Dubbing	Dubbing Picked Out	Medium-to-Light Gray Goose	Gray
Light Sedge	Gold	Tan Fur Dubbing	Ginger	Brown Hen or Widgeon	Light Gray
Additional Patterns					
Little Black Caddis	Silver	Black Seal Fur Dubbing	List or Badger	Dyed Black Goose	Black
Horse Fly	Silver	Gray and Lemon Yellow Dubbing Blended	Sparse Grizzly	Greenish Gray Hackle Tips Paired and Tied Flat	Green
Dubbed Miller	Silver	Rabbit Fur Dubbing	Gray Dun	Gray Goose Tinted Tan	Black
Caperer	Silver	Red-Brown Yarn Dubbing	Scarlet, Sparse	Very Dark Brown Pheasant or Copper Pheasant	Black
Cock Tail	Gold	Brown Dubbing	Brown, Sparse	Light Slate Goose	Orange
Stone Fly	Silver	Rabbit Fur and Yellow Yarn Dubbing Mixed	Ginger	Light Mottled Turkey with Pheasant Tail Feelers	Black

a dark furnace hackle, or coch-y-bondhu hackle, sparsely tied. A wing of dark mottled turkey and a light head will complete this fly. Since the stubs of the dark wing material will affect the color of your light tying thread somewhat, the wrap knot head will appear to be a light gray.

Our second pattern in this stage is the Bright Spec. It is a good example of a pattern that does not specify the material from which the tip is to be made. It may be made with yarn dubbing, as shown on the color plate, or it may be made with chenille, as illustrated in the black-and-white photos. Floss or ostrich herl of the right color could also be used. For this fly, use hot orange tying thread, and after you have made a short gold tag, make the tip a bright orange. Make the body with a dark warm brown yarn dubbing to which a small amount of mohair dubbing of the same color may be added. Use your darkest chocolate brown (havanah) hackle for this fly, and make its wing from strips of dark brown dyed goose or dark brown turkey. You will be delighted with this attractive fly with its dark orange head.

The Female Grannom has a gold tag and a green tip dubbed on green tying thread. The rest of the body is made with dubbing of hare's ear, plucked and spun on a well-waxed thread. This short brindle-colored fur and hair may be plucked from a rabbit mask as well as from an ear. In appearance this dubbing is rougher than dubbing made from yarn. The hackle may be made with a salt-and-pepper hackle, which has a liberal sprinkling of ginger, brown, and black over a white background. Or it may be made with a furnace hackle, chosen for its small, dark center, to create another version of the pattern. Both of these patterns have wings made from paired pheasant tail feathers. For this, use the flues that do not separate at the tips. The heads of these two patterns will be dark green, and both versions are very good wet flies with which to fish.

A Blue Tip, our fourth pattern in this stage of the dubbing-bodied flies, has a silver-tinsel tag. Make its blue tip with bright blue floss. White angora yarn dubbing, or the fluffiest and softest dubbing you can make from the yarn you have, will make the body. Choose for it the palest gray hackle, and make its wings with strips of pale gray

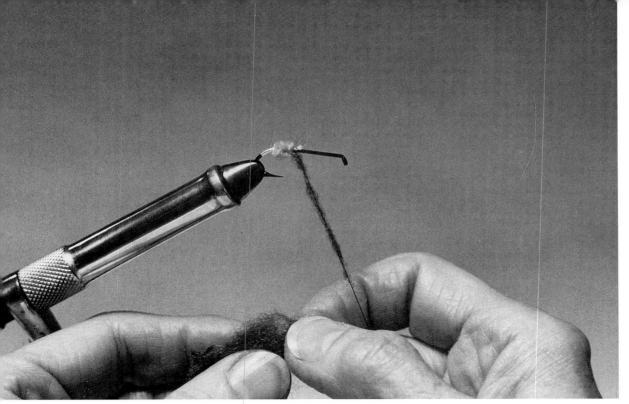

With a tinsel tag and a chenille tip in place, dubbing is spun on the tying thread before winding. It will cover the place where the core of the chenille tip has been bound.

The light-colored chenille tip covers the cut and bound ends of the tinsel tag and, in turn, its cut ends are hidden by the dubbing. The plump little chenille tip forms an attractive end on this dark dubbing body.

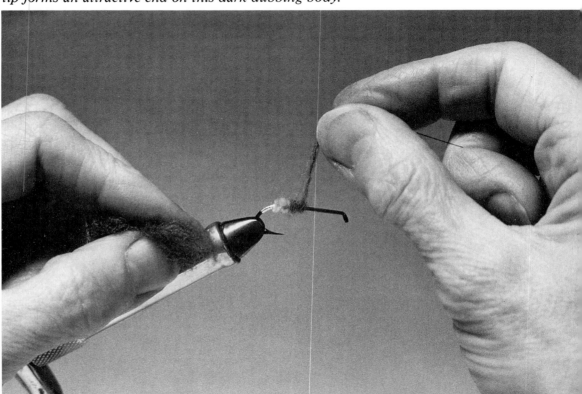

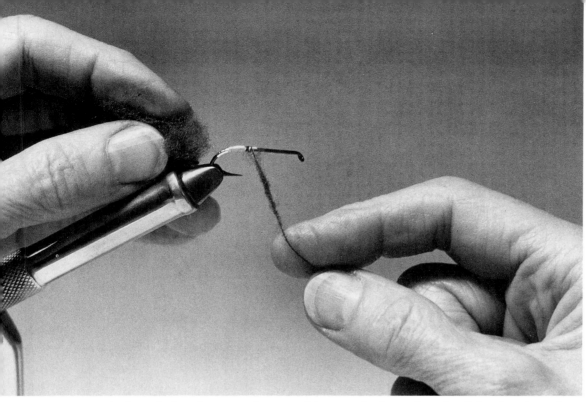

A floss tip has been made smoothly over the bound ends of the tinsel tag for a Fire Fly. The dubbing will cover the tying thread that binds it to the hook.

Determine how long you want the tip to be. If it is to be short, you can cover part of it with the body material. If it is to be longer, as in this example, the dubbing can begin where the floss tip was bound off above the hook point.

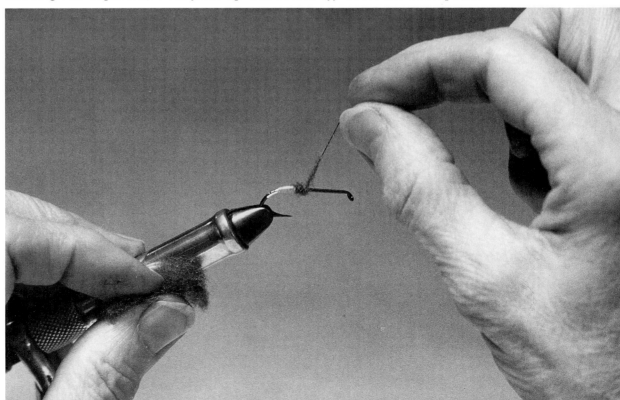

Name of Pattern	Tag	Tip	Body	Hackle	Wing	Head
Small Dark Sedge	Gold	Yellow	Dark Brown Dubbing	Furnace	Dark Mottled Turkey	Light
Bright Spec	Gold	Bright Orange	Dark Brown Dubbing	Havanah Brown	Dark Brown Hen	Orange
Female Grannom	Gold	Green	Hare's Ear Dubbing	Furnace or Salt-and-Pepper	Pheasant	Green
Blue Tip	Silver	Blue Floss	White Angora Dubbing	Light Gray	Light Gray Turkey	Light Gray
Little Light Fox	Gold	Yellow Chenille	Light Cream Dubbing	Yellow Grizzly	Light Gray Goose	Light Gray
Female Gray Gnat	Silver	Yellow Fur	Gray Muskrat Dubbing	Grizzly	Medium Dark Goose	Black
Additional Patterns						
Fire Fly	Gold	Yellow-Green Floss	Dark Gray Dubbing	Short Dark Gray	Gray Goose Tied Flat	Black Herl
Dubbed Grannom	Silver	Blue-Green Floss	Hare's Ear Dubbing	Pale Ginger, Sparse	Partridge Tied Flat	Brown
Orange Tip	Gold	Orange Floss	Brownish Gray Dubbing	Short Gray	Cinnamon Goose	Black
Female Beaverkill	Gold	Yellow Chenille	Gray Dubbing	Brown	Light Gray Goose	Black
English Stone	Silver	Yellow Chenille	Gray Squirrel Dubbing	Brown	Mottled Pheasant	Gray
Dark Partridge	——	Red Chenille	Dark Gray Dubbing	Partridge	Dark Gray Goose	Black

matched turkey, lightly mottled. Gray turkey sometimes has a light, irregular marking of a paler gray or white. These feathers should be paired and put aside for use on a pattern like the Blue Tip. Tie the whole fly with a light gray tying thread.

Use a light gray tying thread for your next fly as well. After a gold tag is in place, use the smallest size of yellow chenille you have for the tip. If it happens that you have a larger chenille to use, it can be carefully trimmed and tapered down after you have tied it on. The tip should be small, and the body made with creamy white fur dubbing. For the hackle, use a light grizzly that has been dyed yellow. Finish this pattern of the Little Light Fox with a wing of light gray goose or duck. (Duck is a little finer in texture than is goose.)

A Female Gray Gnat has a small silver tag. Since the head of this fly will be black, use your very finest black tying thread and carefully dub a small amount of yellow fur on it for making the tip of the body. The black thread should not show through the yellow dubbing. Dub the body with gray muskrat fur. For the hackle, choose a grizzly with fairly short flues that reach only to the bend

of the hook. Wind it on sparingly. Complete this fly with a wing of medium dark gray goose or duck and, of course, the black wrap-knot head.

Among the dubbed patterns in this stage of the fifth fly form, only one has a tip made of floss, one is chenille, the others are dubbed. Among the additional patterns, three have floss tips and three have chenille tips.

Fifth Stage: With Tail

The silhouette for this stage of the dubbing-bodied flies has a tail, indicating a further addition to the patterns in this fly form. The tail for the silhouette, made of a pair of flues, is taken from the short side of goose feathers. A goose feather that has been used for wing material is often discarded, but the other side, with its short flues, can also become a source of material for short tails. Having little or no curve of its own, it can be used on any pattern specifying a short goose-feather tail, and the flues can be paired or used singly. For the following tailed patterns, other feathers are required.

Our first pattern is a Namekagon, and for this

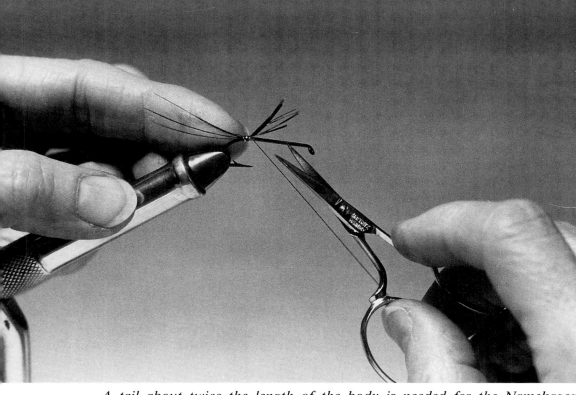

A tail about twice the length of the body is needed for the Namekagon pattern. Three flues from a pheasant tail feather are separated, with the tying thread wound carefully between them and the hook. The cut ends will be trimmed and bound before the body is begun.

or any of the following patterns that do not mention tags, the use of a tag is optional. The tail is made by using three long pheasant tail barbs. For the body, blend orange and green yarn dubbing in equal amounts so that neither color dominates. Spin it on a well-waxed orange tying thread and make a neat oval body. The brown grizzly hackle you choose for this pattern should have flues about the length of the body. This is a beautiful hackle, with alternating bars of light and dark reddish brown. With a wing of white goose and an orange head, this interesting pattern is a worthy addition to any collection of fishing flies.

Our next pattern, the Lady Beaverkill, is a tailed version of the Female Beaverkill found among the additional patterns of the fourth stage. A few wisps of speckled gray mallard make the tail. Tie a small tip of short yellow ostrich herl, and finish the body with a light gray dubbing of fur or yarn. Choose a brown hackle of medium length, with its flues just slightly longer than those for the previous pattern, and complete the fly with wing strips of medium gray goose.

The Green Sack, tied with primrose tying thread, also has a tail of speckled mallard. Use a few more wisps of it than for the Lady Beaverkill. Make the tail as long as the fly body. Fashion a small tip of yellowish green chenille, and dub the body with dark gray muskrat fur. Select a grizzly hackle and use it sparingly. The wing for this pattern is made with mottled gray turkey. The head will be light because of the tying thread.

Use a light yellow or primrose-colored tying thread for the Female Hendrickson. For the tail, use a few fibers of lemon wood duck. Fashion a small tip with yellow floss, and make the rest of the body with tan or fawn-colored fox fur. The undercoat of fox is very fine and spins easily. Select a rusty dun-colored hackle, a feather with subdued ginger-colored flues beyond its light gray center, and use a few turns of it. Lemon wood-duck flues gathered together and tied on in a slender bunch can be made to lie back over the body of the fly as a wing. The angle to which the wing is adjusted is determined by the manner in which you use the tying thread. For this pattern you will want to make the wing tips reach almost to the end of the tail. Trim the stub ends of the lemon wood-

This tail is made of two flues taken from each side of the center tail feather of pheasant. Tied on above the barb, it is carefully divided and the separation maintained with the tying thread. Dubbing body and hackle have been added as for the Dubbed Brown Stone.

Two well-matched hackle points (or hackle tips) are selected and measured for length against the fly body, and . . .

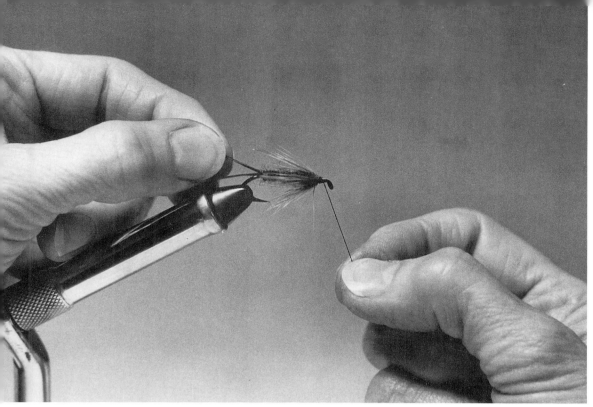

. . . are tied to lie flat over the body. They are then separated to match the V of the tails.

Viewed from the top, the separation of the wings is apparent. They are secured with the tying thread that anchors them firmly in position.

Name of Pattern	Tag	Tail	Tip	Body	Hackle	Wing	Head
Namekagon	——	Three Long Pheasant Tail Barbs	——	Orange and Green Dubbing	Brown Grizzly	White Goose	Dark Orange
Lady Beaverkill	——	Gray Mallard	Yellow Ostrich	Light Gray Dubbing	Brown	Slate Goose	Black
Green Sack	——	Gray Mallard	Green Chenille	Dark Gray Dubbing	Grizzly	Gray Turkey	Primrose
Female Hendrickson	——	Lemon Wood Duck	Yellow Floss	Tan Fox Dubbing	Rusty Dun	Lemon Wood Duck	Primrose
Cahill	Gold	Lemon Wood Duck	——	Hare and Muskrat Dubbing	Brown	Lemon Wood Duck	Primrose
Dubbed Brown Stone	Gold	Two Short Pheasant Tail Barbs	——	Dark Brown Hare with Claret Seal Dubbing	Rusty Dun	Two Narrow Rusty Dun Hackles	Orange
Additional Patterns							
Brown Hen	——	Cinnamon Turkey	——	Brown Seal Dubbing	Red-Brown	Cinnamon	Brown
Dubbed Great Dun	——	Brown Mallard	——	Brown Seal Dubbing	Blue Gray	Slate	Brown
Iron Blue Dun	——	Brown Hackle Wisps	——	Brown and Gray Seal Dubbing	Furnace	Slate	Brown
Red Fox	Gold	Lemon Wood Duck	——	Red Fox Fur Dubbing	Bright Brown	Slate Gray	Black
Marble Fly	——	Speckled Mallard	Yellow Dubbing	Scarlet Dubbing, Picked Out	Yellow	Slate Gray	Brown
Combination	——	Scarlet Goose with Speckled Mallard Flues	Yellow Dubbing, Small	Claret Dubbing, Picked Out	Claret	Slate Goose with Strip of Scarlet and Mallard on Each Side	Black

duck wing and bind them securely, finishing with a light-colored wrap-knot head.

The fifth and sixth patterns have fine gold-tinsel tags, but no tips. For the Cahill, tie on another tail of a few flues or fibers of lemon wood duck, using primrose tying thread. Wax the thread well and spin on dubbing plucked from a hare's ear or mask. Wind it on, fashioning an oval body. Select a brown hackle with flues of medium length and use not more than two turns of it around the hook. Make another lemon wood-duck wing, as you did for the previous pattern, but this time have the tips of it extend only to the end of the hook.

For the Dubbed Brown Stone, when you have made a tag with fine, flat gold tinsel, use two short, paired pheasant tail barbs for its tail and separate them so that they will flare slightly away from each other. Since this pattern, like that for the Cahill, does not specify a tip, make the entire body from a blended mixture of dark brown hare and seal dyed claret. Spin it on a bright brown or dark orange tying thread. Choose a rusty cock's

hackle with flues that will extend only to the end of the hook. Use it sparingly. Two small, narrow hackles of the same rusty dun color will make a fine pair of wings for this pattern. Tie them to lie back over the fly, raised slightly above the body. The wrap-knot head of bright brown or dark orange will complete this pattern handsomely.

In the list of additional patterns, only one has a specified tag. The use of a tag is optional on such patterns, and whether you choose to use gold or silver tinsel, or one of the other colors in which tinsel can be obtained, it is up to you to decide which you want to have on the pattern you are tying. For instance, the Combination could have a gold tag or a tiny bright red tinsel tag beneath its scarlet goose-and-mallard tail to emphasize the brightness of the scarlet strip on each side of its gray-goose wing. It would give an unexpected glint to an otherwise subdued pattern.

Compare the pattern for the Dubbed Great Dun with the pattern of the Great Dun (fifth stage of the fourth fly form). A gold tag for the Great Dun

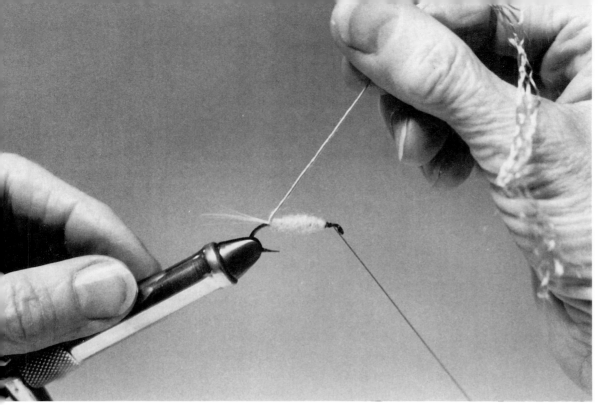

White floss twisted into a fine cord becomes the ribbing for a Pale Sulphur Dun. The light dubbing must be spun very carefully to cover the dark tying thread and prevent it from showing through. For this pattern use a light-colored tying thread.

Keep the floss rib tightly twisted as you wind it around the body and shift it from hand to hand. With windings spaced this closely, seven or eight ribs will be possible on a body this size.

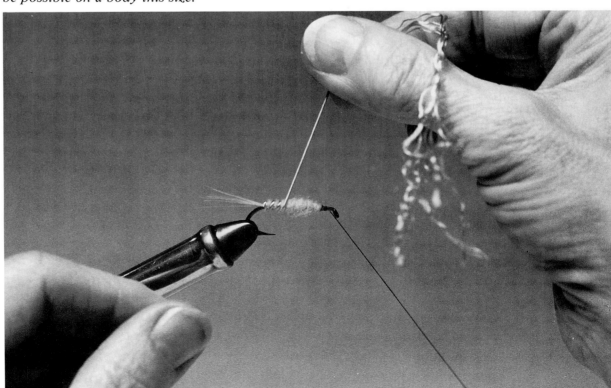

and its body of brown yarn instead of brown seal dubbing mark the only differences between these two patterns.

Sixth Stage: With Ribs

The result of ribbing a dubbed pattern is a little different than the result from winding a tinsel or floss rib over the smooth bodies of yarn and floss. A fine tinsel can become partially embedded in a rough or fluffy dubbing, as well as in herl or a fluffy chenille. Gauge the width of your tinsel to the texture and size of the dubbed body, or wind it on in reverse.

Our first dubbed-body pattern on which we will have a tinsel rib is the Old Irish Iron Blue Dun, a very impressive name for a very good fly. Make the tail about the length of the body with a few wisps from the red breast feather of a golden pheasant. Rib the dubbed blue-gray muskrat body with silver oval tinsel, wound four or five times. Add a naturally black hackle, and make the wing of silvery gray duck or very light gray goose.

Another well-known and well-used pattern is the Gold-Ribbed Hare's Ear. For this fly, make a tiny tag of fine gold tinsel before you tie on a tail of a few brown hackle flues. The same flat tinsel can be used to rib the body as well. The body itself will be made of the hare's ear or mask, from which you will pluck the short fur and guard hair and spin it onto a well-waxed black tying thread. This body should be made slightly more full in the area of the wing and hackle. After you have wound on the tinsel rib and have it securely fastened, pick out some of the dubbing where a hackle would be used, to make a throat for the fly. Let it extend downward as though it were a short hackle, for this is all the hackle this pattern will have. Be very careful while picking the dubbing out because you do not want to disturb or loosen the gold-tinsel rib. Finish this fly with a light slate-colored wing of goose, and a black wrap-knot head.

Our third pattern is a beautiful light fly called the Pale Sulphur Dun, and its name aptly describes its color. Use a primrose or white tying thread for this fly. It has a tail of wisps taken from a white hackle that has been dyed the palest sulphur yellow. The rib for it is made of a fine strand of white floss twisted into a tight and slender cord. Pale sulphur-colored angora or white seal dyed to match will be used for the dubbing body.

For this fly, make sure the wax for the tying thread is completely free of any discoloration and that your fingers are immaculate while you are working with these delicate tints. The fine white floss cord rib will give the light-colored body a palely segmented appearance. A white hackle that has been tinted the same pale sulphur yellow is necessary here. Pick out one with flues that reach only to the barb of the hook and wind it on sparsely, with the flues turning back around the body.

The wing for a Pale Sulphur Dun is made from round tipped white goose feathers that have been tinted to match the dubbing and hackle. If you are interested in dyeing your own materials for flies like this, it is a good practice to select all that you may need of yarns, furs, feathers, and hackles in the sizes you anticipate using, and tint them all in one dyeing session. When they are dry, you can keep them together in a labeled envelope for future use. In this way, they will not contact other materials from which they might pick up minute shreds or filaments of other colors.

Finish the Pale Sulphur Dun with a light-colored wrap-knot head and clear-coat it with head varnish, being careful to prevent any of the varnish from spreading into the wing or hackle.

Our Brown Mallard has a tail of a few fibers of brown mallard feather. The strands should be about the length of the body and gathered together so that the natural tips are even. Tie it on the hook above the barb. (Use black tying thread for this pattern.) The flues in tails like this one will not necessarily stay together, but will spread away from each other a little when they are tied on. The rib for this fly is a narrow gold tinsel, which you will wrap over the brown dubbing body. After the rib is in place, fluff out the body a little between the ribs with the point of your stylet, being careful not to disturb the tinsel. Add two turns of a dark brown hackle. Make the wing with matching strips of a pair of brown mallard feathers and tie them on to arch over the fly in a sickle-shaped wing that reaches almost to the end of the tail, but not beyond. Carefully trim the stubs of the wing into a neat taper, which will be covered by the

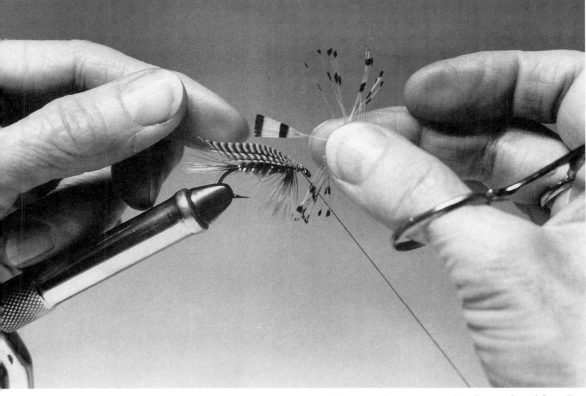

A pattern like a Larry St. John will have a decorative cheek or shoulder. For this fly it is a tippet feather. Only the center flues are used, and remain attached to the central stem of the feather.

Sections of two tippet feathers, gauged to the size of the fly for the right proportion of orange and black, are placed one on each side of the wing. This decorative addition to the wing should not cover more than half of it.

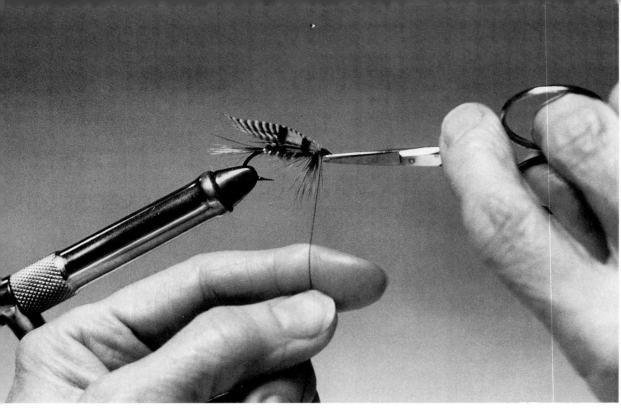

Secure by locking the quills with tying thread. Clip the excess away and finish with a wrap-knot head.

wrap-knot head.

The next pattern has several details in common with the previous one. It also has a brown mallard tail (in this pattern the tail is a little longer than the body), and it has a gold tinsel rib. Make the body with orange dubbing of wool or seal that has been dyed a clear orange. Use a few turns of a light gray hackle. The wing for this pattern is made with a pair of strips of brown mallard. This time, tie them in the shape of the goose wings you have made for many of the flies so far, with the tips turning slightly upward. Make this wing no longer than the length of the hook. When you have finished this pattern with a black wrap-knot head, you will have a Brown Miller.

For our sixth pattern in this stage of the fifth fly form, we will choose the Larry St. John, which is a little more elaborate than those we have already tied. However, it still has their basic structure.

Begin by tying a silver tag, using narrow tinsel. Tie on a slim tail made of a few evenly distributed flues taken in equal amounts from a white and a

black hackle. Tie in a strand of fine gold tinsel to be used for a rib and dub the body with lavender yarn, frayed out for this purpose. After you have wound the rib, use a light grizzly hackle, sparsely tied. Over it, tie a sickle-shaped wing of speckled gray mallard. Carefully trim the stubs of the wing to form a tapered foundation for the head, but do not tie the wrap knot until you have added a small embellishment to the wing, as follows: Select two small central sections from paired tippet feathers. Make sure the flues are evenly divided on each side of the central stem. These sections should be small enough so that one black bar, in addition to the black tips, is visible on each. Place one of these little orange triangles on each side of the wing. These are "shoulders" or decorative "cheeks" for this fly. The quills of the tippets will lie on either side of the head. Bind them there securely. After the ends of the quill stems are clipped away, finish the fly with a black wrap-knot head. You will be delighted with this striking addition to your collection of wet flies.

Name of Pattern	Tag	Tail	Rib	Body	Hackle	Wing	Head
Old Irish Iron Blue Dun	——	Red Breast Feather of the Golden Pheasant	Oval Silver	Blue-Gray Muskrat Dubbing	Natural Black	Light Slate Goose	Black
Gold-Ribbed Hare's Ear	——	Brown Hackle Wisps	Gold	Hare's Ear Dubbing	Hare's Ear	Pale Slate Goose	Black
Pale Sulphur Dun	——	Sulphur Hackle Wisps	White Floss	Pale Sulphur Dubbing	Pale Sulphur	Pale Sulphur Goose	Primrose
Brown Mallard	——	Brown Mallard	Gold	Brown Dubbing	Brown	Brown Mallard	Black
Brown Miller	——	Brown Mallard	Gold	Orange Dubbing	Gray	Brown Mallard	Black
Larry St. John	Silver	White and Black Hackle Wisps	Gold	Lavender Dubbing	Grizzly	Speckled Mallard with Tippet Cheek	Black
Additional Patterns							
Old Brown Stone	Silver	Short Mottled Pheasant or Partridge	Yellow Floss	Yellow-Brown with Hare's Ear Dubbing	Bright Brown, Sparse	Rusty Dun Hackles, Flat	Brown
Summer Imp	——	Three Golden Pheasant Tail Flues	Yellow Floss	Hare's Ear with Beaver Dubbing	Furnace	Dark Gray Goose	Black
Claret and Mallard	——	Tippet Flues	Round Gold	Claret Seal Dubbing	Bright Brown	Brown Mallard	Brown
Carter Harrison	——	Scarlet Goose	Silver	Purple and Black Dubbing, Mixed	Brown	Speckled Mallard	Black

Additional Patterns							
Name of Pattern	Tag	Tail	Tip	Rib*	Body	Hackle	Wing	Head
Maine Jungle	——	Scarlet Goose or Hackle Wisps	Green Floss	Gold	Claret Dubbing	Claret	Jungle Cock Body Feathers	Black
Emmet	Gold	Pheasant Crest	Peacock Herl	Oval Gold	Black Dubbing	Black	Black with Blue Strip on Each Side	Black
Kamaloff	Gold	Brown Mallard	Red Floss	Yellow Floss	Yellow and Gray Dubbing, Mixed	Gray	——	Black

*Over body only

141

Brown Quill	Gray Quill	Dove Quill	Olive Quill	Partridge Quill	Dusty Quill
Claret Smut	Caddis Quill	Quill Cahill	Badger Quill	Mosquito Quill	Equinox Mosquito
Peacock Quill	Ginger Midge	Early Green Quill	Silver Quill	Light Orange Quill	Evening Quill
Black Quill	Blue Quill	Spring Green	Alder Quill	Green Caddis	Roux's Quill
Iron Blue Quill	Bard's Quill	McKensie Quill	Claret Quill	Mallard Quill	Pale Watery Quill
Willow Quill	Ginger Quill	Quill Gordon	Light Cahill Quill	August Dun	Alder Egg Sac

Like a sensitive nerve is the long tapered line
That doth from the tenuous fly rod decline;
And the leap of the fish, with electrical start
Strikes swift thru the hand, on the highest bounding heart.

William Greene, "Angling"

Quill Body
The Sixth Fly Form

First Stage: Body and Hackle

An abundant source of quill is to be found among a fly tyer's materials. Dyed hackles and other dyed feathers furnish quills of many colors. Undyed feathers furnish quills of natural colors: gray, tan, brown, white, and even black. Any feather unsuitable for a particular pattern because of uneven flues, moth damage, or poor color can be a useful source of quill simply by trimming away the imperfect flues along the edges of the central stem. By carefully trimming the flues away from the hackle quill with scissors, the colored surface of the quill will not be damaged. Stripping the flues away will remove some of the surface skin of the quill, and part of its dyed or natural color will be lost.

The quill from feathers that furnish wing material, such as duck, goose, or turkey, can be stripped from the main shaft in a long, narrow piece. Cut through the shiny surface of the quill near the tip of the feather to release it from the pithy core of the shaft and pull it downward with your fingers or pliers toward the base of the shaft. The quill obtained in this way is particularly useful on flies of larger sizes because the surface on the shafts of these feathers is wider than it is on hackles.

Peacock herl and ostrich herl are also sources of quill you can obtain simply by removing the herl entirely. An excellent substitute for feather quills are the hairs of moose mane, both gray and white.

Quill-bodied flies, with their slim silhouettes, are not difficult to tie when the hackle-stem quills are soaked in water before they are wound onto a hook. These quills should be wound on flat, with the smooth colored side uppermost. Since hackle quills have a tendency to turn on edge, flattening them with pliers before you wind them on will help. You will notice that these hackle quills, which are extremely small at the tip end, gradually become wider toward the base. With practice you will be able to determine how much quill will be needed to make the fly body on the hooks you are using. You will eliminate a portion of the thin end of the quill and use the wider part to good advantage. Tie them on while they are still damp.

Use a brown tying thread for the first of the quill-bodied patterns in this stage of the sixth fly form. The body of the Brown Quill is made with peacock strands from which the herl has been removed. Since this body is to be a monotone of brownish gray, the dark strands should be chosen for uniformity of color. (Many peacock-herl quills have a light edge.) Tie the body without overlapping the turns of quill. Choose a grouse hackle with flues that reach just beyond the bend of the hook; three turns of it will be right for this pattern. The brown tying thread will give the Brown Quill a brown head.

A gray tying thread is preferable for the Gray Quill. The gray head of the fly will appear to be a continuation of the body. Take the gray quill for this pattern from a gray hackle that has been carefully trimmed to leave no stubble along the edges. Or use a "quill" of gray moose mane instead. Wind the body smoothly, whichever quill you use, and make sure it is secure before you clip away the excess. Choose a short grizzly hackle with flues that reach only to the barb. Tie it on, and wind two turns of it around the hook. It should be sparse. Finish with the gray head.

Light gray moose-mane "quills" and light grizzly hackle, both materials tinted a light pink, are perfect for the Dove Quill. The result of the tinting will be a pinkish gray, with neither color predominating. After winding on the quill body, choose a hackle with flues which will reach to the bend of the hook. Tie it on sparsely, and complete the pattern with a neat black wrap-knot head.

Materials for the Olive Quill are dyed also. Many of the hackle colors called for in fly patterns can be obtained from companies that furnish fly-tying materials. However, for the subtle tones required for special patterns, it is fun to dye your own materials.

Use an olive-colored quill for the body of this pattern. Tie it on with a brown tying thread. Select an olive brown hackle with flues reaching the bend of the hook. In different light, the hackle will appear to be olive or brown. The brown tying thread, of course, will make a brown head for the Olive Quill.

The Partridge Quill has a slim body made with peacock-herl quill that is light on one edge and dark on the other, resulting in a body alternately light and dark along its length. The delicate light and dark pattern of a partridge hackle makes a subtle continuation of the body shading. Finish

the pattern with a black wrap-knot head.

Once the materials for all of these patterns have been selected and prepared, the method of tying them is exactly the same. With the completion of the Dusty Quill, our next pattern, at least six more excellent patterns have been added to your growing collection of wet flies—more, if you have tied several of each pattern. Tying more than one fly of each pattern makes the tying of each successive one a little easier; the rhythm of tying and the sureness with which the materials are manipulated is increased. Practice is rewarding.

Our Dusty Quill should be tied with a light or cream-colored tying thread because the whole fly has a creamy, dusty appearance. Use white moose mane that has been tinted a light cream color for the body. Or, the quill of a honey dun hackle, which is also a dusty, creamy color, may be used. After the body has been wound, choose a hackle with a gray center and honey-colored or light ginger flues. Use two or three turns of it, with the flues turning back over the light quill body. Finish the tying of this pattern with a light wrap-knot head.

Natural or dyed quills for fly bodies, together with hackles made of different kinds of feathers, both dyed and natural, offer endless combination possibilities to the fly tyer.

Second Stage: With Wings

Beginning with this second stage of the quill-bodied flies, all of the following patterns will be winged.

Our first winged pattern is the Claret Smut, an excellent pattern in #10 and smaller sizes. Use the quill of a hackle that has been dyed a dark claret color. For the hackle itself, use a black one with flues that reach just to the bend of the hook. Use a medium-to-light gray goose for the wet-fly wing, and finish the pattern with a shiny black wrap-knot head.

For a Caddis Quill, use black tying thread for the entire fly. Make the body with peacock-herl quill that shows the light and dark edges. Select a light ginger wet-fly hackle. A ginger hackle that is soft and webby often has a tannish appearance. This is a good choice for your Caddis Quill.

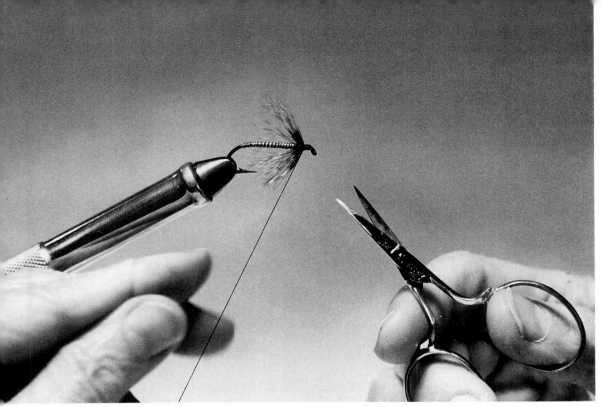

A slim body made of quill becomes an excellent wet fly with just the addition of a hackle. This quill is peacock herl with the herl removed. It shows the light edge as well as the dark, which gives the body a segmented appearance.

Name of Pattern	Body	Hackle	Head
Brown Quill	Peacock-Herl Quill	Grouse Feather	Brown
Gray Quill	Gray Hackle Quill	Short Grizzly	Black
Dove Quill	Light Grayish Pink Quill	Grizzly Tinted Pink	Black
Olive Quill	Olive Hackle Quill	Brown Tinted Olive	Brown
Partridge Quill	Peacock Herl Quill	Partridge Feather	Black
Dusty Quill	Cream Moose Mane	Honey Dun Hackle	Light
Additional Patterns			
Orange Quill	White Moose Dyed Orange	Orange Grizzly	Black
White Quill	White Moose Mane	White	Bright Yellow
Gauze Wing	White Moose Mane Tinted Primrose	Glassy Light Blue-Gray	Green
Bread Crust	Bright Brown Hackle Quill	Grizzly or Brown Grizzly	Brown
Claret Quill	Claret Hackle Quill	Claret	Dark Brown
Green Quill	Green Hackle Quill	Partridge Tinted Green	Dark Brown

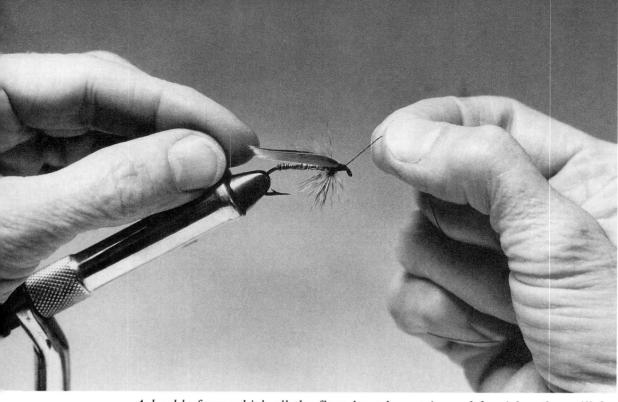

A hackle from which all the flues have been trimmed furnishes the quill for this fly body. A grizzly hackle with short flues is wound on and narrow strips of gray goose make the wings for a Mosquito Quill. In smaller sizes this is an exceptionally effective wet fly under many fishing conditions.

For this fly's wings, use strips of mottled brown pheasant.

Tie a Quill Cahill with a peacock-herl-quill body. Because the head of this fly is light, use a primrose or very light gray tying thread. The hackle flues should reach just to the bend of the hook. Select a reddish brown hackle and tie it on sparingly. Make the wing with lightly speckled lemon wood duck. This well-known fly is one of several variations on the famous Cahill pattern.

A Badger Quill also has a peacock-herl-quill body. For the hackle on this pattern use a badger, or list, hackle with dark tips on its light flues. The dark centers of either hackle should be small for a fly of this size. While you will make the wing for this pattern with lemon wood duck, as you did for the Quill Cahill, choose a feather that has a slightly darker, more pronounced speckling than the one you used for the Quill Cahill. The difference is subtle, but one of the interesting things to note about feathers of the same kind from the same bird is that they are not necessarily identical. Feathers with variations in color or marking should be sorted out and kept together for special use.

The Mosquito Quill's body is a light gray and may be made from the lightest of your peacock-herl quill, without the dark edge, or from a trimmed gray hackle quill. Choose a definitely marked grizzly hackle with short flues, and when you tie it on, use it sparingly. Make the wings from slender strips of light gray goose and let them extend no more than the width of the gape beyond the bend of the hook.

Another mosquito pattern is the Equinox Mosquito, with a body this time made of a single dark gray "quill" of moose mane. Choose a fairly light bluish gray hackle with flues just a trifle longer than for the Mosquito Quill, and wind on one or two turns of it. For the slender wing on this pattern use the speckled gray teal or mallard.

The red macaw, specified for the Bradley Quill, does not commonly appear in wet-fly patterns. It is a dull brownish red and has extremely short flues along the edges of its strands that are not removed when a strand of it is used for a quill

146

Name of Pattern	Body	Hackle	Wing	Head
Claret Smut	Dark Claret Quill	Black	Medium Light Gray	Black
Caddis Quill	Peacock-Herl Quill	Tan	Mottled Brown Pheasant	Black
Quill Cahill	Peacock-Herl Quill	Red-Brown	Lemon Wood Duck	Light
Badger Quill	Peacock-Herl Quill	Badger or List	Dark Wood Duck	Black
Mosquito Quill	Light Gray Quill	Short Grizzly	Light Slate Goose	Black
Equinox Mosquito	Dark Moose Mane	Light Blue-Gray	Teal or Mallard	Black
Additional Patterns				
Black Quill Gnat	Black-dyed Hackle Quill	Black-dyed	Dark Slate Goose	Black
Bradley Quill	Red Macaw Quill	Furnace and Blue Grizzly	Furnace Hackles, Small	Black
Dark Olive Quill Gnat	½ Olive, ½ Peacock-Herl Quill	Furnace	Blue-Gray Hackles, Small	Black
Light Quill Cahill	Light Gray Hackle Quill	Ginger	Lemon Wood Duck	Black
Tailless Widdicomb	Peacock-Herl Quill	Golden Badger	Light Blue Dun Hackles, Spent	Black
Winged Orange Quill	White Moose Mane Dyed Orange	Grizzly Dyed Orange	Light Slate Goose	Black

body. A good substitute for it is a strand of short-flued white ostrich herl dyed a brownish red, or a strand of dyed swan.

Third Stage: With Tag

The use of a tinsel tag may create a small problem when used on a quill-bodied pattern. The cut ends of the tinsel and the tying thread that binds them must be covered to make a flat foundation for the quill. While this is not difficult to do with materials such as herl, yarn, dubbing, or floss, extra care must be taken when quill patterns are being tied. Use as fine a tying thread as possible in order to prevent the underlying turns of thread from causing unwanted ridges as the smooth quill is wound over them. Keep the windings close together. Make the foundation uniformly flat for the quill that is to cover it.

A padding of yarn or floss, which may be used on large flies to equalize the foundation over which a quill body is wound, is impractical on flies of #10 size or smaller.

Use a fine, flat gold tinsel for the tag on a Peacock Quill. Select a peacock-herl quill that still has some very short and very sparse herl clinging to it. Wind it on, making sure that it covers the place where the tinsel tag ended as smoothly as possible. When the quill has been wound on and secured, wind on a few turns of a black hackle with flues that reach to the barb of the hook. When the hackle is in place, tie on a wing of darkest gray goose and finish with a neat black wrap-knot head.

Examine the way the quill covers the cut and bound ends of the tinsel tag. When the quill proceeds smoothly along the hook from its first turn, you have made a good foundation for it. A few extra turns of thread along the hook beneath the body material of a wet fly are all right as long as they do not overlap and form unnecessary ridges.

A Ginger Midge needs a fine, flat gold tag and a

black quill body. This quill may be obtained from a dyed black hackle that has been trimmed of its flues, or from a moose-mane "quill" dyed black. Select a bright ginger hackle with flues that reach to the bend of the hook and use two or three turns of it. Over this, tie on a wing of medium-to-dark gray goose. Tie it all with a fine black tying thread to make a beautiful wrap-knot head. This is an excellent fly to tie in very small sizes.

An Early Green Quill has a narrow, flat silver-tinsel tag, and its body is made with bright green quill. This quill may be taken from a hackle that has been dyed a bright green. Trim the flues away with your scissors, leaving no trace of stubble along the edges. Complete your Early Green Quill with a light yellow hackle, a wing of gray speckled teal or mallard, and a shiny black head.

Our fourth pattern is a Silver Quill. Make a short tag with your fine, flat silver tinsel. Carefully trim away the flues from a grizzly hackle that has a stem showing the dark gray-and-white bars of the feather. This barring on the quill will show alternately along the body as you wind it on. Select another grizzly with short flues for a few turns of hackle and make the wing for the Silver Quill

from silvery duck or the very lightest gray goose.

Our fifth quill pattern in this stage dates from about 1921: the Light Orange Quill. The tag for this fly is a fine, flat gold tinsel, and is tied with light yellow tying thread. The body is a bright orange quill, obtained from a very large dyed and trimmed hackle in order to have a wide quill. A strip of dyed goose quill could also be used. Remember that a quill from a hackle should be flattened and soaked well in water before it is wound on a hook. Incidentally, duck-billed pliers are very useful for flattening the quills of trimmed hackles.

Use a sparsely tied light ginger hackle for the Light Orange Quill, and make its wing of goose dyed a light yellow. You will have tied a bright and effective fly. Compare this pattern with the Orange Quill in the additional patterns of the first stage, and note the differences between them.

An Evening Quill has a silver tag and a body of pale yellow quill. Its bluish gray hackle extends just a trifle beyond the bend of the hook. The wing for this pattern is built with a narrow strip of blue laid over the main strip of slate goose. These wings can be put together before the fly is tied in order to facilitate the tying. Be sure to make more than one

Name of Pattern	Tag	Body	Hackle	Wing	Head
Peacock Quill	Gold	Peacock-Herl Quill	Sparse Black	Dark Gray Goose	Black
Ginger Midge	Gold	Black Quill	Ginger	Slate Gray Goose	Black
Early Green Quill	Silver	Bright Green Quill	Light Yellow	Teal or Mallard	Black
Silver Quill	Silver	Grizzly Hackle Quill	Grizzly	Light Duck or Goose	Black
Light Orange Quill	Gold	Orange Quill	Light Ginger	Yellow Goose	Light Yellow
Evening Quill	Silver	Light Yellow Quill	Bluish Gray	Blue Over Gray Goose	Light Gray
Additional Patterns					
Phantom Quill	Silver	White Moose Mane	Light Straw-Colored	White Goose	White
Silver Bowman	Silver	Natural Gray Quill	Gray Dun	Light Gray Duck	Black
Red Quill	Small Gold	Red-Brown Hackle Quill	Long Red-Brown	Light Gray Goose	Brown
June Quill	Small Gold	White Goose Quill	Maroon, Short and Sparse	Maroon Goose	Black
August Quill	Silver	Peacock-Herl or Gray Mallard Quill	Ginger, Short and Sparse	Light Gray Goose	Orange
Golden Quill	Gold	Brown Quill	Bright Ginger Grizzly	Cinnamon Goose	Brown

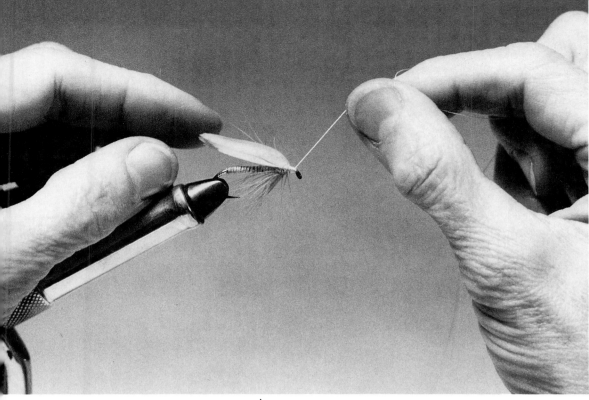

When pale-colored quills are used, a light tying thread is a good choice to use on the entire fly. For the Phantom Quill, a white head is specified.

pair of wings at a time to have them uniform and ready for additional flies of the same pattern. Tie the Evening Quill with a light gray tying thread.

Fourth Stage: With Tip

All of the patterns in this stage of the sixth fly form have a small tip at the end of their quill bodies. A fine black chenille is used for the tip of the Black Quill and easily covers the cut and bound ends of the short, fine gold-tinsel tag specified for this pattern. Quill for the body may be dark moose mane, a strip of gray goose quill, or peacock-herl quill on which a minute amount of very short and sparse herl remains. Sparsely tied black hackle and a wing of dark gray goose complete this pattern. A head of black tying thread finishes the tying.

A Blue Quill has a fine silver-tinsel tag. Make the tip for this fly with light gray floss. Moose mane dyed blue is needed for the body, and since this pattern will have a gray head, use a light gray thread for the entire fly. Select a bluish gray hackle with flues that reach just to the bend of the hook. Two turns of it are sufficient. Make the wing with strips of medium gray goose. The

light gray head of the finished fly matches the light gray tip.

From your floss file, select a dark yellow-green floss for the Spring Green. Lay out the tinsel, floss, quills, hackles, and feather wings to have them ready before you begin to tie. In this way the rhythm of tying is not interrupted by stopping to prepare the materials for each fly separately. Use light yellow tying thread. Tie a flat gold-tinsel tag securely, and make a short tip for this pattern with the floss you selected. Make the body with a bright green hackle quill from which the flues have been trimmed. A very light yellow hackle, with flues that reach only to the barb, is needed. Two turns of the hackle are sufficient. Make the wing for this fly with strips of your lightest gray goose and complete the tying with a light yellow wrap-knot head. This attractive light-colored fly has proven to be surprisingly effective under adverse conditions.

A light gray tying thread will make a gray head for the Alder Quill, our fourth pattern. No tag is required, so we will begin with a short tip of primrose floss, a light, pale greenish yellow. The body is a true orange. This may be white moose-mane "quill" dyed, or the quill from a dyed hackle. This

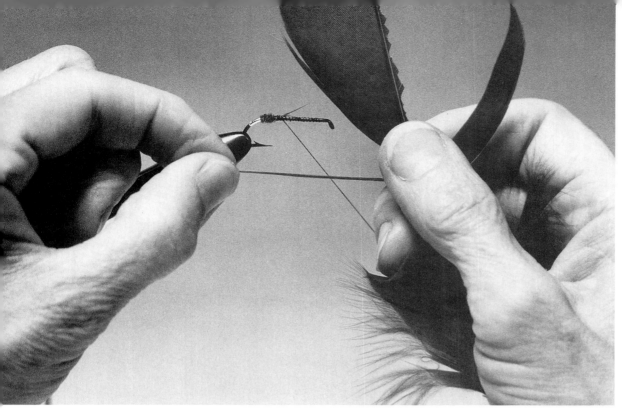

With a tinsel tag in place, a strand of dyed swan makes an interesting tip. The herl along the edges of the strand is minute and on very small flies can be used for an entire body.

A strand of ostrich herl is used for this tip, and covers the ends of a tinsel tag. These strands, like those of peacock herl, can be chosen for the width of herl along the edges. Here, a strand with very short herl has been selected.

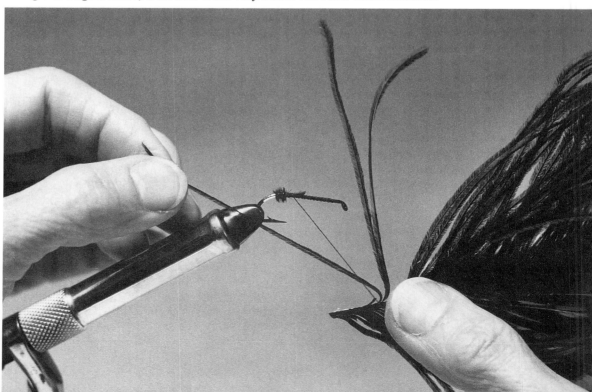

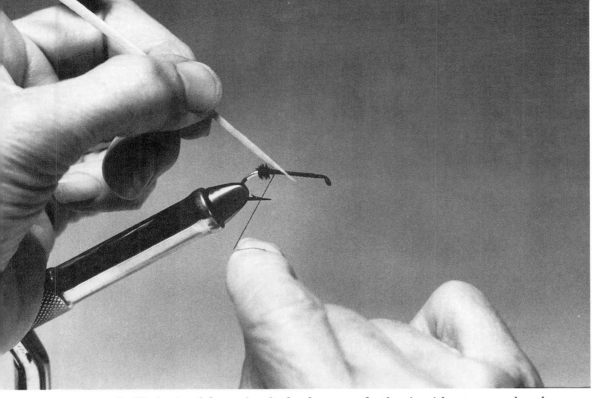

Quill obtained from the shaft of a goose feather is wide at one end and narrow at the other. Here, the narrow end has been trimmed to a slim point where it will be tied on the hook just in front of the herl tip.

Bound securely to the hook, the slim tip of the quill creates no bulk where the first turns of the quill begin.

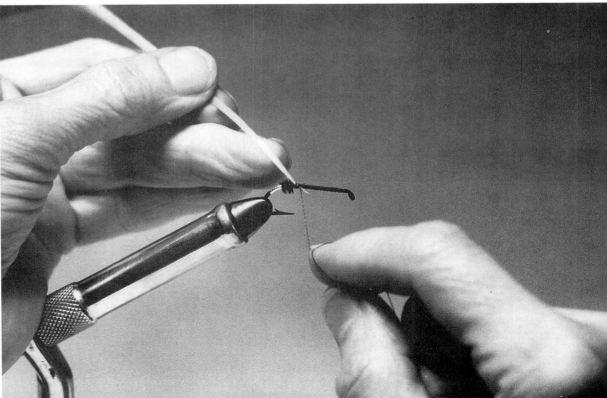

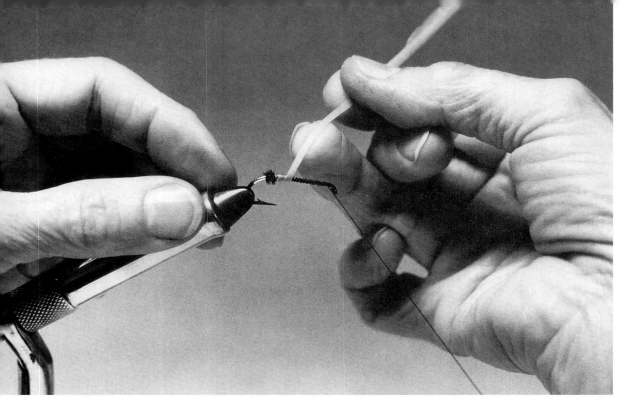

Keep the quill flat as it is being wound on. The edges of goose quills may overlap very slightly to make a smooth body.

The unused portion of the goose quill may be saved for another fly.

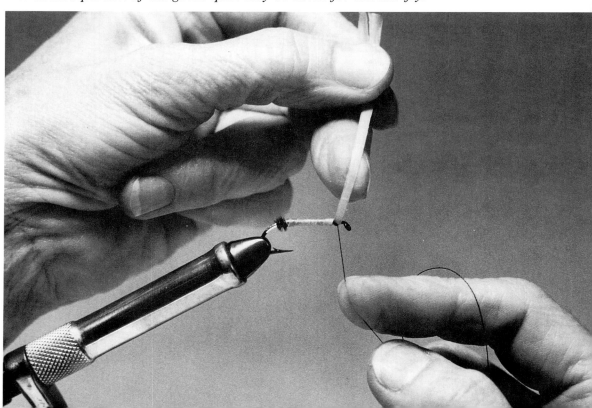

Name of Pattern	Tag	Tip	Body	Hackle	Wing	Head
Black Quill	Gold	Black Chenille	Gray Goose Quill	Black	Dark Gray	Black
Blue Quill	Silver	Gray Floss	Blue-Gray Moose Mane	Blue-Gray	Medium Gray Goose	Gray
Spring Green	Gold	Yellow-Green Floss	Bright Green Quill	Yellow	Pale Gray Goose	Light
Alder Quill	———	Primrose Floss	Orange Quill	Orange and Light Gray	Pale Gray Goose	Light Gray
Green Caddis	———	Bright Green Chenille	Peacock-Herl Quill	Olive	Woodcock	Brown
Roux's Quill	———	Black Floss	Brown Quill	Furnace	Black with Brown Over	Black
Additional Patterns						
Silver Brown	Silver	Brown Floss	Dark Gray Quill	Brown Grizzly	Light Duck	Brown
Barred Quill	Silver	Black Swan	Light Gray Quill	Partridge	Barred Wood Duck	Black
Sierra Quill	Silver	Light Green Chenille	Peacock-Herl Quill	Light Olive	Brown Mouse Deer, Tied Flat	Black
Yellow-Tip Quill	———	Bright Yellow Chenille	Black-Dyed Quill	Furnace	Brown Hen	Black
Gray Moose Quill	Silver	Small Dark Moose Mane	Black-Dyed Quill Shading to Light	Grizzly	White-Tipped Turkey	Black
Scarlet Quill	Gold	Small Yellow Chenille	Bright Scarlet Goose Quill	Gray	Brown Turkey	Black

fly has a double hackle. Select an orange one with flues that reach just to the bend of the hook and use two turns of it. Secure it, clip away the excess, and, immediately ahead of it, tie on a light gray hackle with flues the same length as the orange one. Two turns of the gray one, as close to the first hackle as possible, are enough. In tying on these two hackles, be sure to estimate enough space for them without crowding the eye of the hook, for you still have a wing to tie on. Make the wing with strips of light gray goose, and finish the pattern with a light gray head.

Tie the Green Caddis with a coppery brown tying thread. Make its small tip with a fine bright green chenille. The body is peacock-herl quill from which all of the herl has been removed. Choose those strands of it that show a definite light and dark stripe. Wind the quill on edge-to-edge with each turn so the stripes will show. The hackle for this pattern is olive. The dark brown wing is woodcock, mottled with a lighter brown. With its brown head this is a very attractive fly to add to your impressive collection of patterns.

Our sixth pattern is another beautiful one. A Roux's Quill is a combination of black with brown, in this manner: make a small tip of black floss. Select a light brown hackle quill from which all of the flues have been trimmed and tie the body with it. Pick out a furnace hackle with a black center that will occupy about one-third of the length of the flues. These in turn should reach just to the bend of the hook. Build the wing with a strip of black-dyed goose, and to the top attach a very narrow strip of brown goose to match the body. Make several pairs of these wings before tying the fly in order to have a supply on hand for tying several more, and to have a reserve for later use. The more often you make built-wings, the easier it becomes. This handsome dark fly is an excellent one with which to fish.

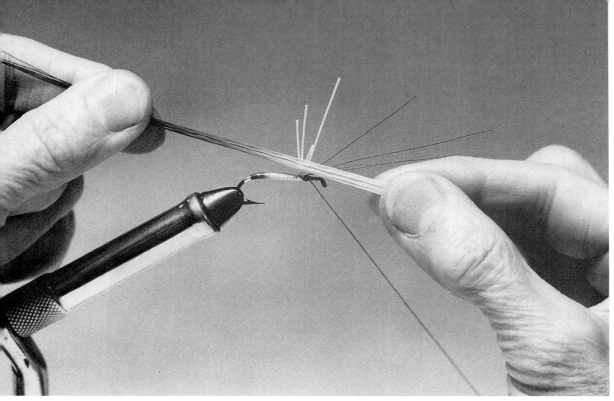

These "quills" of moose mane were carefully chosen for their shading. Laid together like this, and with the dark end tied in first, they will make a dark tip on a light body as they are wound around the hook. Reverse them, and you will have a light tip on a dark body. Built-in tips!

Sometimes a hackle will be very webby near the base of its central shaft. This end makes an excellent hackle for a wet fly.

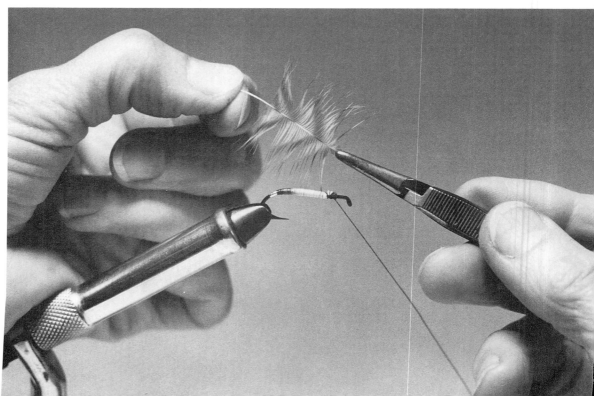

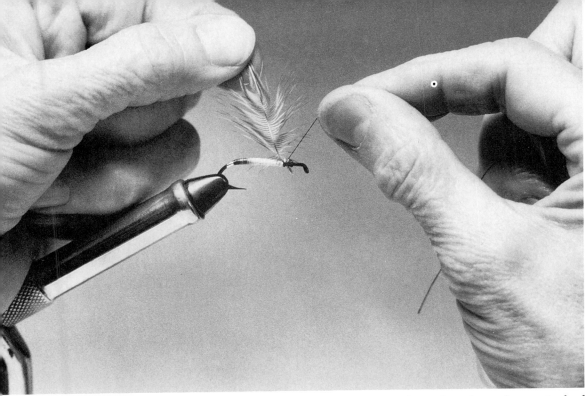

The strong webby flues cling together, even when they have been stroked backward against the direction of their growth. Add a wing of white-tipped turkey and you will complete this pattern of a Gray Moose Quill.

Fifth Stage: With Tail

With or without tags or tips, the following patterns in this stage all have tails. Our first quill pattern to have a tail is the Iron Blue Quill. And for this fly, all of the material required should be of the same color, dyed an iron blue: dark, almost black. Make the tail as long as the body, with matching strips of about three flues of dyed goose. Make the body with dyed quill taken from the same feathers that furnished flues for the tail and that will provide wing strips for this pattern also. Three or four turns of hackle with flues that reach to the bend of the hook will give this fly a slightly heavier hackle than you have used for other patterns. Tie on the wing, making sure that it extends no farther than the center of the tail, and complete the fly with a shiny black wrap-knot head.

Bard's Quill is as light a pattern as the Iron Blue Quill is dark, but it can be tied with a black thread. Make a short tip of silver tinsel. Select a list hackle and use a few of those flues for the tail, which is as long as the hook. The dark center of the tail flues should show as a tiny spot behind the body, so be careful in your selection of the hackle and be sure the flues are not too long. Tie the body

with white moose-mane quill. The hackle for this fly is also a list, and its dark tips should extend just beyond the hook bend. Three turns of it are ample. Use light gray goose for the wing and finish this fly with a neat black wrap-knot head.

A rusty badger hackle will furnish flues for the tail of your McKensie Quill. This pattern does not specify a tag, but a gold one is optional and is a nice addition. After the tail is tied on, use dark moose-mane quill for the body. The proportions for this fly are the same as those for the Bard's Quill. Use the rusty badger hackle now, with a slightly darker gray wing of goose than you used for the Bard's Quill. You can tie the McKensie Quill with a dark gray tying thread and complete the fly with a dark gray wrap-knot head. Comparison of these two patterns shows the McKensie Quill to be a darker version of the Bard's Quill. Whoever tied either pattern "first" or "invented" them may not have been aware of the other one at all. Both are good flies.

A Female Claret Quill has no tag, but it does have a tip. The tail is a narrow strip of goose that has been dyed claret, and the tip is made with a fine, light yellow-green chenille. Make the body

Name of Pattern	Tag	Tail	Tip	Body	Hackle	Wing
Iron Blue Quill	———	Dark Iron Blue	———	Dark Iron Blue Quill	Dark Iron Blue	Dark Iron Blue
Bard's Quill	Silver	List or Badger	———	Light Moose Mane	List or Badger	Light Gray
McKensie Quill	———	Rusty Badger	———	Dark Moose Mane	Rusty Badger	Dark Gray
Female Claret Quill	———	Claret Goose	Yellow Chenille	Claret Ostrich Quill	Claret	Dark Gray
Mallard Quill	———	Brown Mallard	———	Peacock-Herl Quill	Havanah Brown	Brown Mallard
Pale Watery Quill	———	Light Yellow Hackle Flues	Light Yellow Chenille	Light Peacock-Herl Quill	Light Yellow	Pale Gray
Additional Patterns						
Female Red Quill	———	Dark Brown Hackle Flues	Lemon Yellow Floss	Dyed Red Quill	Red-Brown	Mallard
Brown Winged Quill	———	Light Brown Hackle Flues	———	Gray Quill	Light Ginger	Brown Mallard
Female Spinner Quill	———	Six Long Dark Brown Hackle Flues	Yellow Chenille	Gray Quill	Red-Brown	Narrow Speckled Mallard
Female Dark Olive Quill	———	Yellow Olive Flues	Yellow Ostrich	Olive Green Quill	Yellow Olive	Blue-Gray Hackles
Hairwing Quill	———	White Hackle Flues	Red Chenille	Peacock-Herl Quill	List	Black Squirrel
Grieg's Quill	———	Dark Badger Flues	———	Peacock-Eye Quill	Dark List	Lemon Wood Duck

for this fly with fine ostrich herl that has been dyed claret, and from which the very short herl has not been removed. This will give the body a velvety appearance. The flues of your claret hackle should reach just to the bend of the hook. Make the wing the same shade of gray goose that you used for your McKensie Quill.

Compare the Female Claret Quill with the Claret Quill in the Additional Patterns of the first stage of this fly form. The basic structure of body and hackle have been embellished now with a tail, a tip, and a wing. Both are good flies for fishing.

Dark brown mallard furnishes both tail and wing for our next pattern, the Mallard Quill. Seven or eight of the flues are all we will need to make the tail. Make the body with peacock-herl quill and select a short hackle of chocolate (called havanah) brown. This very dark brown hackle matches the dark brown of the mallard feather wing. The entire fly may be tied with black tying thread, but it is also very handsome if a dark

brown tying thread is used, making a chocolate brown wrap-knot head.

Our next pattern will have a small yellow chenille tip. A small silver tag is optional, and not specifically required. The Pale Watery Quill has a rather short tail made of a few light yellow hackle flues. For this fly, use light yellow tying thread. Tie the peacock quill body so that the light stripe of the quill will predominate. Select a hackle that is a little lighter tint than the tail, and tie it on sparingly. Make the wing from your palest gray goose or duck. The head, even though it has darkened a bit (from the wax and handling) will still be light in appearance.

Sixth Stage: With Ribs

A Willow Quill will be our first quill-bodied pattern to have a rib. The beginning for this fly is a short gold-tinsel tag tied on with black tying thread. Use a few flues of brown mallard for the tail. Tie in a strand of very fine round gold tinsel for the rib. Expose the core of threads before you tie it on, making sure the tinsel and threads are flattened against the hook with the tying thread. Use a brown hackle quill for the body of the fly and wind it on smoothly. When the quill is secure, wind the round gold tinsel over it, spacing the windings evenly along the body. Secure the rib where you will wind the hackle before you add a wing.

Choose a light bluish gray hackle, with flues that reach only to the hook barb. Wind sparingly. Make the wing of brown mallard. This may be done in two ways: the mallard may be bunched and tied on to lie back over the fly body; or, you can use strips of mallard to make a regular wet-fly wing, as you did in the second stage of this fly form. Finish tying this fly with your now-familiar wrap-knot head in black.

This version of the famous Ginger Quill pattern, tied as a wet fly, has a short, fine, flat gold-tinsel tag. The tail is made with a few wisps of finely marked lemon wood duck, with or without a few flues of ginger hackle intermingled. Use a gold wire rib tied in reverse over the body of this fly. For the quill body, trim the flues from a bright ginger hackle. When the body is wound, wind the gold wire over it, crossing the quill from the opposite direction of the quill windings. Select a ginger hackle and wind on two turns of it. Make the wing with a pair of matched lemon wood duck feathers, or a good substitute. This is a very useful, popular pattern to make and rely on in many fishing situations, and a valuable addition to your wet-fly collection.

For another very famous pattern called a Quill Gordon, use a short, fine, flat gold tinsel for its tag. It, too, has a tail of lemon wood duck flues and a rib of gold wire wound in reverse over the body. Make the body for this fly with peacock-herl quill that shows the light and dark edges as you wind it on the hook. Select a smoky blue hackle. Wind it on sparingly, and make the wing as you did for the Ginger Quill, from a matched pair of lemon wood duck feathers. With its black wrap-knot head, this fly also is very useful.

A Light Cahill Quill has a short, fine, flat gold-tinsel tag. It also has a tail of lemon wood duck flues and a fine gold wire rib wound in reverse over a body of peacock-herl quill. Make the wing with strips from matched feathers of lemon wood duck. This time the hackle is a light gray dun with a brownish overcast, the color to match as closely as possible the color of the lemon wood duck wing.

The three preceding patterns are very similar in appearance, yet have subtle differences. The interesting thing about them is that one may work very well under some fishing conditions while the other two may be ignored entirely. It is well to have several of each of them in assorted sizes, for if one doesn't produce, one of the others surely will.

Compare the Light Cahill Quill with the Quill Cahill in the second stage of the sixth fly form, and notice how it has been developed with a tag, a tail, and a rib.

Tie on another gold tag and a tail of lemon wood duck for the beginning of the August Dun. For this pattern, choose a lemon wood duck feather that has a bolder or more defined marking. Tie in a strand of gold wire for the rib and a bright brown hackle quill for the body. When you have wound the quill body, again wind the wire rib in reverse over it. Select a bright brown hackle with flues that reach only to the point of the hook and wind on a few turns of it. For the wings, use a pair of pale blue hackle tips, or small hackles with short flues. Tie the pair on flat with their dull sides down, over the body of the fly, to arch back only slightly separated.

A fly such as our next pattern, the Alder Egg Sac, is made of several materials that are tied on and then wait to be used in their turns. How to cover the stub ends of all the materials is explained.

When a pattern specifies a slim body with a rib, the stub ends of tag, tail, rib, and body material must be covered in such a manner as to keep the body slim. In the case of the Alder Egg Sac, the stub ends of all of these materials will be covered by a chenille tip. When the chenille is wound on to make the tip, it will cover the stub ends of the other materials as well as its own.

Begin by using a brown tying thread for the Alder Egg Sac. Tie on a short tag of flat gold tinsel. For the tail, use brown hackle flues about the length of the hook. Next, with their stub ends pointed toward the bend of the hook, tie on a brown hackle quill for the body and a length of gold wire for the rib. Bind them to the hook by winding the tying thread back over them to the base of the tail. Clip off these stub ends carefully.

The tying thread, which is now at the base of the tail, is in readiness to bind on the core of the chenille tip. Use a strand of bright orange chenille for this. Tie it on in the usual way; this will bring the tying thread to the right again. Wind on the chenille tip. Catch the core with the tying thread where the rib and body material wait. These can easily be moved out of the way to the left to facilitate your binding down the core of the chenille. Now, continue to wind the tying thread along the hook, in close turns, toward the hook eye. This will make a smooth foundation for the quill body.

Next, keep the wire rib out of your way, again by moving it to your left, while you wind on the quill body. Make the first turn of quill around the hook as close to the chenille tip as possible. (There should be no gap between the tip and the quill.) Wind it along the hook, covering the core of the chenille tip and the foundation of tying thread. When the quill body is secure, pick up the wire rib. Begin winding it in reverse, with the first turn around the hook at the place where tip and body meet. Continue to wind it on, making an evenly spaced spiral over the quill body.

Select a bright brown hackle for the Alder Egg Sac, with flues that reach just to the bend of the hook. Use two or three turns of it. Select a pair of small, light bluish gray hackles with short flues for the wings. Hold them with their dull sides together and measure them against the fly for the correct length. Their tips should reach about halfway to the end of the tail—no farther. Transfer the pair of hackles to your left hand now, and tie them edge-on to the hook. Be sure to lock-tie the stems of all such hackle wings so that the thin stems of the feathers will not pull out from under the windings at the head of the fly.

Finish this pattern with a bright brown wrapknot head, and you will have completed another fine fly of which you can be proud.

Among the additional patterns, one pattern has been included that requires the use of a golden pheasant crest feather for a tail. This naturally curved feather is not an obstreperous one when you know what to expect of it. The shape of its quill tends to make it slip toward one side of the hook or the other as your tying thread is tightened across it. To overcome this, clip the flues on each side of the quill where the tying thread will cross it, and at that place crease the quill with your thumbnail. The crest feather can then be bound onto the hook in an upsweeping golden arc with little or no difficulty, making a beautiful tail.

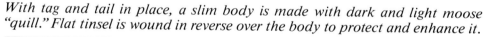

With tag and tail in place, a slim body is made with dark and light moose "quill." Flat tinsel is wound in reverse over the body to protect and enhance it.

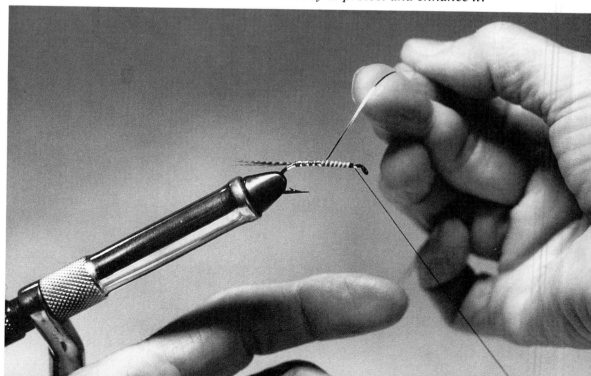

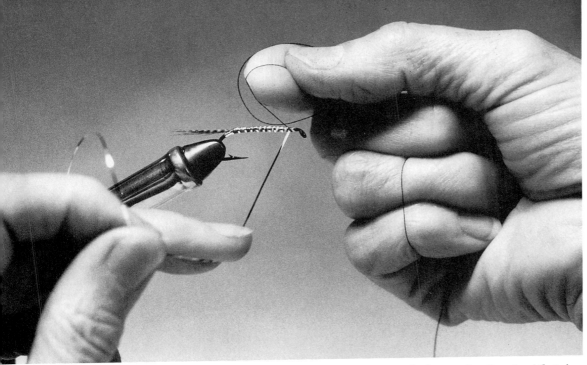

Tinsel wound in reverse must be carefully secured. Cross the tinsel with tying thread, as shown here. Then, bring the tinsel up and across the tying thread. Cross the tinsel once more with the tying thread in order to lock the tinsel before clipping the loose end away.

Also included with these patterns is a hairwing version of the famous Ginger Quill, which substitutes a wing of fitch hair for the use of lemon wood duck. Yet another pattern adds an egg sac to the equally famous and popular Quill Gordon, thereby making it a female version of that well-known pattern. It also substitutes smoky blue hackles for the lemon wood duck wings. These changes have given us two other excellent wet-fly patterns based on more familiar ones.

Name of Pattern	Tag	Tail	Rib	Tip	Body	Hackle	Wing	Head
Willow Quill	Gold	Brown Mallard	Round Gold	——	Brown Hackle Quill	Blue-Gray	Brown Mallard	Black
Ginger Quill	Gold	Lemon Wood Duck and Ginger Hackle Flues	Flat Gold, Reversed	——	Ginger Hackle Quill	Ginger	Lemon Wood Duck	Black
Quill Gordon	Gold	Lemon Wood Duck	Gold Wire, Reversed	——	Peacock-Herl Quill	Smoky Blue	Lemon Wood Duck	Black
Light Cahill Quill	Gold	Lemon Wood Duck	Gold Wire, Reversed	——	Peacock-Herl Quill	Light Brown-Gray	Lemon Wood Duck	Black
August Dun	Gold	Lemon Wood Duck	Gold Wire, Reversed	——	Brown Quill	Brown	Light Blue Hackles, Small	Black
Alder Egg Sac	Gold	Brown Hackle Wisps	Gold Wire, Reversed*	Orange Chenille	Brown Quill	Brown	Light Blue-Gray	Black
Additional Patterns								
Hairwing Ginger Quill	Gold	Lemon Wood Duck and Ginger	Flat Gold	——	Peacock-Herl Quill Dyed Ginger	Ginger	Fitch Hair	Black
Campbell's Quill	Gold	Golden Pheasant Crest	Oval Gold	——	Peacock-Herl Quill	Coch-y-bondhu	Barred Teal	Black
Female Quill Gordon	Gold	Light Blue Dun Wisps	Flat Gold, Reversed*	Yellow Ostrich	Peacock-Herl Quill	Smoky Blue	Smoky Blue Hackles	Black
Blue Olive Quill	Gold	Dark Olive Wisps	Flat Gold, Reversed*	Yellow Ostrich	Olive Brown Quill	Pale Olive	Blue Dun Hackles	Black
Female Brown Quill	——	2 Pheasant Barbs	Flat Gold, Reversed*	Yellow Floss	Brown Quill	Ginger	Gray Tinted Brown	Black
Lady Hamlin	Gold	Pale Olive-Blue with Brown Mallard	Flat Gold, Reversed*	Orange Floss	Dark Moose Mane	Black, Small	White Goose	Black

*Over body only

Brown Hackle Silver	Silver Grizzly	Black and Silver	Silver List	Grouse and Copper	Silver Partridge
Silver Brown	Silver Queen	West Branch	Red Start	Copper Sand Fly	Brookie Fin
Honey Dun	Silver Knight	Ranger	Davis	Silver Green	Red Evening Fly
Red-Tipped Silver Brown	Black Prince	Silver Wraith	Blue and Brown	Black and Silver Ant	Brown Ant
Silver Montreal	Bloody Butcher	Preston's Fancy	Slim Jim	Perch Fly	Tasche's Golden Lady
Turkey and Silver	Fish Hawk	Golden Drake	Dr. Burke	Alexandria	Tippet and Silver

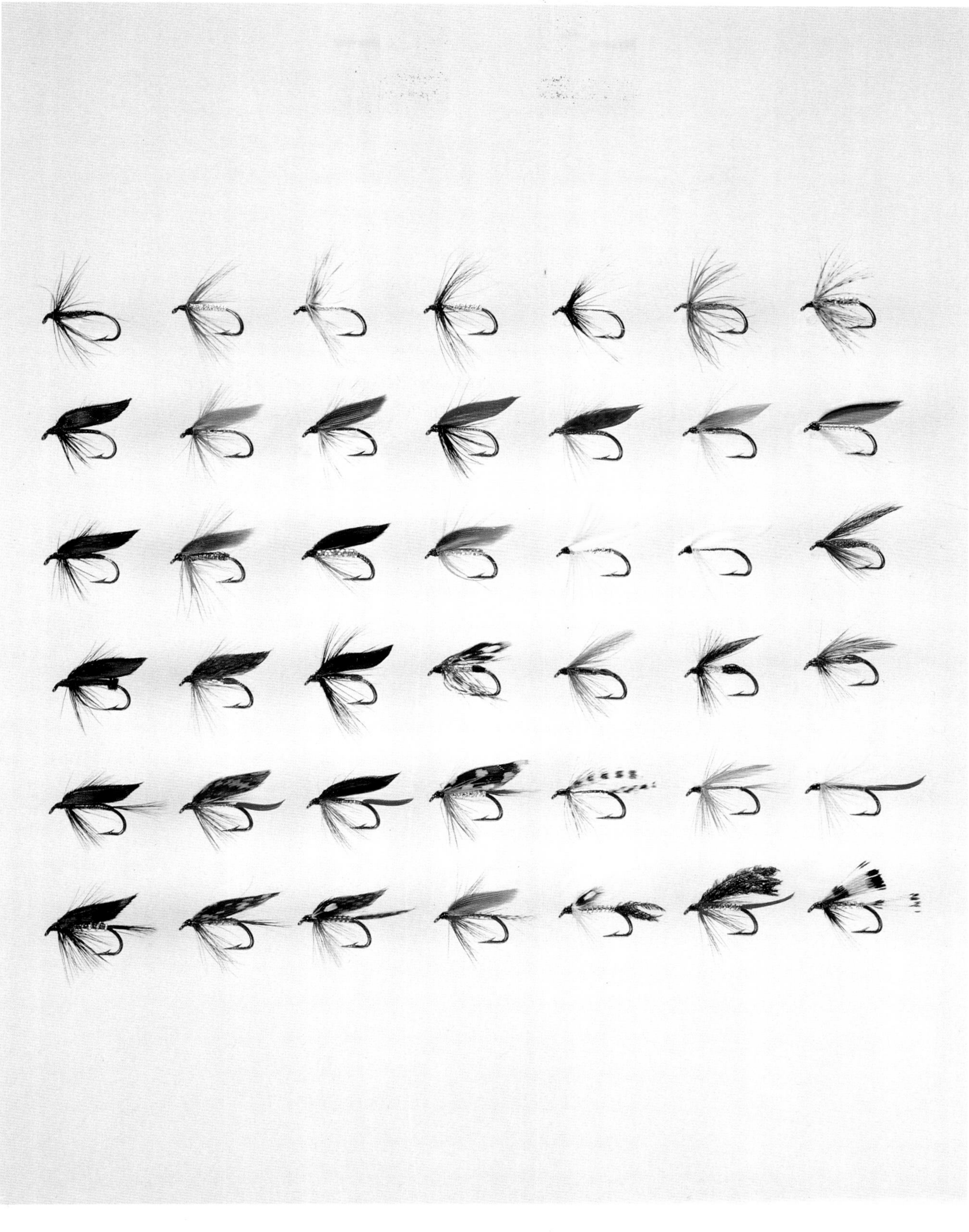

Oh! The gallant fishers' life is the best of any.
'Tis full of pleasure, void of strife,
and 'tis beloved by many.

Izaak Walton, "The Angler"

Tinsel Body
The Seventh Fly Form

First Stage: Body and Hackle

Fly fishermen are in accord on one point: They seldom outgrow the love of fishing, and interest in it deepens with the years. Fly tying helps to perpetuate that love and interest.

There are two schools of thought concerning the relative merits of the "exact imitation" as opposed to an "approximation" of the food fish find attractive. Those who hold that the exact imitation of an insect is the only fly to use are opposed by those who know from their own experience that an "approximation" can represent a whole family of naturals. The latter believe that an exact copy of any individual insect is self-defeating because the fish can detect the fraud immediately. Since fly tying began, the "exact imitation" has been found unnecessary by many an ardent angler, and many a successful fly pattern has no counterpart whatever in nature. However, the "exact" imitations dressed by skillful tyers are a joy to behold, creations of infinite patience and observation. The basic techniques employed are the same for both the imitators and the approximators.

As we come to the seventh fly form, we know that in nature no insects are found with metallic bodies. We also know that tinsel-bodied fly patterns are very effective for fishing. The tinsels we will use are plain flat ones in different widths, or round and oval ones with thread cores, also in different sizes. Then there are the embossed tinsels, available not only in different widths, but in an assortment of colors as well as embossed patterns.

All except one of the patterns in this stage are made with black tying thread. All except one have hackles with flues long enough to extend a little beyond the bend of the hook.

Our first tinsel-bodied pattern is the Brown Hackle Silver. Like the flies in the first stage of the first fly form, the name is a description of the materials from which the fly is tied. Make the body with a medium-width embossed silver tinsel. Coat it lightly with clear lacquer after the body is tied—as you will coat all of the tinsel-bodied flies—and when that is dry wind on a brown wet-fly hackle. Finish with a shiny black wrap-knot head. Coat the head with clear lacquer also, making sure it does not flow into the hackle. Several very thin coats of lacquer are preferable to a single heavy coating.

The second tinsel-bodied pattern is a Silver Grizzly. It too has a body of embossed silver tinsel, but this time use a narrower one than before and notice the difference in the appearance of.the body. Use a light grizzly hackle on this fly and finish it with a neat black head.

A Black and Silver has a body made with a wide embossed Tinsel, which gives it a heavier appearance than that of either of the first two patterns. Its hackle is black. All but one of these tailless and wingless patterns use hackles just a little longer than those generally found in the rest of the patterns in this fly form. Finish the Black and Silver with the familiar neat black wrap-knot head you have mastered. Remember that half-hitches cannot replace the wrap knot for the head of a fly.

Our fourth pattern is the Silver List. The list hackle you select for this pattern should have definite tips of black on its flues and a black center that will end about at the point of the hook after it has been tied on. The interruption of color on this hackle gives it an interesting effect of being disconnected, with only the sheen of the light flues showing between the dark center and the dark tips. Tie the body for this fly with a flat silver tinsel of medium width, and wind on two or three turns of the list hackle. If a badger hackle without the dark tips were used instead, the fly would then be called a Badger Hackle or a Silver Badger.

For the Grouse and Copper, use a fine copper wire for the body. Tie this fly with a copper-colored or bright orange tying thread, for this is the one pattern in this stage that does not have a black head. Select a brown grouse feather for the hackle and wind on about three turns of it. Make a neat wrap-knot head and give it several coats of thin, clear lacquer.

The Silver Partridge has a slightly heavier body than any of the tinsel-bodied flies we have tied. This time, select a wide, oval silver tinsel. As with all of the tinsels that have a thread core, unwind the tinsel until the core is exposed. By easing the threads of the core evenly around the hook the bulk of the material will be distributed and an even foundation for the body will be made. The oval tinsel can then be wound on as smoothly as possible.

Wind this tinsel on, as with all tinsels, edge-to-edge, without gaps and without overlapping the turns. When you have the oval tinsel securely fastened and the excess trimmed away, coat it several times with clear lacquer. Wind on a few turns of a partridge feather for the hackle and complete this pattern with your neatly tapered wrap-knot head.

One material that can be used for tinsel-bodied flies is a piece of electrical wire from which the outer sheath has been removed to reveal many fine copper strands.

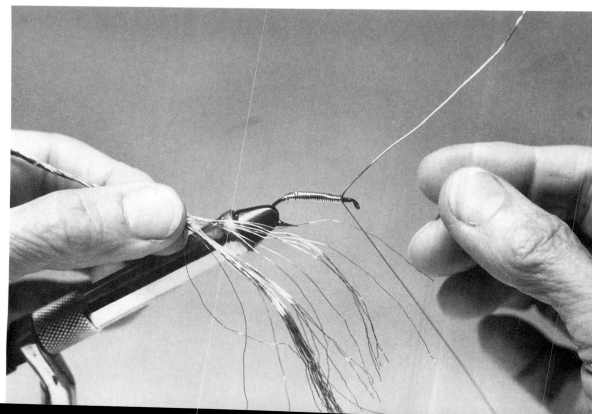

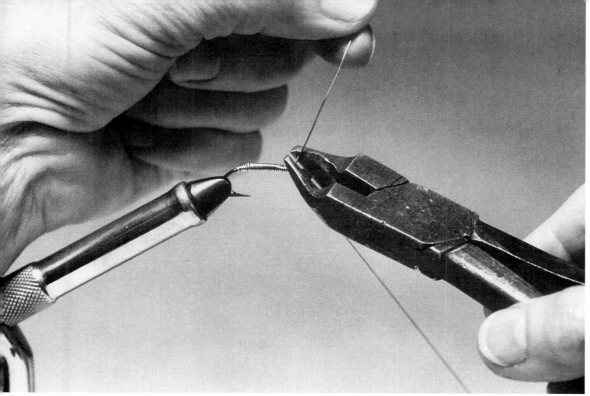

With a tip made of fine fly-tying wire, the remainder of this body is wound with a strand of salvaged copper wire. Although the solid fly-tying wire is fine enough to be cut with fly-tying scissors, heavier wires should be cut with a pair of wire clippers.

Duck-billed pliers are useful for flattening the heavier wires to prevent sharp edges from cutting the tying thread.

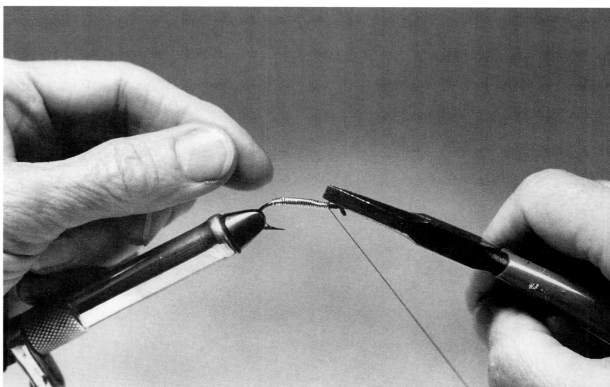

Fly-tying pliers act as an extension of the fingers when it is necessary to grip a short feather quill.

Oval tinsel provides many light-reflecting facets for this fly body. A small partridge feather has been tied on the hook by its stem. The tip of the short hackle is held with fly-tying pliers in order to facilitate winding.

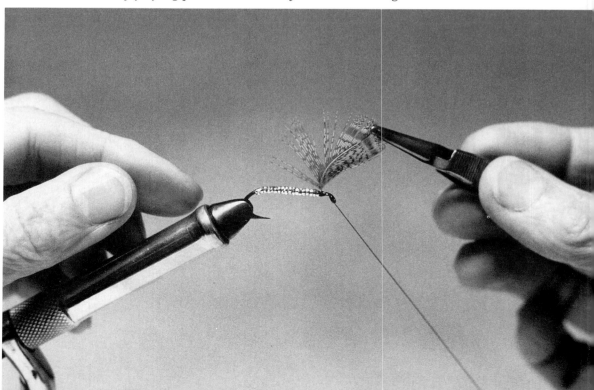

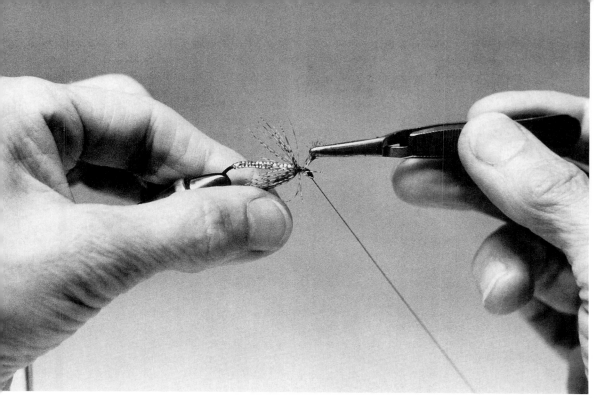

A partridge-feather hackle adds its own delicate pattern to make an attractive tinsel-bodied, wingless wet fly.

Plain, flat tinsel wrapped on edge-to-edge gives the hook an almost plated appearance. The lower end of a hackle, with its heavily webbed flues, is excellent for wet-fly patterns. Although it may be short, it is still a useful material.

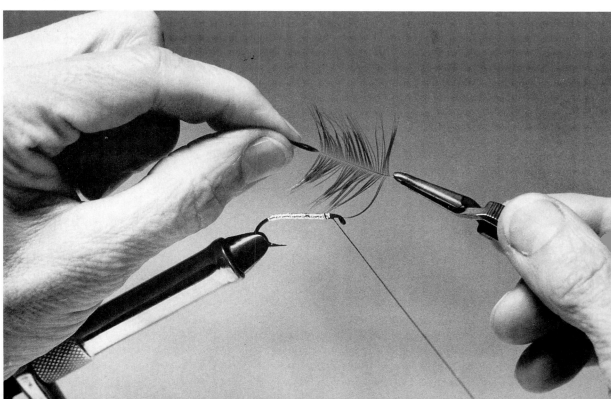

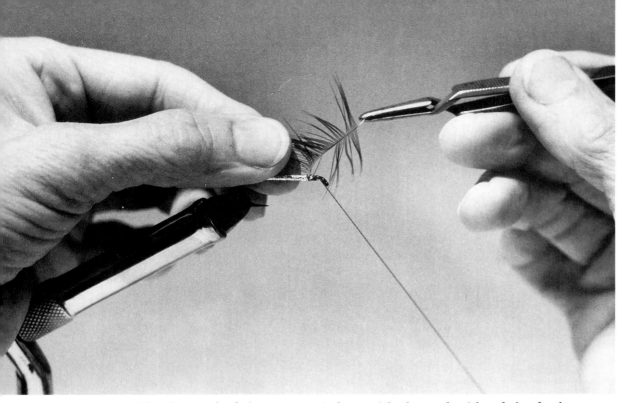

The thin end of the stem is tied on with the underside of the feather away from the hook eye. Its other end can be gripped firmly with hackle pliers, which become extensions of your fingers.

As the hackle is wound on, the webbed flues turn back naturally over the body in fine traditional wet-fly fashion.

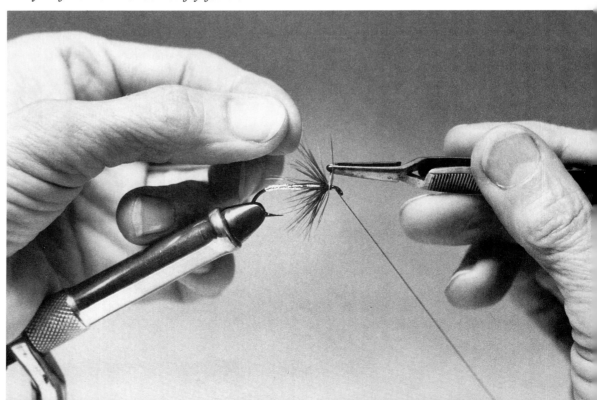

Name of Pattern	Body	Hackle	Head
Brown Hackle Silver	Medium Embossed Silver Tinsel	Brown	Black
Silver Grizzly	Narrow Embossed Silver Tinsel	Grizzly	Black
Black and Silver	Wide Embossed Silver Tinsel	Black	Black
Silver List	Medium-Width Flat Silver Tinsel	List	Black
Grouse and Copper	Fine Copper Wire	Grouse	Copper-Colored or Orange
Silver Partridge	Wide Oval Silver Tinsel	Partridge	Black
Additional Patterns			
Golden Hackle	Medium-Width Gold Tinsel	Gray	Yellow
Scarlet Gnat	Red Embossed Tinsel	Scarlet	Red
Fiery Gold Gnat	Fine Embossed Gold Tinsel	Furnace	Black
Summer Green	Fine Embossed Green Tinsel	Long Sparse Orange	Black
Purple Prince	Fine Embossed Purple Tinsel	Ginger with White Center	Black
Blue Tinsel Gnat	Narrow Bright Blue Tinsel	Black	Black

Second Stage: With Wings

Wings for the tinsel-bodied flies are, with a few exceptions, like those you have been tying for the patterns in the previous fly forms. Measurements for the wings are standard for all of these unless a specific change is indicated.

Our first winged silver-bodied pattern is a Silver Brown. Use plain silver tinsel for the body, then select a brown hackle with flues that reach only to the bend of the hook. Use light gray goose for the wing, and when you measure it for length make it just a trifle shorter than the length of the wings you have been making. Compare this fly with the Brown Hackle Silver (first stage). Minute differences are noticeable: in the length of the brown hackle, and the effect of an embossed silver-tinsel body as against a plain silver body. With a wing added, the Brown Hackle Silver becomes a Winged Brown Hackle Silver, and different from the Silver Brown.

Our second pattern is a Silver Queen. On a plain silver body, use a light grizzly hackle. Make a regular wet-fly wing with strips of medium gray goose and finish the pattern with a shiny black and tapered wrap-knot head.

Our West Branch has a body of plain silver tinsel also, and a glossy dyed-black hackle that reaches to the bend of the hook. Make the wing for this attractive fly with goose that has been dyed a bright red.

Tie the Red Start with red tying thread. Use embossed red tinsel for the slim body. Select a bright light ginger hackle and use two or three turns of it. Make the wing with mottled turkey that has been dyed red. This wing is darker than the one for the West Branch. Finish the pattern with a neat red head. Coat it several times with clear lacquer.

The body for a Copper Sand Fly is just a little different in construction, but is based on the same principle as the others. Starting above the barb of the hook, tie on a fine copper wire and cover about three-quarters of the body length with it. Tie it off carefully to make a smooth foundation for the remaining quarter of the body, which you will cover with a strand of flat gold tinsel. Flatten the copper wire where the strand of gold will be tied on. Wind the flat gold carefully over the foundation you have made for it. Coat the entire body with clear lacquer and permit it to dry thoroughly before tying on a few turns of a light ginger hackle. For the wing this time use cinnamon turkey, or goose that has been dyed cinnamon.

The sixth pattern in this second stage is also just a little different. Although the body for this fly is made with plain silver tinsel, the pattern for the Brookie Fin calls for the extra protection of a wire wound in reverse over its body.

Until now you have worked with patterns that had tails tied on before the rib was added. This pattern has no tail, and the wire must be tied on as securely and as inconspicuously as possible. In order to do this easily, tie on the wire above the barb, allowing the stub end of it to reach as far forward as the wing position. This bound wire will underlie the entire body. Keep the wire on top of the hook as you bind it down with the tying thread. Keep the thread windings close together for the full length of the body. Now, you will tie on your strand of plain silver tinsel at the wing position. Wind it back toward the end of the hook, without overlapping the turns of tinsel, until you reach the place where the wire was tied on. Carefully wind the tinsel forward again, over itself, edge-to-edge, to the tying thread at wing position. Here you will secure it and trim away the excess strand of tinsel.

Now you are ready to wind the protective wire in reverse, over the tinsel body. Begin by bringing the wire toward you. Carry it down beneath the body and up on the far side, continuing in this manner, spacing the turns evenly along the body, until you reach the wing position again. Secure the wire, clip away the excess, and coat the body with clear lacquer.

By keeping the wire on top of the hook and the windings of tying thread close together, you have minimized the presence of the wire underlying the tinsel body and made a smooth foundation for it.

The hackle for this fly is made with a small tuft of polar bear hair. It does not go all around the hook, but is kept beneath it, forming a "throat."

Let the tips of the hair cover the point and barb of the hook.

The wing for our Brookie Fin is a built-wing. This time it is made with four strips of different colors of goose, three of which have been dyed. The main strip of the wing is orange. Above it is a narrow strip of red; above that, a narrow strip of black; and over it all you will use a narrow strip of white. The exact number of flues for each color depends on the width of the finished wing for the particular size of hook you are using. The feathers from which you take the strips of flues for the wing also have some bearing on how many or how few you will need. Some goose pointers have wider flues than others. Suffice it to say that the strips of flues above the main part of the wing are narrow by comparison. The four colored strips together should not be any wider than the width of a wing made of a single colored strip. See the color plate for the correct proportions of the different flues that make up this lovely wing.

This is an exceptionally good wet-fly pattern, producing strikes when other patterns may prove to be ineffectual under many fishing conditions.

Third Stage: With Tag

A tinsel-bodied Honey Dun is our first pattern in this fly form to sport a tinsel tag. Make a short tag with your fine, flat silver. Use oval gold tinsel for the body and coat both tag and body with clear lacquer before tying on the hackle. Select a ginger hackle with a gray center for this fly. The flues should extend just a little beyond the bend of the hook. Use strips of medium gray goose for the wing. Use black tying thread for this pattern, as well as for all of the others in this stage.

The Silver Knight has a rather long purple tinsel tag and a body of oval silver tinsel. Use a few turns of a reddish purple hackle. Separate it on top of the hook and draw it down beneath the hook to form a throat. Anchor it there with the tying thread. Finish this pattern with a wing of black-dyed goose and a black wrap-knot head.

The short tag for a Ranger is made with fine, flat silver tinsel. Make this body with an oval silver tinsel, as you did for the Silver Knight. Select a light gray hackle and use light gray goose or duck

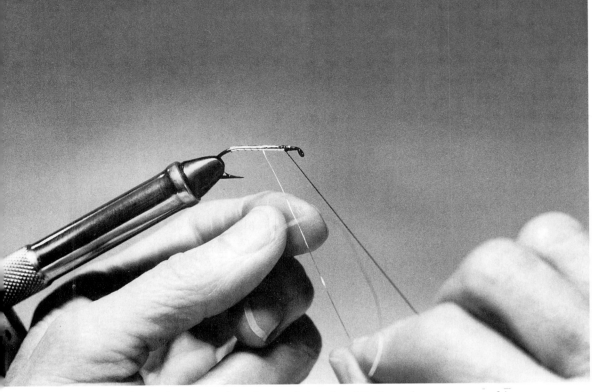

A fine wire, or oval and round tinsels with thread cores, wound in reverse over a plain tinsel body serve the dual purpose of enhancing and protecting it. This is additional insurance against damage to any tinsel body and may be used without altering a pattern.

This pattern requires a throat of polar bear. The hairs of polar bear are stiff and shiny. Where the hair is covered by the fuzzy undercoat, it is thinner than at its tips and ties in well.

From a small, select tuft of polar-bear hair, all of the undercoat at its base is removed, leaving the shiny hairs free. Make the tips of the hair even.

Hold the tips of the tuft of hair beneath the hook. Measure for length, with the tips reaching the bend. Transfer the tuft to your left hand and tie it on, keeping it beneath the hook.

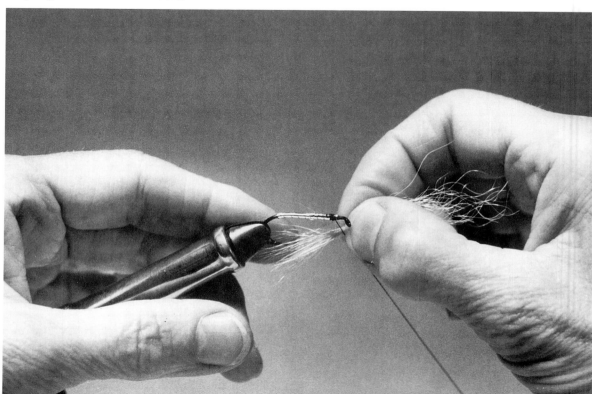

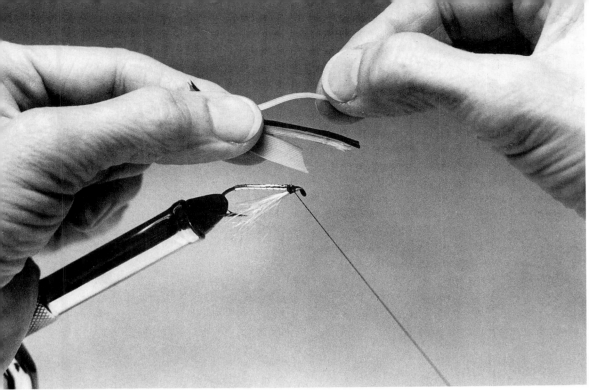

With a throat of polar-bear hair securely in place beneath the hook, the body of the Brookie Fin is ready for its wings. Built with four colored flues from matching feathers, each side of the wing becomes a unified strip. Several pairs of these married-feather wings can be made at one time and stored for future use.

Name of Pattern	Body	Hackle	Wing	Head
Silver Brown	Silver Tinsel	Brown	Light Gray Goose	Black
Silver Queen	Silver Tinsel	Light Grizzly	Medium Gray Goose	Black
West Branch	Silver Tinsel	Black	Bright Red Goose	Black
Red Start	Embossed Red Tinsel	Light Ginger	Turkey Dyed Red	Red
Copper Sand Fly	3/4 Copper Wire, 1/4 Flat Gold Tinsel	Light Ginger	Cinnamon Turkey or Goose	Black
Brookie Fin	Flat Silver Tinsel with Silver Wire Over	Polar Bear, Throat	2/3 Orange Goose, 1/9 each Red, Black and White	Black
Additional Patterns				
Golden King	Oval Gold Tinsel	Guinea Dyed Brown	Small Ginger Hackles	Black
Silver Gnat	Silver Tinsel	Black	Dark Slate Goose	Black
Kingfisher	Silver Tinsel	Brown	Brown Turkey	Black
Golden Nail	Flat Gold Tinsel	Gray Badger	Jungle Cock Eyed Feathers	Black
Teal and Silver	Flat Silver Tinsel	Light Grizzly	Barred Teal	Black
Golden Grouse	Wide Flat Gold Tinsel	Grouse Feather	Goose Dyed Brown	Black

for the wing, matching the two grays as closely as possible.

Another pattern, this time with an embossed silver-tinsel body, is the Davis. Begin by making a short tag with narrow flat gold. Taper the end of the embossed tinsel before you tie it on, and make sure it is secure before you wind it. Use a yellow hackle, sparsely tied, for this fly. Make the wing with strips of white goose.

Our fifth pattern in this stage is a Silver Green. Here "green" refers to the tag, which is made with a narrow green tinsel, while the body is made with flat silver tinsel. The green tag is the only color on this fly, for the rather long hackle and the wing of goose are both white. This becomes another interesting pattern when it is tied with a bright green tying thread, giving it a green head as well as a green tag.

The sixth pattern is a Red Evening Fly. It has a tag made with narrow embossed gold tinsel. The body is made with embossed red tinsel. Both the

hackle and the wing are brown. Make the wing with a pair of small and narrow hackles. Hold them with their dull sides together while you measure them for length against the hook, and tie them edge-on to the hook, to ride at an angle of about forty-five degrees above the body. Their position can be adjusted and secured with the tying thread before the wrap-knot head is made. Be sure to lock-tie the quill of the wing hackles, to prevent their pulling out of the thread winding later on. Coat the head with several applications of clear lacquer, being careful to prevent the lacquer from spreading into the hackle or the wings.

In the additional patterns, the hackle called "straw" is a very light-colored ginger with a gray center. For the wing of the Muench, a carefully chosen tail of fitch can supply hair close in color to that of lemon wood duck. With tips ending in a creamy color, its fine, soft undercoat ranges from cream to a warm rusty ginger and is excellent for use as dubbing.

Name of Pattern	Tag	Body	Hackle	Wing	Head
Honey Dun	Silver	Oval Gold Tinsel	Honey Dun	Gray Goose	Black
Silver Knight	Purple	Oval Silver Tinsel	Purple Throat	Black-Dyed Goose	Black
Ranger	Silver	Oval Silver Tinsel	Gray	Slate Gray Goose	Black
Davis	Gold	Embossed Silver Tinsel	Yellow	White Goose	Black
Silver Green	Green	Silver Tinsel	White	White Goose	Black or Green
Red Evening Fly	Gold	Embossed Red Tinsel	Havanah Brown	Narrow Brown Hackles	Black
Additional Patterns					
Fox Squirrel	Gold	Embossed Gold Tinsel	Brown	Rusty Squirrel	Black
Muench	Embossed Gold	Copper Wire	Straw	Fitch Hair	Black
Mystery	Gold	Embossed Silver Tinsel	Bright Ginger	White Goose	Black
Cinnamon and Gold	Silver	Embossed Gold Tinsel	White	Cinnamon Goose	Black
Golden Brown Gnat	Gold	Flat Gold Tinsel	Brown	White Goose Dyed Brown	Black
White-Winged Scarlet Gnat	Silver	Embossed Red Tinsel	Scarlet	White Goose	Black

Fourth Stage: With Tip

The Red-Tipped Silver Brown is a long but descriptive name for our first tinsel-bodied pattern to have a tip. First of all, it has a short silver tag. Make its short tip with a bright red floss. The body itself is made with flat silver tinsel of a width suitable for the size fly you are tying. Choose a brown hackle with flues that will reach to the bend of the hook. Tie it on sparsely, and over it tie on a wet-fly wing of dark brown mottled turkey. When you compare this pattern with the third additional pattern in the second stage of this fly form, you will find that your Red-Tipped Silver Brown is a Kingfisher with a red tip.

Our second pattern is a Black Prince. This fly also has a short silver tag. Make the tip with a slightly darker red floss and somewhat shorter than the one for the previous pattern. The body is made with a flat silver tinsel. Select a black hackle with longer flues for this fly and make the wing with black-dyed goose. Finish the fly with a black wrap-knot head.

A Silver Wraith will have a short silver tag and a tip of black floss. This time the body is made with embossed silver tinsel. The hackle of guinea fowl should have flues that extend a little beyond the hook. This pattern calls for a wing made with paired jungle fowl feathers. With the scarcity of jungle fowl, substitutes for those lovely feathers become important. Narrow black hackles with a small cream-colored spot painted at the tip are acceptable alternatives. The interruption of the blacks and whites on this fly make it a very interesting and effective one with which to fish.

An equally interesting pattern is the Blue and Brown. Use black tying thread for this fly. Make a short tag with narrow green tinsel and a short tip with brown floss. Tie the rest of the body with a narrow blue tinsel; both hackle and wing are brown. Make the wing with a pair of short-flued narrow hackles, or hackle tips, and tie them edge-on to the hook to stand at an angle of about forty-five degrees from the body. Finish with a wrap-knot head. This becomes a very handsome pattern when a brown tying thread is used, giving it a rich brown head.

Our fifth pattern is the Black and Silver Ant. The last two patterns in this fourth stage are with-out tags. Make the tip for this fly with black floss. Carefully build it up into a larger diameter than the tinsel body. Keep it tapered where it rises from the hook. Permit the floss to spread a little, as you taper the tip down again to the hook shank, before securing it. This swollen tip should occupy about one-third of the body length. Keep the floss taut so that its individual fibers will not slip. Use embossed silver tinsel for the remaining two-thirds of the body. Coat both tip and tinsel with clear lacquer, and permit it to become thoroughly set before tying on a few turns of a rather short black hackle. Have the flues of this hackle just long enough to reach to the barb of the hook. The narrow black hackles for the wing should be slim and extend only to the bend of the hook. Tie this wing at a forty-five degree angle from the body, and secure it there with the tying thread. Lock-tie the quills of the hackle wings and finish the fly with a wrap-knot head.

Our Brown Ant will have a brown head, so use a brown tying thread. Make its tip with brown floss, using the same proportions for tip and body as you did for the Black and Silver Ant. For the remainder of this body use fine copper wire. Choose a bright coppery brown furnace hackle, with flues that reach to the barb.

Select a pair of narrow brown hackles for the wings and tie them on in the manner of most of our wet-fly wings, to lie back over the body. These wings are tied edge-on to the body, but are not set at the elevated angle of the two preceding patterns. The hackle wings should extend beyond the hook in an amount equal to the gape of the hook. Measurements such as these are not arbitrary, but are intended as guidelines for uniformity when more than one fly of a pattern is tied.

The Silver Doctor Ant of the additional patterns has a body that is the same as that of the Black and Silver Ant. Here, the hackle has extremely short flues—so short as to be almost negligible. Use about two turns of it, no more. The end of the wing will be just about even with the bend of the hook. The wing is made of fine calf-tail hair, in four colors. The first sparse layer above the hook is white, the next is yellow, and above that is red. Over it all is a layer of light bright turquoise blue. The layers of colored hair

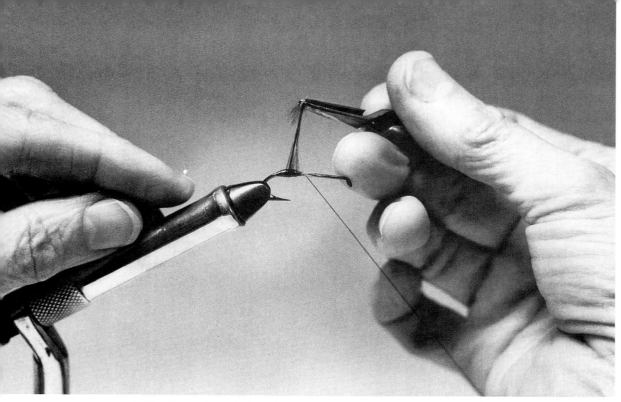

This floss tip is being built up for an ant pattern. Other tips for tinsel-bodied flies may be made of different kinds of herl and chenille. Small tapered tips can also be made with floss.

A fine wire has been attached in front of the swollen tip and is being wound forward over the closely wound tying thread on the hook shank.

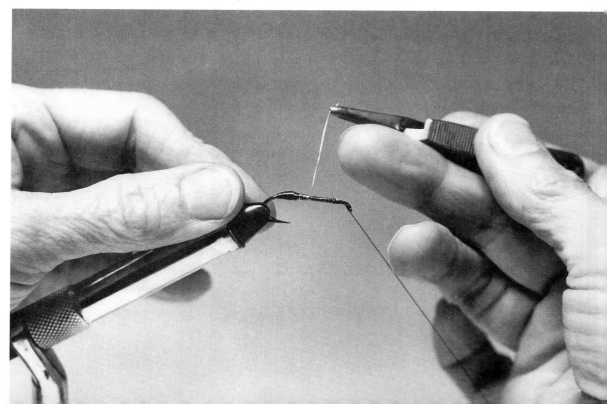

Name of Pattern	Tag	Tip	Body	Hackle	Wing	Head
Red-Tipped Silver Brown	Silver	Red Floss	Silver Tinsel	Brown	Brown Turkey	Black
Black Prince	Silver	Dark Red Floss	Silver Tinsel	Black	Black Goose	Black
Silver Wraith	Silver	Black Floss	Embossed Silver Tinsel	Guinea	Short Jungle Cock	Black
Blue and Brown	Green	Brown Floss	Blue Tinsel	Brown	Brown Hackles	Black or Brown
Black and Silver Ant	———	Black Floss	Embossed Silver Tinsel	Black	Black Hackles	Black
Brown Ant	———	Brown Floss	Copper Wire	Coppery Furnace	Brown Hackles	Black
Additional Patterns						
Copper Olive	Gold	Olive Floss	Copper Wire	Grouse	Light Mottled Turkey	Brown
Silver Doctor Ant	———	Black Floss	Embossed Silver Tinsel	White	Hair Wing	Black
Gold and Green	Gold	Bright Green Floss	Gold Tinsel	Green	Slate Goose	Black
Golden Day	Silver	Bright Orange Floss	Gold Tinsel	Yellow	White Goose	Black
Natty Jack	Gold	Warm Yellow Floss	Silver Tinsel	Black	Narrow Yellow Hackles	Black
Golden Partridge	Gold	Green Peacock Herl from Eye	Gold Tinsel	Partridge	Dark Brown-Dyed Goose	Black

should show definite stripes, and all of them together should create a normal hair wing that is not bulky.

As each colored layer is added, each stripe will make a little wider angle from the hook shank than did the previous one, so that the tips of the turquoise blue stripe will be at a forty-five-degree angle above the bend of the hook. The effect of all four stripes is fan-shaped, with the fan rising above the bend of the hook—not spreading sideways. The whole hair wing should be no wider than the fly body. Where this hair wing is tied on, of course, the hair will be no thicker than for a hair wing of one color. Carefully trim the stub ends of the hair to taper the foundation for the head. This has proved to be an exceptionally effective hairwing wet fly over many years, although what trout take it to be is anyone's guess. Be sure to add it to your collection of wet flies in #10 and #12, which have proven to be the best sizes.

Fifth Stage: With Tail

Although tags may be optional, they are omitted for the following patterns that do not specify them. All of the patterns are tied with black thread.

For the first pattern, tie on a tail of red goose, about three flues in width, and no longer than the length of the body. Make the body with plain silver tinsel. For the hackle, select one that has been dyed a dark claret. Use dark brown mottled turkey for the wing, and when you have completed the wrap-knot head you will have added a Silver Montreal to your stock of wet flies.

The Bloody Butcher is next, with a tail and body the same as the Silver Montreal, but this time the dyed hackle is a bright red to match the tail of red goose. For the wing of this pattern, cut two matching strips from the dark purplish blue of a mallard covert feather and tie the pair on with the deep color on the outside. (The "wrong," or dull, sides of these strips are gray.)

Preston's Fancy has a tail of brown hackle wisps. Make the body for this pattern with embossed gold tinsel. Select a brown hackle with flues that reach to the bend of the hook and tie it on sparingly. For the wing, use matching strips of guinea fowl. The wing may be a trifle wider than

A pair of narrow, well-matched hackles will make a fine wing for a tinsel-bodied wet fly. Four hackles may also be used—two on each side—for a slightly heavier double wing.

the one for the Bloody Butcher in order to show several of the white spots on the Guinea feather.

The next two patterns have slender wings made with small and narrow hackles with short flues, or with the tips of small hackles. The first of these two is a Slim Jim. Select two very small and narrow grizzly hackles for the tail, which extends no farther than the width of the gape beyond the hook. Use a flat tinsel for the silver body, and for the sparse hackle select a dark grizzly with flues that reach only to the barb. Tie a pair of very slender grizzly hackle wings edge-on over the body, permitting their tips to reach about to the center of the tail. Lock-tie the hackle quills before you trim away the excess, and finish the fly with a tapered black head. This has proven to be a very popular wet fly over time.

The Perch Fly is our fifth pattern in this stage of the tinsel-bodied flies, and it is the second pattern to have the slender hackle wings. Make the tail with a few wisps of orange hackle flues, and its body with a fine, flat gold tinsel. The flues of its orange hackle should reach only to the barb of the hook. Use one or two more turns of it around

the hook than you did for the hackle of the Slim Jim. The wing for this pattern is made with four narrow hackles: the two center ones are white, and an orange one is on each side. Tie the four on together, edge-on to the hook, lock-tying their quills before you clip off the excess. Finish with a tapered black wrap-knot head.

This wing of four hackles is not difficult to tie on after you have laid them together—the two inner white ones with their dull sides together, and the orange ones with their bright sides on the outside. The orange hackles, carefully matched for size, completely hide the white ones sandwiched in between. Their movement in the water will separate and unite the feathers intermittently. This pattern can also be tied with yellow in place of the orange, and in both colors these flies are excellent for crappie and perch, as well as for trout.

Tasche's Golden Lady has always been a very successful wet-fly pattern. Tie on a long slender tail of red goose, as long as the hook is overall. Make the slender body with flat gold tinsel. Select a bright golden ginger hackle with flues that reach to the bend of the hook after it is tied on. Make

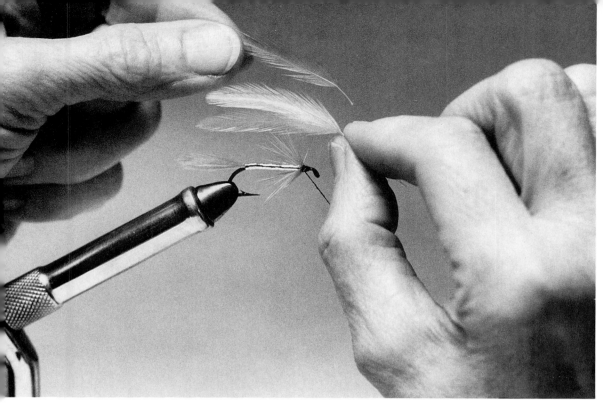

A tail of short hackles, or hackle tips, is in place on a tinsel body. The hackle has been tied on. The wing for this fly is being made with four narrow hackles: the central two are white, and a colored feather will be placed on each side of the white pair.

With wings of this type, tied edge-on to the hook, your small wet fly becomes a feather-winged streamer in miniature.

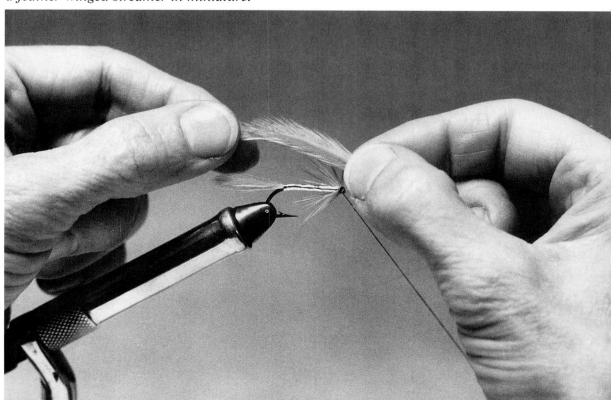

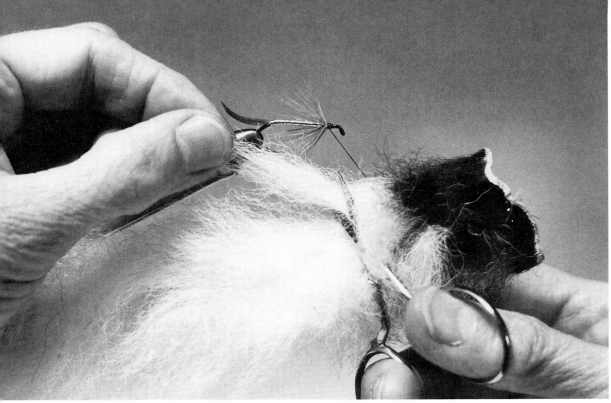

With tail, tinsel body, and hackle in place, select a tuft of calf-tail hair, instead of feather, for the wing.

the wing for this pattern with a sparse tuft of calf-tail hair from which all of the soft undercoat has been removed. Sort the hair to make the tips even. Before you tie the wing on, measure it for length against the fly body. The tips of the hair wing should extend to the center of the tail. Keep the wing flat from side to side, and tie it on to be fan-shaped over the fly body. When this fly has been in the water, all of the hair in the wing will lie close to the tinsel body in the manner of a streamer wing. Tie several different sizes of this pattern, for it is an excellent one to use in fast water in sizes from #12 through #6.

Sixth Stage: With Ribs

While many fly patterns do not specify a rib, there are those whose beauty is enhanced by one. The following patterns all have ribs. This time we have tinsel over tinsel and floss over tinsel for the ribbing. Although tags may be optional, they are not indicated here.

Our first pattern is a Turkey and Silver. Make the tail for this fly with a few wisps of scarlet hackle flues. Select a very fine oval silver tinsel for

the rib. On smaller hooks use a fine round tinsel. Expose the thread core before you tie it on the hook, making sure to catch the end of the tinsel as well as the threads of the core with your tying thread. Use your flat silver tinsel for the body. Since you will make few turns around the body with an oval tinsel rib, try to space them evenly, and where possible cover the joined edges of the flat tinsel with a rib. Carefully coat the ribbed tinsel body with clear lacquer before you wind on the hackle. When the lacquer is thoroughly dry, tie on a dark claret-colored hackle and wind it on sparsely. Finish the pattern with a dark brown wing of mottled turkey.

Compare your finished fly with the first pattern in the fifth stage. The only differences between your Turkey and Silver and the Silver Montreal are the rib and the material from which the tails were made.

The Fish Hawk has a slender tail of dark brown turkey flues. This fly has a rib of brown floss. Since a full strand of floss would be much too bulky for a #10 hook, divide the strand, using only a part of it for the rib. Tie it in and bind it

Flues from peacock sword feathers are carefully selected to have the same natural curve in all of the strands used for the wing of the same fly.

Name of Pattern	Tail	Body	Hackle	Wing
Silver Montreal	Red Goose	Silver Tinsel	Dark Claret	Dark Brown Mottled Turkey
Bloody Butcher	Red Goose	Silver Tinsel	Red	Purple-Blue Mallard
Preston's Fancy	Brown Hackle Wisps	Embossed Gold Tinsel	Brown	Guinea Fowl
Slim Jim	Grizzly Hackles	Silver Tinsel	Grizzly	Grizzly Hackles
Perch Fly	Orange Hackle Wisps	Silver Tinsel	Orange	White Hackles between Orange Hackles
Tasche's Golden Lady	Red Goose	Gold Tinsel	Bright Ginger	White Calf Tail
Additional Patterns				
Crappie Fly	Yellow Hackle Wisps	Silver Tinsel	Yellow	White Hackles between Yellow Hackles
Silver Miller	Narrow White Hackles	Silver Tinsel	White	White Goose
Golden Stork	Gray Mallard	Gold Tinsel	Brown	Brown Mallard
Silver and Black	Tippet	Silver Tinsel	Black	Black Goose
Silver Drake	Gray Mallard	Silver Tinsel	Badger or List	Gray Mallard
St. Patrick	Peacock Sword or Green Goose	Silver Tinsel	Light Blue-Gray	Peacock Sword

smoothly to the hook to make the foundation for the body of flat gold tinsel. Lacquer the tinsel body and let it dry, but keep the floss strand for the rib out of the way until it does. When the lacquer has thoroughly set, wind on the floss rib. Keep the strand twisted into a firm cord as you wind it over the tinsel body. This pattern has a brown hackle and a wing of the dark brown turkey to match the tail. If you have a pair of very small jungle cock eyed feathers, place one on each side of the wing for a "cheek," and secure their little quills before making the wrap-knot head. If you do not have the jungle cock, select two matching strips of guinea fowl that have a white spot at the tip. Or use a little black hackle on which you have painted a small white or cream-colored spot.

On a Golden Drake, use a few wisps of barred teal as the tail. Use a fine oval or round gold tinsel for the rib, and make the body with a flat gold tinsel. This fly has a bright red hackle and is complete when you have added a wing of light gray goose and finished the black wrap-knot head with a coating of lacquer.

The pattern for a Dr. Burke has a tail of peacock-sword feathers. With their fine herl along both edges, the flues are heavier than those from hackles, goose or turkey. A pair of matched flues of the peacock swords makes a bulky little tail that will slim down somewhat when the fly has been in the water. Use your fine oval silver tinsel for ribbing, over the flat silver tinsel body. Use care in lacquering this body to keep the lacquer from spreading into the peacock swords of the tail. Select a short yellow hackle with flues that reach to the barb of the hook; a few turns of it are all that is required for this pattern. Tie on a wet-fly wing of white goose, and from your precious stock of small jungle-cock feathers (or with a pair of sub-stitutes) make a small cheek on each side of the white wing. Finish this pattern with your well tied wrap-knot head.

An Alexandria also uses peacock-sword feather flues—this time for the wing. But before the wing can be tied, make the tail for this fine pattern with a few flues of red goose. The rib is a round silver tinsel evenly spaced over a flat silver-tinsel body. When you lacquer this body, again try to keep it from spreading into the tail. Wind on a bright red hackle, and over the body and hackle arch a wing of matched peacock swords. Select these swords to curve in the same direction, and measure them for length so that they reach almost to the end of the tail. Tie them on, carefully trimming the stubs into a tapered foundation for your wrap-knot head.

A Tippet and Silver has a tail made of flues from the orange and black tippet feathers that adorn the cape of a golden pheasant. Choose matching flues that are short enough so that the black bar will show behind the body of the fly and the whole tail will be no longer than the hook. For the rib, use a fine oval silver tinsel and wind it in reverse over a flat silver-tinsel body. Select a badger hackle with flues that reach to the bend of the hook and wind it on sparsely.

The wing for this pattern is also made with tippet feathers. Choose a matching pair, and tie them on so that their black tips will be above the black bar of the tippet tail. Only a tiny spot of orange should show between the black bar on the wing and the black wrap-knot head of the fly.

A handsome variation of this pattern is made with a badger hackle that has been dyed orange. The orange tips of the hackle beneath the hook then appear to be a continuation of the bright orange color in the tippet wing above.

Name of Pattern	Tag	Tail	Rib	Body	Hackle	Wing
Turkey and Silver	———	Scarlet Hackle	Oval Silver Tinsel	Flat Silver Tinsel	Dark Claret	Dark Brown Turkey
Fish Hawk	———	Brown Turkey	Brown Floss	Flat Gold Tinsel	Brown	Dark Brown Turkey
Golden Drake	———	Barred Teal	Oval or Round Gold Tinsel	Flat Gold Tinsel	Scarlet	Gray Goose
Dr. Burke	———	Peacock Sword	Oval Silver Tinsel	Flat Silver Tinsel	Yellow	White Goose
Alexandria	———	Red Goose	Round Silver Tinsel	Flat Silver Tinsel	Scarlet	Peacock Sword
Tippet and Silver	———	Tippet	Oval Silver Tinsel	Flat Silver Tinsel	Badger (or Badger Dyed Orange)	Tippet

Additional Patterns							
Name of Pattern	Tag	Tail	Tip	Rib	Body	Hackle	Wing
Silver Gray	———	Tippet	———	Round Silver Tinsel	Flat Silver Tinsel	Blue-Gray	Barred Teal
Cinnamon and Gold	———	Tippet	———	Gold Wire, Reversed	Flat Gold Tinsel	Ginger	Cinnamon Turkey
Blue Jay	———	Lemon Wood Duck	Blue Chenille	Flat Silver Tinsel over Body	Embossed Silver Tinsel	Black	Blue Jay
Tomah Joe	Silver	Yellow Goose	Peacock Herl	Round Silver Tinsel over Body	Flat Gold Tinsel	Scarlet and Yellow	Barred Wood Duck
Silver Ibis	Silver	Red Hackle or Goose	Green Herl from Eye	Silver Wire over Body	Flat Silver Tinsel	Red	Red Goose
Flamer	———	Crimson Hackle	Brown Chenille	Silver Wire over Body	Flat Gold Tinsel	Brown	Crimson Goose

181

Index